TOURISM PLANNING AND MANAGEMENT

TOURISM PLANNING AND MANAGEMENT

Vikas Choudhary

CENTRUM PRESS
NEW DELHI-110002 (INDIA)

CENTRUM PRESS

H.O.: 4360/4, Ansari Road, Daryaganj,
New Delhi-110002 (India)
Tel: 23278000, 23261597, 23255577, 23286875

B.O.: No. 1015, Ist Main Road, BSK IIIrd Stage,
IIIrd Phase, IIIrd Block, Bangalore-560085 (INDIA)
Tel: 080-41723429

Email: centrumpress@gmail.com
Visit us at: www.centrumpress.com

Tourism Planning and Management

First Edition, 2010

ISBN 978-93-80540-76-4

PRINTED IN INDIA

Printed at Balaji Offset, Delhi.

Contents

Preface

Tourism impacts are multifaceted and therefore are difficult to plan for and manage. As tourism activity in Asia continues to grow at a fast rate so do the expectation of tourists for high quality service and environments. Many destinations operate within highly competitive environments where customers have a wide range of choices even within a country or a region. The challenge is for destinations to develop a service culture, physical environment and a set of products that can satisfy not only first-time visitors but attract repeat visitors. Destinations refer to the place where the tourists spend their time while they are on vacation. There are a wide range of geographical scales of destinations from small communities to a region of a country to an entire city. Working at the destination scale in an integrated manner is crucial since this is where the entire visitor experience is delivered. Most of the interactions and impacts of tourism activity occur at the destination level making it the ideal unit for tourism and visitor planning and management.

Due to the obstacles of ensuring a quality destination experience many communities are missing significant opportunities to create productive employment for the residents and realize opportunities for poverty reduction due to the ineffective planning and management.

While there are no magic panaceas for destination management there has evolved a good understanding of the key components of the destination management process.

Destination management requires a strong commitment and collaboration amongst the major stakeholders, a good understanding of the market potential of the destination for both domestic as well as international tourism, working with both the public and private sectors in providing a high level of visitor care and attention and constantly updating the product and attractions in order to meet changing consumer preferences and requirements.

This book has provided the basis of tourism telling us of the tourism particulars and different ways of marketing this composite commodity.

—*Vikash Choudhary*

1

Marketing of Tourism

Introduction

Tourism is one of many activities in a community or region that requires planning and coordination. This bulletin provides a simple structure and basic guidelines for comprehensive tourism planning at a community or regional level. Planning is the process of identifying objectives and defining and evaluating methods of achieving them. By comprehensive planning we mean planning which considers all of the tourism resources, organizations, markets, and programs within a region. Comprehensive planning also considers economic, environmental, social, and institutional aspects of tourism development.

Two Sides of Tourism Planning

Tourism planning has evolved from two related but distinct sets of planning philosophies and methods. On the one hand, tourism is one of many activities in an area that must be considered as part of physical, environmental, social, and economic planning. Therefore, it is common to find tourism addressed, at least partially, in a regional land use, transportation, recreation, economic development, or comprehensive plan.

The degree to which tourism is addressed in such plans depends upon the relative importance of tourism to the community or region and how sensitive the planning authority is to tourism activities.

Tourism may also be viewed as a business in which a community or region chooses to engage. Individual tourism businesses conduct a variety of planning activities including feasibility, marketing, product development, promotion, forecasting, and strategic planning. If tourism is a significant component of an area's economy or development plans, regional or community-wide marketing plans are needed to coordinate the development and marketing activities of different tourism interests in the community. A comprehensive approach integrates a strategic marketing plan with more traditional public planning activities. This ensures a balance between serving the needs and wants of the tourists versus the needs and wants of local residents. A formal tourism plan provides a vehicle for the various interests within a community to coordinate their activities and work toward common goals. It also is a means of coordinating tourism with other community activities.

Steps in the Planning Process

Like any planning, tourism planning is goal-oriented, striving to achieve certain objectives by matching available resources and programs with the needs and wants of people. Comprehensive planning requires a systematic approach, usually involving a series of steps. The process is best viewed as an iterative and nagging one, with each step subject to modification and refinement at any stage of the planning process. There are six steps in the planning process:

1. Define goals and objectives.
2. Identify the tourism system.
   (a) Resources.
   (b) Organizations.
   (c) Markets.
3. Generate alternatives.
4. Evaluate alternatives.
5. Select and implement.
6. Monitor and evaluate.

Step One: Defining Goals and objectives. Obtaining clear statements of goals and objectives is difficult, but important. Ideally, tourism development goals should flow from more general community goals and objectives. It is important to understand how a tourism plan serves these broader purposes. Is the community seeking a broader tax base, increased employment opportunities, expanded recreation facilities, better educational programs, a higher quality of life? How can tourism contribute to these objectives?

If tourism is identified as a means of serving broader community goals, it makes sense to develop plans with more specific tourism development objectives. These are generally defined through a continuing process in which various groups and organizations in a community work together toward common goals. A local planning authority, chamber of commerce, visitors bureau, or similar group should assume a leadership role to develop an initial plan and obtain broad involvement of tourism interests in the community. Public support for the planning process and plan is also important. Having a good understanding of tourism and the tourism system in your community is the first step toward defining goals and objectives for tourism development. The types of goals that are appropriate and the precision with which you are able to define them will depend upon how long your community has been involved in tourism and tourism planning. In the early stages of tourism development, goals may involve establishing organizational structures and collecting information to better identify the tourism system in the community. Later, more precise objectives can be formulated and more specific development and marketing strategies evaluated.

Step Two: Identifying Your Tourism System When planning for any type of activity, it is important to first define its scope and characteristics. Be clear about exactly what your plan encompasses. A good initial question is, "What do you mean by tourism?" Tourism is defined in many ways. Generally, tourism involves people travelling outside of their community for pleasure. Definitions differ on the specifics of how far people must travel, whether or not they must stay overnight, for how long, and what exactly is included under travelling for "pleasure". Do you want your tourism plan to include day visitors, conventioneers, business travellers, people visiting friends and relatives, people passing through, or seasonal residents?

Which community resources and organizations serve tourists or could serve tourists? Generally, tourists share community resources with local residents and businesses. Many organizations serve both tourists and locals. This complicates tourism planning and argues for a clear idea of what your tourism plan entails. You can begin to clarify the tourism system by breaking it down into three subsystems:

(1) tourism resources,

(2) tourism organizations, and

(3) tourism markets.

An initial task in developing a tourism plan is to identify, inventory, and classify the objects within each of these subsystems.

Tourism Resources are any (1) natural, (2) cultural, (3) human, or (4) capital resources that either are used or can be used to attract or serve tourists. A tourism resource inventory identifies and classifies the resources available that provide opportunities for tourism development. Conduct an objective and realistic assessment of the quality and quantity of resources you have to work with.

Tourism Organizations combine resources in various proportions to provide products and services for the tourist. It is important to recognize the diverse array of public and private organizations involved with tourism.

The most difficult part of tourism planning is to get these groups to work toward common goals.

You should develop a list of these organizations within your own community and obtain their input and cooperation in your tourism planning efforts. Setting up appropriate communication systems and institutional arrangements is a key part of community tourism planning.

Natural Resources

* Climate-seasons.
* Water resources-lakes, streams, waterfalls.
* Flora-forests, flowers, shrubs, wild edibles.
* Fauna-fish & wildlife.
* Geological resources-topography, soils, sand dunes, beaches, caves, rocks & minerals, fossils.
* Scenery-combinations of all of the above.

Cultural Resources

* Historic buildings, sites.

* Monuments, shrines.
* Cuisine.
* Ethnic cultures.
* Industry, government, religion, etc.
* Anthropological resources.
* Local celebrities.

Human Resources

* Hospitality skills.
* Management skills.
* Seasonal labour force.
* Performing artists-music, drama, art, storytellers.
* Craftsman and artisans.
* Other labour skills from chefs to lawyers to researchers.
* Local populations.

Capital

* Availability of capital, financing.
* Infrastructure-transportation roads, airports, railroads, harbours & marinas, trails & walkways.
* Infrastructure: utilities water, power, waste treatment, communications.

Tourism Management Organizations and Services

Off-Site: Coordination, planning, technical assistance, research, regulation:

* Federal & state departments of commerce, transportation, & natural resources.
* Federal, state, regional, & local tourism associations.
* Educational organizations & consultants, e.g., Travel & Tourism Research Association; U.S. Travel Data Centre; Travel Reference Centre, Univ. of Colorado, Boulder; Travel, Tourism, & Recreation Resource Centre, Michigan State University.
* Travel information & reservation services On-Site: development, promotion and management, of tourism resources:

- Federal agencies, NB. departments of commerce, transportation, & land management agencies.
- State agencies, NB. departments of commerce, transportation, & land/facility management agencies.
- Local government organizations, e.g., visitor information, chamber of commerce, convention & visitor's bureaus, parks.

* Businesses: Accommodations: Hotels, motels, Lodges, resorts, bed & breakfast cabins & cottages, Condominiums, second homes, Campgrounds-Food & Beverage: Restaurants, Grocery, Bars, nightclubs.

Fast Food, Catering Services

- Transportation: Air, rail, bus; Local transportation: taxi, limo, Auto, bicycle, boat rental; Local tour services.
- Information: Travel agencies, Information and reservation services, Automobile clubs.
- Recreation Facilities & Services: Winter sports: ski, skating, snow mobile areas; Golf courses, miniature golf; Swimming pools, water slides, beaches; tennis, handball, racquetball courts, bowling alleys; Athletic clubs, health spas; Marinas, boat rentals and charters; hunting & fishing guides; Horseback enterprises; Sporting goods sales & rentals.
- Entertainment: Nightclubs, amusement parks, spectator sport facilities; Gambling facilities: casinos, horse racing, bingo; video arcades; art galleries and studios, craft shops, studios, demonstrations; performing arts: theatre, dance, music, film; historic & prehistoric sites; museums: art, history, science, technology; arboreta, zoos, nature centres.
- Special festivals and events-Support services: Auto repair, gasoline service stations; boat & recreation vehicle dealers and service; retail shops: sporting goods, specialties, souvenirs, clothing; health services: hospitals, clinics, pharmacies; laundry and dry cleaning; beauty & barber shops; baby-sitting services; pet care; communications: newspaper, telephone; banking and financial services.

Tourism Markets: Tourists make-up the third, and perhaps most important subsystem. Successful tourism programs require a strong market orientation.

The needs and wants of the tourists you choose to attract and serve must be the focus of much of your marketing and development activity.

Therefore, it is important to clearly understand which tourism market segments you wish to attract and serve. Tourists fall into a very diverse set of categories with quite distinct needs and wants. You should identify the different types of tourists, or market segments that you presently serve or would like to serve.

This may involve one or more tourism market surveys. A visitor survey identifies the size and nature of the existing market and asks the following questions:

* What are the primary market segments you presently attract?
* Where do they come from?
* What local businesses and facilities do they use?
* What attracted them to the community?
* How did they find out about your community?
* How satisfied are they with your offerings?

A market survey (usually a telephone survey) also can be conducted among households in regions from which you wish to attract tourists. This type of study helps identify potential markets, and means of attracting tourists to your area.

Tourism Market Segments

In a general tourism plan, some clear target tourism market segments should be identified. You might begin by defining the market area from which you will draw most of your visitors. The size of your market area depends upon the uniqueness and quality of your "product", transportation systems, tastes and preferences of surrounding populations, and your competition.

Identifying the market area will help target information and promotion and define transportation routes and modes, competition, and characteristics of your market. Next, divide your travel market into the following trip length categories:

* day trips from a 50 mile radius,
* day trips from 50 to 200 miles away,
* pass-through travellers,

* overnight trips of 1 or 2 nights (most likely weekends), and
* extended overnight vacation trips.

After you have an idea of your market area and kinds of trips you will be serving, begin defining more specific market segments like vehicle campers, downhill skiers, sightseers, family vacationers, single weekenders, and the like. These segments can be more clearly tied to particular resources, businesses, and facilities in your community.

What kinds of products and services are likely to attract each of these groups? Tourist needs as well as their impact on the local community are quite different for day tourists versus overnight tourists. Areas catering primarily to weekend traffic will experience large fluctuations in use. In deciding the relative importance of these different segments, communities need to assess both their ability to provide required services (do you have enough rooms?), as well as the demand for different types of trips relative to the supply and your competition.

The Environment: A tourism plan is significantly affected by many factors in the broader environment. Indeed, one of the complexities of tourism planning is the number of variables that are outside of the control of an individual tourism business or community. These include such things as tourism offerings and prices at competing destinations, federal and state policy and legislation, currency exchange rates, the state of the economy, and weather. These factors are discussed more fully in Extension bulletin E-1959 as part of the market environment analysis.

Local populations also must be considered in tourism planning. As they compete with tourists for resources, they can be significantly affected by tourism activity, and they are an important source of support in getting tourism plans implemented. A survey of local residents can be conducted to assess community attitudes toward tourism development, identify impacts of tourism on the community, and obtain local input into tourism plans.

Public hearings, workshops, and advisory boards are other ways to obtain public involvement in tourism planning.

Local support and cooperation is important to the success of tourism programs and should not be overlooked.

Tourism Market Segments

I. Geographic market areas.

II. Trip categories.

Day Trips:

* short-within 50 miles.
* long-up to 200 miles.

Pass through traffic:

* day visitors.
* overnight stays.

Overnight Trips:

* weekend.
* vacation.

III. Activity or trip purpose Outdoor Recreation:

* Water-based Activity:
  - Boating: sail, power, cruise, row, canoe, water ski.
  - Swimming: pool, beach, sunbathing, scuba.
  - Fishing: charter, sport, from pier, boat, shore, ice.
* Land-based Activity:
  - Camping: back packing, primitive, developed.
  - Hiking: climbing, beachcombing, spelunking.
  - Hunting.
  - Skiing: downhill, cross country.
  - Snowmobiling.
  - Bicycling.
  - Horseback riding.
  - Picnicking.
* Air-based Activity:
  - Aeroplane rides, hang gliding, ballooning, parachuting.
* General:
  - Nature study.
  - Photography or landscape painting.
  - Viewing natural scenery.

Sightseeing & Entertainment:

* Visiting particular sites or areas:
  - historic or prehistoric.
  - cultural.
  - amusements.
  - scenic.
* Attending particular events, shows, or demonstrations:
  - ethnic festivals.
  - sporting events.
  - performances.
  - agricultural fair or festival.
  - boat show.
  - shopping.

Other Primary Purpose for Trip:

* Visiting Friends & Relatives.
* Convention & Business/Pleasure.

Step Three: Generating Alternatives. Generating alternative development and marketing options to meet your goals requires some creative thinking and brainstorming. The errors made at this stage are usually thinking too narrowly or screening out alternatives prematurely. It is wise to solicit a wide range of options from a diverse group of people. If tourism expertise is lacking in your community, seek help and advice outside the community. Tourism planning involves a wide range of interrelated development and marketing decisions. The following development questions will get you started:

* How much importance should be assigned to tourism within a community or region?
* Which general community goals is tourism development designed to serve?
* Which organization(s) will provide the leadership and coordination necessary for community tourism planning?

What are the relative roles of public and private sectors? Tourism marketing decision questions include:

* *Segments:* Which market segments should be pursued; geographic markets, trip types, activity or demographic subgroups?

* *Product:* What kinds of tourism products and services should be provided? Who should provide what?
* *Place:* Where should tourism facilities be located?
* Promotion: What kinds of promotion should be used, by whom, in which media, how much, when? What community tourism theme or image should be established?
* *Price:* What prices should be charged for which products and services. Who should capture the revenue?

Step Four: Evaluating Alternatives. Tourism development and marketing options are evaluated by assessing the degree to which each option will be able to meet the stated goals and objectives. There are usually two parts to a systematic evaluation of tourism development and marketing alternatives: (1) Feasibility analysis, and (2) Impact assessment.

These two tasks are interrelated, but think of them as trying to answer two basic questions: (1) Can it be done?, and (2) What are the consequences? A decision to take a specific action must be based both on feasibility and desirability.

***Feasibility Analysis*:** First, screen alternatives and eliminate those that are not feasible due to economic, environmental, political, legal, or other factors. Evaluate the remaining set of alternatives in more detail, paying particular attention to the market potential and financial plan. Make a realistic assessment of your community's ability to attract and serve a market segment or segments. This requires a clear understanding of the tourism market in your area and how this market is changing. Also carefully identify your competition and evaluate your advantages and disadvantages compared to the competition.

Plan toward the future because it takes time to implement decisions and for your actions to take effect. Therefore, look at the likely market and competition for several years to come. Review forecasts for the travel market in your area, if available. Careful tracking of tourism trends in your own community can help identify changes in the market that you will have to adapt to.

***Impact Assessment*:** When evaluating alternative development and marketing strategies it is important to understand the impacts, both positive and negative, of proposed actions. A classification of economic, environmental, and social impacts associated with tourism development. The types of impacts and their importance vary across different communities and proposed actions. Generally, the size, extent, and nature of tourism impacts depend upon:

* volume of tourist activity relative to local activity.
* length and nature of tourist contacts with the community.
* degree of concentration/dispersal of tourist activity in the area.
* similarities or differences between local populations and tourists.
* stability/sensitivity of local economy, environment, and social structure.
* how well tourism is planned, controlled, and managed.

Look at both the benefits and costs of any proposed actions. While tourism development can increase income, revenues, and employment, it also involves costs. Evaluate benefits and costs of tourism development from the perspectives of local government, businesses, and residents.

Impacts of Tourism

Economic Impacts:

* Sales, revenue, and income.
* Employment.
* Fiscal impact-taxes, infrastructure costs.
* Prices.
* Economic base & structure.

Environmental Impacts:

* Lands.
* Waters.
* Air.
* Infrastructure.
* Flora & fauna.

Social Impacts:

* Population structure & distribution.
* Values & attitudes.
* Education.
* Occupations.

* Safety & security.
* Congestion & crowding.
* Community spirit & cohesion.
* Quality of life.

Impacts on Local Government Local government provides most of the infrastructure and many of the services essential to tourism development, including highways, public parks, law enforcement, water and sewer, garbage collection and disposal. Evaluate tourism decisions with a clear understanding of the capacity of the local infrastructure and services relative to anticipated needs, and take into account both the needs of local populations and tourists.

A fiscal impact analysis evaluates the impact of tourism on the community's tax base and local government costs. It entails predicting the additional infrastructure and service requirements of tourism development, estimating their costs, deciding who will pay for/provide them, and how. Will tourism generate increased local government revenue through fees and charges, local sales or use taxes, increased property values or property tax rates, or larger local shares of federal and state tax revenues?

Impacts on Business and Industry Businesses that are directly serving tourists benefit from sales to tourists. Through secondary impacts, tourism activity also benefits a wide range of businesses in a community. For example, a local textile industry may sell to a linen supply firm that serves hotels and motels catering primarily to tourists. A local forest products industry sells to a lumberyard where local woodcarvers or furniture makers buy their supplies. They in turn sell to tourists through various retail outlets. All of these businesses benefit from tourism. If most products and services for tourists are bought outside of the local area, much of the tourist spending "leaks" out of the local economy. The more a community is "self-sufficient" in serving tourists, the larger the local impact.

Impacts on Residents

Local residents may experience a broad range of both positive and negative impacts from tourism development.

Tourism development may provide increased employment and income for the community. Although tourism jobs are primarily in the service sectors and are often seasonal, part time, and low-paying, these characteristics, are neither universal nor always undesirable. Residents may value opportunities for part time and seasonal work. In particular, employment opportunities and work experiences for students or retirees may be desired. Residents may also benefit from local services that otherwise would not be available. Tourism development may mean a wider variety of retailers and restaurants, or a better community library. It may also mean more traffic, higher prices, and increases in property values and local taxes. The general quality of the environment and life in the community may go up or down due to tourism development. This depends on the nature of tourism development, the preferences and desires of local residents, and how well tourism is planned and managed.

Steps Five and Six

Implementation, and Monitoring and Evaluation. We will not attempt a complete discussion of decisionmaking, plan implementation, and monitoring, but these are critical steps in the success of a tourism plan. A set of specific actions should be prescribed with clearly defined responsibilities and timetables. Monitor progress in implementing the plan and evaluate the success of the plan in meeting its goals and objectives on a regular basis. Plans generally need to be adjusted over time due to changing goals, changing market conditions, and unanticipated impacts. It is a good idea to build monitoring and evaluation systems into your planning efforts.

Concluding Remarks

Successful tourism planning and development means serving both tourists and local residents. The bulletins in this series stress the importance of a market orientation for attracting and serving tourists. This market orientation must be balanced with a clear view of how tourism serves the broader community interest and an understanding of the positive and negative impacts of tourism development. Remember, tourism should serve the community first and the tourist second. Tourism development must be compatible with other activities in the area and be supported by the local population. Therefore, the tourism plan should be closely coordinated with other local and regional planning efforts, if not an integral part of them.

2

Economic Development of Tourism

Time is a valuable commodity for today's travellers. Dual-income families find it difficult to schedule vacation time; family members often have jobs or activities that conflict; or an individual's job makes long vacations impractical. As a result, more families and individuals are taking long weekend or holiday vacations, or extending business trips into short getaway vacations. Packaging is a popular technique used for attracting these customers, because packages make travel easier and more convenient. In the hospitality and tourism industry, "packaging" is the process of combining two or more related and complementary offerings into a single-price offering. A package may include a wide variety of services such as lodging, meals, entrance fees to attractions, entertainment, transportation costs (air, auto, train, cab or bus), guide services, or other similar activities. Packaging can also create a variety of benefits for participating businesses. This publication will: Identify reasons for the increased popularity of packaging. Address issues a business should consider when developing a package. Describe the components of successful packages. Discuss the process of pricing a package.

Why Packages are Popular

Travel packages have become increasingly popular over the years. They are attractive because they benefit both the customer and participating businesses; packaging provides convenience and value to the customer, and added revenue for participating businesses.

Items to Consider in Developing a Package

Before developing a tourism packaging program, the business should devise a marketing plan through practical marketing research. The business owner should ask him/herself the following questions: Are you willing to do market research to determine who your customers are and what they want? What are the potential attractions, businesses, or marketing service firms that could provide a part of the package? Meet with the managers of these businesses and public attractions to discuss their interests and ideas. What are potential marketing and promotional networks that will help spread the word about your product?

Convention and visitors bureaus, chambers of commerce, retail travel agents, clubs and organizations, state offices of tourism, and other attractions or travel businesses all have the potential to play an important role in merchandising your package. Will the physical appearance and service skills of your business match the target audience? Does your business have the ability to manage and service the customers you generate through your packaging program? Are you prepared for a risk? Because you will be including customer service activities that are not under your direct control, you will be required to develop formal, written agreements between the cooperating businesses.

Benefits to the Customer

Packaging can be an effective marketing tool to provide several customer benefits. These may include: Ability to budget for trips. Packages include most of the components a customer must pay for during a trip. The customer pays at one time and has a good idea of the trip's total cost. Increased convenience. Trips can be time consuming and difficult to arrange. Several telephone calls and letters may be required to arrange for tickets, accommodations, reservations, and other components of a trip. A package allows a customer to arrange many components of a trip with one call or letter and one payment, saving the customer time and aggravation.

Greater economy. Businesses that package can frequently purchase tickets, meals, and other package components at wholesale prices. The business can add in the cost of packaging and still provide a competitive price to the customer. Thus, the cost to the customer is usually more economical than purchasing the package components individually. Popular programs and activities. Visitors and travellers are often unfamiliar with many of the activities and attractions in an area: a package can help customers find them easily.

Specialized interests. Packaging provides a unique opportunity to design components of a package for specialized interests. These so-called "benefit bundles" can include a package component not readily available to individual customers. For example, a package weekend may feature a cooking demonstration by a well-known chef or a lecture by a well-known author. Benefits to Participating Businesses Packaging can be used by businesses to help improve profitability and build customer volume. Examples include:

Improved profitability. During peak or high-demand periods, use packaging to add value to an existing product. Purchasers may be required to stay a prescribed period or purchase a combination of goods and services. Packaging may also allow a business to price its product at a premium by adding special goods and services. Smooth business patterns. Use packaging during low demand periods to add attractive features to the business's service or product, thus generating additional business. Other businesses may also be willing, to discount their services during this time. Adding these services to the existing product mix may generate new business.

Joint marketing opportunities. Packaging can allow the business to reduce marketing costs or start a new program one could not normally afford by joining with one or more businesses to conduct a marketing or advertising program. This strategy can be especially effective if the businesses involved have similar customers. Improved target marketing. Packaging can be an effective tool to tailor tourism and travel products for specific target markets. Examples can be ski, sports, or theatre weekends. Good market research is needed so an appropriate mix of tourism and travel services will meet the needs and desires of a target group of customers.

Greater holiday weekend business. Packaging can be used to highlight special holiday weekends by developing services appropriate to the theme of the weekend. New Year's, Valentine's Day, or Mother's Day are just a few of the holidays that can be used to develop special programs for parties, couples, or family gifts. Unique recurring events. Businesses can create their own events that can occur throughout the year. Events could be tournaments such as chess or bridge or crime re-enactments that let guests do the detective work. Events of this type will require imagination and inventiveness to take advantage of the wide variety of activities that take place in the community. This technique is often called "programming."

Redirected traffic to lesser-known attractions. Directing visitors to often overlooked attractions can help in two ways: heavily visited attractions may be offered some relief, while newly discovered attractions may thrive and prosper. Businesses can use many different strategies in designing a package product. Success will depend on good market research, an understanding of existing customers, research, an understanding of existing customers, and a good knowledge of the community and its activities.

Pricing a Package

Lodging or transportation—the most expensive parts of a package product-are usually the first contact points for customers who purchase a packaged vacation or travel product. Lodging operations or travel agents are usually the key to organizing a packaging program, even though an area's attractions may bring visitors to a community. Although accommodations and transportation are the basic ingredients of a package, tickets to attractions, dining, and other services are other key parts of the product mix that make the package marketable. It is necessary for a business to understand its target market and conduct basic practical market research in order to develop a successful package. Experimenting with a set of packages can also help you identify which sets of activities are most attractive to your customers.

Issues to consider when pricing a package include: The package must be a good value and competitive in the market. Customers should not be able to purchase separate items in the package for less than the package price. A large user of package components should be able to receive discounts from businesses that provide them. Evaluate the role packaging can play in the business's marketing program. While packaging can be used to implement many different strategies, the basic intent is to generate additional business. Determine if the package is feasible by applying a break-even analysis to help determine how many packages a business must sell before earning a profit.

Break-Even Analysis

Break-even analysis is a tool used to determine total sales needed to recoup costs, hence the name "break-even." This analysis technique can also be used to evaluate alternative pricing levels.

Elements of a Successful Package

Putting together a successful package is not easy. However, by following the suggestions listed below, the chances of success will be greater. Include attractions or demand generators. Every package needs one or more core attractions. These could be tickets to a special event, specialized programming, or reduced prices. Provide value to the customer. Many travellers buy packages because they perceive they will receive greater value for the travel dollars they spend. For some, this translates into a package that costs less than the sum of the regular prices of individual elements. Almost everybody is interested in getting something for nothing or next to nothing. Be well planned and coordinated. A successful package must be well planned and coordinated. Each element should flow naturally from one to the next. Use a theme to hold the package together and create a positive experience for the tourist.

Offer consistent quality and compatibility among elements. Many customers buy packages because they expect consistency in quality. Combine only package components that are compatible and enhance the overall quality of the traveller's experience. Customer dissatisfaction with one part of the package will often spoil the entire experience. Provide a distinctive customer benefit. The best packages provide customers something they would not get if they purchased package elements separately. Sometimes this benefit is the offer of value, but in other cases, it is a component that is not readily available to individual customers.

This might involve incorporating special lectures or appearances, unique dining experiences, or other activities. Cover all the details. The temptation might be to throw a package together, but the close attention to detail makes some packages more successful than others. Remember, it is often the little things a business does for guests that matter the most. Some things to consider include a policy on refunds and cancellations and complete information on all package elements included in the price, as well as items not included. Generate a profit. Clearly, packages offer a unique way to satisfy traveller needs and wants. Of course, the package should also be designed to generate a profit. The ideal time to offer packages is when demand is low and when the package will not displace customers who may generate higher revenues.

Tourism Contribution to Economic Conservation

The main positive economic impacts of tourism relate to foreign exchange earnings, contributions to government revenues, and generation of employment and business opportunities. These are discussed briefly here; further information on economic contributions from tourism can be found at the World Travel & Tourism Council's home page.

Foreign Exchange Earnings

Tourism expenditures and the export and import of related goods and services generate income to the host economy and can stimulate the investment necessary to finance growth in other economic sectors. Some countries seek to accelerate this growth by requiring visitors to bring in a certain amount of foreign currency for each day of their stay and do not allow them to take it out of the country again at the end of the trip.

An important indicator of the role of international tourism is its generation of foreign exchange earnings. Tourism is one of the top five export categories for as many as 83% of countries and is a main source of foreign exchange earnings for at least 38% of countries.

Contribution to Government Revenues

Government revenues from the tourism sector can be categorized as direct and indirect contributions. Direct contributions are generated by taxes on incomes from tourism employment and tourism businesses, and by direct levies on tourists such as departure taxes. Indirect contributions are those originated from taxes and duties levied on goods and services supplied to tourists.

The United States National Park Service estimates that the 273 million visits to American national parks in 1993 generated direct and indirect expenditures of US$ 10 billion and 200,000 jobs. When visits to land managed by other agencies, and to state, local, and privately-managed parks, are added, parks were estimated to bring around US$ 22 billion annually to the US economy. These expenditures also generate significant tax revenues for the government. The World Travel and Tourism Council estimates that travel and tourism's direct, indirect, and personal tax contribution worldwide was over US$ 800 billion in 1998-a.

Employment Generation

The rapid expansion of international tourism has led to significant employment creation. For example, the hotel accommodation sector alone provided around 11.3 million jobs worldwide in 1995. Tourism can generate jobs directly through hotels, restaurants, nightclubs, taxis, and souvenir sales, and indirectly through the supply of goods and services needed by tourism-related businesses. According to the WTO, tourism supports some 7% of the world's workers.

Stimulation of Infrastructure Investment

Tourism can induce the local government to make infrastructure improvements such as better water and sewage systems, roads, electricity, telephone and public transport networks, all of which can improve the quality of life for residents as well as facilitate tourism.

Contribution to Local Economies

Tourism can be a significant, even essential, part of the local economy. As the environment is a basic component of the tourism industry's assets, tourism revenues are often used to measure the economic value of protected areas.

For example, Dorrigo National Park in New South Wales, Australia, has been estimated to contribute 7% of gross regional output and 8.4% of regional employment. The importance of tourism to local economies can also be illustrated by the impacts when it is disrupted: the catastrophic 1997 floods that closed Yosemite National Park in California cause locally severe economic losses to the areas around the park. In the most heavily impacted county, Mariposa County, 1997 personal income was reduced by an estimated US$1,159 per capita (US$18 million for the entire county)-a 6.6% decline. The county was also estimated to have lost US$1.67 million in county occupancy and sales tax revenues, and 956 jobs, a significant number in a county of fewer than 16,000 residents.

There are other local revenues that are not easily quantified, as not all tourist expenditures are formally registered in the macroeconomic statistics. Money is earned from tourism through informal employment such as street vendors, informal guides, rickshaw drivers, etc. The positive side of informal or unreported employment is that the money is returned to the local economy, and has a great multiplier effect as it is spent over and over again. The World Travel and Tourism Council estimates that tourism generates an indirect contribution equal to 100% of direct tourism expenditures.

The Economic Impacts of Ecotourism

There are two related, but distinct, economic concepts in Ecotourism: economic impact and economic value. This issues paper focusses on economic impact, which refers to the change in sales, income, jobs, or other parameter generated by Ecotourism. A common Ecotourism goal is the generation of economic benefits, whether they be profits for companies, jobs for communities, or revenues for parks. Ecotourism plays a particularly important role because it can create jobs in remote regions that historically have benefited less from economic development programs than have more populous areas. Even a small number of jobs may be significant in communities where populations are low and alternatives are few. This economic impact can increase political and financial support for conservation.

Protected areas, and nature conservation generally, provide many benefits to society, including preservation of biodiversity, maintenance of watersheds, and so on. Unfortunately, many of these benefits are intangible. However, the benefits associated with recreation and tourism in protected areas tend to be tangible. For example, divers at a marine park spend money on lodging, food, and other goods and services, thereby providing employment for local and nonlocal residents. These positive economic impacts can lead to increased support for the protected areas with which they are associated. This is one reason why Ecotourism has been embraced as a means for enhancing conservation of natural resources. Several studies in Australia and elsewhere have assessed the economic impacts of Ecotourism.

Predictably, the level of benefits varies widely as a result of differences in the quality of the attraction, access, and so on. In some cases, the number of jobs created will be low, but in rural areas even a few jobs can make a big difference. Still, Ecotourism benefits should not be oversold, or there may be a backlash as reality fails to live up to expectations. The impacts of Ecotourism, or any economic activity, can be grouped into three categories: direct, indirect, and induced. Direct impacts are those arising from the initial tourism spending, such as money spent at a restaurant. The restaurant buys goods and services (inputs) from other businesses, thereby generating indirect impacts. In addition, the restaurant employees spend part of their wages to buy various goods and services, thereby generating induced impacts. Of course, if the restaurant purchases the goods and services from outside the region of interest, then the money provides no indirect impact to the region — it leaks away. By identifying the leakages, or conversely the linkages within the economy, the indirect and induced impacts of tourism can be estimated.

In addition, this information can be used to identify what goods are needed but are not being produced in the region, how much demand there is for such goods, and what the likely benefits of local production would be. This enables policy makers to determine priorities for developing inputs for use by the tourism or other industries. How, then, are these direct, indirect, and induced impacts to be estimated? For small areas with non-diverse economies, there are relatively few indirect and induced impacts, and there are relatively little data available for modelling these impacts. Therefore, surveys of visitors, residents, and/or businesses often are used to identify tourism's direct impacts. For larger areas, such as states or countries, economists have developed various techniques for estimating indirect and induced impacts, including computable general equilibrium (CGE) and input-output (IO) analysis.

Negative Economic Impacts of Tourism

There are many hidden costs to tourism, which can have unfavourable economic effects on the host community. Often rich countries are better able to profit from tourism than poor ones. Whereas the least developed countries have the most urgent need for income, employment and general rise of the standard of living by means of tourism, they are least able to realize these benefits. Among the reasons for this are large-scale transfer of tourism revenues out of the host country and exclusion of local businesses and products.

Leakage

The direct income for an area is the amount of tourist expenditure that remains locally after taxes, profits, and wages are paid outside the area and after imports are purchased; these subtracted amounts are called leakage. In most all-inclusive package tours, about 80% of travellers' expenditures go to the airlines, hotels and other international companies (who often have their headquarters in the travellers' home countries), and not to local businesses or workers. In addition, significant amounts of income actually retained at destination level can leave again through leakage. A study of tourism 'leakage' in Thailand estimated that 70% of all money spent by tourists ended up leaving Thailand (via foreign-owned tour operators, airlines, hotels, imported drinks and food, etc.). Estimates for other Third World countries range from 80% in the Caribbean to 40% in India.

Source: Sustainable Living

Of each US$ 100 spent on a vacation tour by a tourist from a developed country, only around US$ 5 actually stays in a developing-country destination's economy.

There are two main ways that leakage occurs: Import Leakage: This commonly occurs when tourists demand standards of equipment, food, and other products that the host country cannot supply. Especially in less-developed countries, food and drinks must often be imported, since local products are not up to the hotel's (i.e. tourist's) standards or the country simply doesn't have a supplying industry. Much of the income from tourism expenditures leaves the country again to pay for these imports.

The average import-related leakage for most developing

countries today is between 40% and 50% of gross tourism earnings for small economies and between 10% and 20% for most advanced and diversified economies, according to UNCTAD. Even in developed regions, local producers are often unable to supply the tourism industry appropriately even if good will is present: the 64-room hotel "Kaiser im Tyrol" in Austria, an award-winning leader in sustainable practices, cannot find organic food suppliers in the local farming networks in the appropriate quantity, quality and reliability, as production cycles and processes are not compatible with its needs.

Source: Austrian Preparatory Conference for the International Year of Ecotourism, September 2001 Export leakage Multinational corporations and large foreign businesses have a substantial share in the import leakage. Often, especially in poor developing destinations, they are the only ones that possess the necessary capital to invest in the construction of tourism infrastructure and facilities. As a consequence of this, an export leakage arises when overseas investors who finance the resorts and hotels take their profits back to their country of origin.

A 1996 UN report evaluating the contribution of tourism to national income, gross levels of incomes or gross foreign exchange, found that net earnings of tourism, after deductions were made for all necessary foreign exchange expenditures, were much more significant for the industry. This report found significant leakage associated with: (a) imports of materials and equipment for construction; (b) imports of consumer goods, particularly food and drinks; (c) repatriation of profits earned by foreign investors; (d) overseas promotional expenditures and (e) amortization of external debt incurred in the development of hotels and resorts.

The impact of the leakage varied greatly across countries, depending on the structure of the economy and the tourism industry. From the data presented in this study on the Caribbean, St. Lucia had a foreign exchange leakage rate of 56% from its gross tourism receipts, Aruba had 41%, Antigua and Barbuda 25% and Jamaica 40%.

Source: Caribbean Voice

Enclave Tourism: Local businesses often see their chances to earn income from tourists severely reduced by the creation of "all-inclusive" vacation packages. When tourists remain for their entire stay at the same cruise ship or resort, which provides everything they need and where they will make all their expenditures, not much opportunity is left for local people to profit from tourism.

The Organization of American States (OAS) carried out a survey of Jamaica's tourist industry that looked at the role of the all-inclusives compared to other types of accommodation. It found that 'All-inclusive hotels generate the largest amount of revenue but their impact on the economy is smaller per dollar of revenue than other accommodation subsectors.'

It also concluded that all-inclusives imported more, and employed fewer people per dollar of revenue than other hotels. This information confirms the concern of those who have argued that all-inclusives have a smaller trickle-down effect on local economies.

The cruise ship industry provides another example of economic enclave tourism. Non-river cruises carried some 8.7 million international passengers in 1999. On many ships, especially in the Caribbean (the world's most popular cruise destination with 44.5% of cruise passengers), guests are encouraged to spend most of their time and money on board, and opportunities to spend in some ports are closely managed and restricted.

3

Managing Tourism Services

There is an interrelationship between the nature or characteristics of the tourism services and the marketing mix. Hence, there is a need to take into consideration the 7 key issues while determining the criteria of the Marketing Mix (4 Ps).

The Marketing Mix

The most important factor is consumer perception of price

- o Consumer may choose not to buy when offering is perceived to be of lesser value than the asking price. Hence, bookings or visits will decline.
- o If price is low in relation to value offered, then demand will be difficult to manage and revenue loss could be substantial.

The marketer's task is to maintain a balance between; Value Perceived (Quality) & Price.

Price and Demand

- o Price has little to do with cost, and far more to do with what customer arc prepared to pay for a product.
- o How well a changed in price affect a change in total demand— price elasticity of demand.
- o In a market where the product is unique, or without satisfactory substitute, or where-the product is manufactured by a company that enjoys a monopoly or near monopoly, price will be set high.
- o In setting the prices, the company will want to know what levels of demand it is likely to experience at different prices. For a new product this is hard to gauge. The

- two most common methods of assessing demand are:
- Asking potential customers what they would be willing to pay for service
- Test marketing the product at different prices in different regions.

How can price be used to control consumer demand?

- o Maximize access.
- o Restrict access.
- o Control demand in time.
- o Control demand in space.

Pricing Methods

Cost-plus Pricing

- o A standard mark-up is added to the cost of the product.
- o E.g. A bottle of wine that costs $14 may sell for $28, a 100% mark-up on cost.

Going Rate Pricing

- A strategy of going-rate pricing is the establishment of price based largely on those of competitors, with less attention paid to costs or demand.
- The firm might charge the same, more, or less than its major competitors. Some firm might charge a bit more or less, but they hold the amount of difference constant.

Skimming Pricing

- Price skimming is setting a high price when the market is price insensitive. (Higher-end market).
- To be used when:
  - o Highly differentiated product.
  - o Inelastic demand.
  - o Maximize shortrun profit when product has short life cycle or demand exceeds supply over a short time period.
  - o Premium product with added value.

Penetration Pricing

- o Companies set a low initial price to penetrate the market quickly and deeply, attracting many buyers and winning a large market share.

- o To be used when:
  - Little product differentiation.
  - Many competitive substitutes.
  - Inferior product.

Place

- o It is place that represents distribution of and access to the product.
- o In tourism industries, distribution systems are used to move the customer to the product: hotel, restaurant cruise ship or aeroplane.
- o Various distribution channels or intermediaries are used to market tourism services.
- o Distribution channels or Intermediaries are used to describe any dealer who acts as a link in the chain of distribution between the company and its customers.

Distribution Channel Functions

(1) *Information*-gathering and distributing marketing research and intelligence information about the marketing environment.

(2) *Promotion*-developing and spreading persuasive communication about an offer.

(3) *Contact*-finding and communicating with prospective buyers.

(4) *Matching*-shaping and fitting the offer to the buyers' needs.

(5) *Negotiation*-agreeing on price and other terms of the offer so that ownership or possession can be transferred.

(6) *Physical distribution*-transporting and storing goods.

(7) *Financing*-acquiring and using funds to cover the cost of channel work.

(8) *Risk taking*-assuming financial risks, such as the inability to sell inventory at full margin.

Why do companies choose to deal with intermediaries?

(1) It is cheaper for a company to deal through intermediaries

than to set up its own network of retail shops or sell its product directly in any other way By paying a commission or other agreed form of financial remuneration to their intermediaries, companies buy the use of distributive network.

(2) The system also acts as a convenience to consumers as they can choose from a range of different products under one roof, instead of having to visit each producer's shop in turn to select their product.

(3) Through their contact, experience and specialization, intermediaries normally offer more than a firm can on its own Managing, Monitoring and Modifying Channels Channel systems will require periodic review and modification to meet changing market needs. Organizations will need to review the success of their channel systems regularly and determine is all the participants are performing at an acceptable level. It may be necessary to:

- Either expand or reduce membership at various levels or drop some existing channel members who are no longer performing.
- Change direction or consider totally new ways of looking at the business.

This is happening as the interest in call centres grows and hotels are reviewing the need for hotel representatives where call centres might be able to achieve the same results more cost effectively. Similarly, major changes are taking place in computer reservations systems with every advance in technology.

Promotion

- o Is an aspect of general marketing that promotion management deals with explicitly.
- o It includes the practices of advertising, personal selling, sales promotion, publicity and point-of-purchase communications.

Why promotional activities are carried out?

All marketing communication efforts are directed at accomplishing one or more of the following objectives:

1. Build product category wants.
2. Create brand awareness.
3. Enhance attitudes and influence intentions.
4. Facilitate purchase.
5. Promotional Mix Strategies.

Most leisure and tourism organisations use a combination of promotional activities including:

1. *Advertising:* the paid-tor sponsorship of a message in a commercially available medium. The media (press, broadcast: television and radio, posters/billboards, cinema) task is essentially to choose and buy the most economical combination of advertising space and/or time to reach defined audiences sufficiently frequently and with sufficient impact to convey the agreed messages effectively.
2. *Sales Promotion:* Those marketing activities other than personal selling and advertising and publicity that stimulate purchasing and dealer effectiveness, such as displays, shows and exhibitions, demonstrations and various non-recurrent selling efforts not in ordinary routine. Sales Promotion can be targeted at consumers, the trade and the company.
3. *Public Relations:* PR in tourism is about how people who matter to a tourism organisation think about it and how their perceptions, attitudes and behaviour can be kept or made positive. *External PR* involves everything an organisation does that impinges on people's perceptions including: its products; its employees; its communication programmes and media coverage, its overall corporate identity; its financial reputation; its promotional activities; the buildings in which it transacts business – in short everything that contributes to the *image* of an organisation. *Internal PR* is used to build and maintain morale within an organisation through such things as good communication practices, incentive benefits, sportsman activity provision, etc.
4. *Direct Marketing:* Tourism organisations make heavy use of promotional materials mailed out or given away to customers or passed on to them by intermediaries

Photographs are a crucial element of mass tour brochures. Also, maps, a critical part in tourism promotion in generating interest in a destination. One of the most difficult things to achieve in brochures aimed at the mass market is competitive differentiation.

5. *Personal Selling:* An interpersonal process whereby the seller ascertains, activates and satisfies the needs and wants of the buyer so that both the seller and buyer benefits. It is a method of influencing the purchase. The selling sequence include prospecting and qualifying, planning and delivering sales presentations, overcoming objections and closing the sale.

Product

Problems in Managing Services

The effectiveness of planning the marketing mix depends as much on the ability to select the right target market as on the skill in devising a product which will generate high levels of satisfaction. Hence, the decision depends very much on the capability of the marketers to tackle the following issues concerning tourism services:

Intangible Nature of Business

Customer cannot physically evaluate or sample most services: they tend to rely on other people's experiences with these services Customers place great value on the advice of hospitality and travel experts, such as travel agents Implications:

- o Tourism marketers tend to 'tangibilize' the tourism offering in brochures and videos-visual displays of the real thing.
- o Marketers tend to generate positive "word-of-mouth" among the customers.

Variability in Production Methods

Quality control of services is neither as precise nor as easy to achieve because of the human factors that are involved in supplying them All staff members cannot consistently provide the same level of service as their colleagues

* Although standardised service is an admirable target that all organisations should try to achieve it is unrealistic.

* The same standardisation cannot be provided since the actions of service staff, other+customers and the customers themselves make the experience more variable.
* Hotels, restaurants, airlines, theme parks and travel agencies are some of the 'factories' in the business. Behaviour of one customer can ruin the service experience of others.
* Implications:
    - o Tourism marketer design processes to minimise differences in service encounters and provision between different outlets or between different shifts at a hotel. Example: Provision of uniforms and of similar physical surroundings illustrates evidence of standardisation.

Perishability

* Service is highly perishable-"like a running tap in a sink with no plug".
* An unoccupied seat on a train or bed in a guesthouse is lost forever.
* Services and the time available to experience them cannot be stored.
* Implications:
    - o The management task emphasises managing demand and capacity to a degree of time tuning. Example: Airlines offer stand by fares to those willing to fill unexpected empty seats at short notice.

Distribution Channels

There is no physical distribution system in tourism industry. Instead, there are many intermediaries in the hospitality and travel industry where the items are being purchased.

Cost Determination

Services are both variable and intangible. Some customers might require more attention than others.

Relationship of Services to Providers

* Some services are inseparable from the individuals who provide them.

* Example: Restaurant-whose chefs or owners have developed unique reputations for their food, personalities or both.
* Implications:
  - o Marketers attempt to devise delivery systems which ease interaction and invest in campaigns to educate staff and consumers as to how to get the best from the interaction.
  - o Training in hotels emphasises how staff can manage the interaction.

Target Marketing

- o In tourism industry, we need to acknowledge that not all individuals would want to buy from us.
- o ;e might not have the services that they may be looking for.
- o And hence, it is important to consider targeting the right market to ensure success of our business.
- o Marketing is about developing the right product/service to the right market/people so that they will be satisfied with what they receive.
- o Target marketing can be defined as:
  - Seller identifies market segments (groups), selects one or more and develops products and marketing mixes tailored to each selected segments.

Market Segmention

- o Involves dividing market into distinct groups of buyers who requires different products or marketing mixes.
- o There is no single way to segment a market
- o MaNor variables include.
  - (a) Geographic Segmentation divide market according to location e.g. nations, regions, states, countries, cities.
  - (b) Demographic Segmentation divide market into groups, based on demographic variables e.g. age, gender, family life cycle, income, occupation, education, religion, race/culture, nationality.
  - (c) psychographic Segmentation divide buyers into

(d) Behaviour Segmentation buyer is divided into groups, based on knowledge, attitude, usage rate, and response.

different groups, based on social class, lifestyle, and personality characteristics.

Refers to the buying behaviour of final customers (individuals and households) to buy goods and services for personal consumption MaNor factors influencing buying behaviour include.

E Ypxyvi Jegxsvw

Culture comprise of the basic values, perceptions, want and behaviour that a person learns continuously in a society Culture is expressed through tangible items such as food, buildings, clothing and art. e.g. the culture shift toward greater concern about health and fitness has resulted in many hotels adding exercise rooms/ health clubs. e.g. KFC, piazza and Burger King in Israel adapted their menus to make them kosher for Passover (.ewish) Subculture groups of population with shared value system base oncommon experiences and situations Social classesare relatively permanent and ordered divisions in a society whose members share similar values, interests and behaviours e.g. income, occupation, education, wealth Social classes show distinct product and brand preferences in such areas as food, travel and leisure activity. e.g. CE3, managers and directors organizations often indulge in golfing activities.

Reference Group

A personvs refer group consists of all the groups that have a direct/indirect influence on the personvs attitude/behaviour e.g. artist, idol Family Marketers have examined the role and influence of the husband, wife and children on the purchase of different products and services.

Roles and Status: A person position in each group can be defined in terms of role and status a role consists of the activities that a person is expected to perform each role carried a status e.g. pinna parents daughter Family wife/mother Company staff.

B9=ER DECISI32 4R3CESS

This model emphasizes that the buying process starts long before and continues long after the actual purchases It encourages marketer to focus on the entire buying process rather than Nust the purchasing decision.

Problem Recognition

The buying process starts when the buyer recognizes a problem or need.

The need can be triggered by internal and external stimuli. They should research customers to find out what kinds of needs/ problems, led them to purchase an items, what brought these needs about, and how they led consumers to choose a particular product. E.g. SPA Travel relaxation/need to get out of city life.

Information Search

1. The strength of drive.
2. The amount of initial information.
3. The ease of obtaining the information.
4. The value placed on additional information.
5. The satisfaction one gets from search.

Consumer can obtain information from several sources personal sources family, friends, neighbours, acquaintances Commercial sources z sales person, packaging, advertising, dealers, displays public sources z restaurant reviews, editorials in the travel section Therefore, a company must design its marketing mix to make prospects aware of and knowledgeable about the features and benefits of its products/brands.

E.g. TRA:E0 Fair

(1) promote in newspaper (create awareness).

(2) initial information (from newspaper or a call to travel agent).

(3) obtain information from internet, visit travel agents.

(4) value (are the information of high quality trustworthy).

(5) satisfaction (are consumers happy with the search).

Evaluation of Alternatives

- o This is the stage where consumer makes an assessment of the goods/services offered and is considering the alternatives.
- o The marketer must ensure that his product/service is on the list of alternatives.
- o The buyer must be convinced of its suitability before the buyer can proceed to the buying/purchase decision.

- o The product/service must be readily available to the consumer.

Purchase Decision

- o The buyer would have made a decision by now as to which product/service is suitable to fulfil his/her needs.
- o The ideal product would have all the attributes/ characteristics that the customer is looking for:
  - Then the decision to purchase is made, the product that is thought to be most suitable will be selected.
  - However, 2 factors can influence the purchase intention and the purchase decision.
    - (i) Attitudes of others (getting information from relatives/family members).
    - (ii) Unexpected situational factors (e.g. earthquakes, flood, SARS, effect of tsunami).

Post Purchase Behaviour

- o Feelings felt by the buyer towards the product offer that has been purchased.
- o To avoid post purchase dissonance, there must be no gap between the expectations of the buyer and the actual product performance.
- o The buyervs decision to buy the product again later will depend on the buyervs satisfaction with the product performance.

Paper on Community Travel and Tourism Marketing

Every community if affected by visitors. While many communities recognize opportunities for growth in the tourism industry, options at the local level expand when travellers are included. Travellers are people away from home temporarily. In collecting data, sometimes "more than miles away from home" further defines a traveller.

This travel may result from a variety of sources: a pleasure vacation, business and convention purposes, friends and relatives, special events and festivals, sport recreation, historic sites, specific attractions, or when people pass-through headed for another destination. The cash register doesn't sort out travel purchases this way, and in reality it is impractical to separate tourists from travellers. All visitors are important to the travel and tourism industry.

Minnesota is experiencing a boom in communities organizing to attract and host visitors as a way to diversify and boost economies. The impact of travel and tourism on the local economy goes beyond first level expenditures at food, lodging, gas, entertainment, and retail establishments. Travel spending brings in outside dollars that "turn over" in the community. Even if you do not have direct contact with travellers, the money filters through the entire economy as residents re-spend travel dollars. But the increased interest in tourism translates to fierce competition in the marketplace.

Key to gaining the attention of potential tourists is development of a community marketing, not a selling approach. Marketing is a continuous, coordinated set of activities associated with efficiently distributing products to high potential markets. It involves making decisions about product, price, promotion, and distribution. Marketing focuses on providing customer benefits and satisfying needs better than the competition. It is based on the principle that consumer buying resistance will be overcome if the product satisfies buyer needs.

In contrast, selling focuses on the product offered rather than satisfying customer needs. It assumes that the main thing necessary to sell the product is to overcome purchase resistance. A statement reflecting the selling approach is "we will attract tourists to Our City because we want tourists and everyone would want to visit. Selling is only a small part of marketing. The formal marketing process involves six steps:

- Analyse your current situation.
- Identify product(s).
- Select target market(s).
- Set objectives.
- Carry out promotion strategies.
- Evaluate results.

When the structure to support tourism is in place-1) attractions, 2) services and facilities, 3) an information/direction/interpretive system, and 4) transportation linkages-communities can move to market their unique tourist and travel experiences. This publication outlines one approach for preparing a marketing that describes how you will get visitors to stop, to stay, to tell others, and to return.

Analyse your Current Situation

What does your community have that travellers want? The first step in the marketing process is to conduct an inventory and analysis of the travel and tourism industry and its potential within your area. Tourism isn't just a community or collection of small businesses with an interest in attracting visitors. Tourism is an entire "region" organizing to draw and host travellers-it's an overall view with a wide angle lens. Analysis answers the question "what is?" As a basis for "what could be?" Ten crucial questions for a community to answer on a regular basis include:

1. What attractions exist that will entice people to stop and visit?
2. What hospitality services and facilities are available?
3. What experiences are visitors having in the community?
4. What promotion methods are used? How well do they work?
5. What are the current markets?
6. What is the competition for your community?
7. How is tourism related to the community lifestyle and goals?"
8. What roles do community organizations play in tourism development?
9. What are trends that affect the tourism industry?
10. What are the community strengths and weaknesses, problems and opportunities in serving visitors?

Attractions (Question 1)

Through fate or creativity, most communities have tourist attractions that draw visitors. A community's basic assets may include:

- Natural resources, or a scenic setting;
- Human-made attractions such as racetracks, museums, or resorts;

- Historical sites;
- Cultural and ethnic resources;
- Recreation opportunities;
- Special events and festivals;
- Availability of high quality personal services such as shopping, medical care and education; or
- Local industries and economic base.

Describe each attraction, including quality. How many of each type of attraction are there? Look forward and list potential visitor resources that could be enhanced or used more fully. The Minnesota Extension Service publication "So Community Wants Tourism" outlines the range of travel attractors that determine a community's capability to bring travellers.

As you develop a community tourism campaign, it is useful to separate "core" attractions that are a prime reason for travel, from secondary "supporting" attractions that enhance a visitor's experience once they are there. There are infinite reasons to visit Minneapolis and St. Paul, but Twin Cities Attractions Council is organized to promote the plus theatres, museums, special events, and other core attractions that draw large audiences. This distinction is useful when you are selecting an image for your marketing program. The Spicer area tourism committee has developed a four-tier list of tourism assets: most important (includes Green Lake, resorts, 2 hours to Twin Cities); important (Sibley State Park, fishing, golf course); significant (fall colours, hunting, July 4 celebration); and contributing (antique shops, sailing regattas, farm tours). Spicer's marketing theme reflects this ranking.

Hospitality Services (Question 2)

The economic impact of tourism largely comes from spending in the hospitality sector primarily composed of private commercial businesses. The U.S. Travel Data Centre estimates tourist dollar expenditures on a state wide basis by category (1985):

* Food $0.26,
* Public transportation.25,
* Auto transportation.17,
* Lodging.15,
* Entertainment & recreation.09,

* Retail and other.08,
* $1.00.

It is useful to have local or regional expenditure data to track the travel industry and develop public support for this economic sector. However, data collection requires a visitor survey, and study and questionnaire design are complex. Seek assistance from industry professionals in developing a data base that accurately represents spending patterns.

Good restaurants and sufficient overnight lodging capacity are essential. Describe the mix of establishments, their occupancy, and their services. For example, do motels have facilities for families such as pools and playgrounds, or are they positioned to attract business meetings where evening entertainment may be a factor in the decision to make reservations? Grocery stores, specialty retail shops, entertainment and service stations also support the visitor industry.

Questions about the adequacy of public services come into play. Transportation issues such as roadway congestion, parking and signing, restroom availability, and utilities (sewage and trash disposal) assume importance as the industry expands. Plans for a proposed megamall in the Twin include construction to widen roads in the area.

Tourism Today (Questions 3, 4, and 5)

The tourism experience your community promotes now, whether or accidental, is generally a good indicator for the future. It is often easier to modify and market a travel experience that has evolved over time and is built on local flavour, than Do introduce and develop a new form of tourism that does not match local culture, environment, and heritage. Mississippi Rivertown Rendezvous, an organization promoting the towns along the river corridor from Hastings to Winona, builds upon a common heritage and landscape.

Describe the visitor experience your community offers both in terms of tangibles: the resorts, the boating, the location, as well as the intangibles. Talk about customer benefits when you think about intangibles: rest and relaxation, friendliness, excitement. Then outline and valuate promotion strategies now in use to envision future options. Through survey or observation, determine who is buying your community's experience now. Customers who have visited (even though there may have been no major promotion campaign) are a good clue about the target market your community naturally appeals to.

Outside Influences (Questions 6 through 9)

Tourism marketing occurs within a competitive marketplace that goes well beyond the community boundaries. There are many forms of competition for your customers and their dollars-but neighbouring communities generally are not one of them. A number of strong travel-oriented communities, working together on regional promotion, results in a stronger destination image, a greater variety of attractions and facilities, wider market exposure, and a healthy degree of competition that spurs improvements. The Land of Legends group-a ring of communities within 60 miles of Itasca State Park could not promote itself as a major destination without the involvement of many Chambers of Commerce. This "critical mass" of diverse attractions and quality services also enables the Land of Legends area to attract and host "fam" (familiarization) tours for travel writers and tour brokers as part of an overall marketing program.

More important, there is competition for how consumers spend their discretionary dollar. The purchase of a VCR, buying a more expensive car, or saving for a college education means less money is available for leisure and travel. You also have to be concerned with other destination areas on a national level. Consumers have worldwide choices today; you must understand your competition and their strategies to market your competitive advantages.

In promoting certain visitor experiences, assess what type of tourism is compatible with local lifestyles. For example, many residents of northwestern Minnesota enjoy the hunting opportunities. They use the same resource nonlocal hunters use. Conflicts over resource use must be negotiated before hunting is promoted as a primary visitor attraction. In other areas, emphasis on scattered small town activities is more appropriate than major new construction and facility development. The latest brochure for Southeastern Minnesota Historic Bluff Country emphasizes small-scale tourism businesses such as canoe rental, locally made arts and crafts, bed and breakfasts, and a lefsa factory tour. It is a format designed to encourage travellers to wander and explore the area, rather than directing everyone to a few major sites. In addition, specify the roles various community organizations play in development and promotion, and understand social trends that influence your market position. React quickly when they occur. For example, the move toward shorter getaway mini-vacations is radically changing travel industry strategies.

Where are We Now? (Question 10)

Summarize findings on community attractions, services and facilities, the current travel industry and outside influences in a Written summary statement. Combine relevant in an outline of community strengths and weaknesses, problem opportunities for tourism. Spend sufficient time on this step: analysis is the basis for subsequent decisions about marketing your community's unique visitor experiences.

Identify Product

What is your community marketing? One main reason people travel is to experience a new and different environment. After the situation analysis, most communities find they are faced with multiple options for attracting tourists. The challenge is to choose one dominant identity among all these alternatives. You can not and should not promote all of the community attributes equally. In a tourism marketplace where consumers are faced with diverse choices, need an "edge" to set yourself apart from the competition. You need to create a unique product with a theme or identity that characterizes major promotion efforts. Red Lake Riverlands-Red Lake Falls, Thief River Falls, Crookston, East Grand Forks-features river uses like tubing and boat tours, and nearby food and lodging services. The thirteen Iron Trail United Communities capitalize on the unique mining characteristics and strong ethnic heritage of the Range. Iron world, with its train and festival series, Hill Annex Mine and Tower-Soudan State Park are the core attractions that support the mining theme. A region-wide visitor newspaper and radio information network are part of this cooperative marketing approach.

An example from the private sector is three ski resorts that offer the same hills, the same snow, and the same lift equipment. One business bills itself as a "mountain of hospitality," another is a family resort and the third sells serious, technical skiing.

A marketing theme is the one main idea or message you want to communicate. It should be based on satisfying visitor needs. Theme development requires creativity, and there are advertising agencies that specialize in "positioning" a product in the marketplace and developing a parallel marketing campaign. Consult the Minnesota Extension Service sheet "Creating a Tourism Promotional Theme.

Select Target Markets

Who will buy the product your community is marketing? One certain way to fail is to try to please everyone. A target market is a group of individuals sharing common characteristics, toward whom marketing efforts will be directed. The process of dividing the total market into high-potential target markets is called market segmentation and involves these steps:

- Identifying and describing the different segments that make up the total market;
- Evaluating the economic potential of each segment;
- Choosing one or more market segments on which to focus.

Current visitors are a good indication of target markets attracted to your community. New prospects are likely to have many of the same characteristics unless you are planning a product shift. Target markets can be defined by several factors: geography, demographics, and behaviour.

Geography refers to potential visitors: where they live and they travel. Negative travel time and positive attraction factors are recognized widely as the two main variables that determine what customers choose to see and where they choose to go. Travel time and distance can be negative factors for potential visitors, but the power of an area's tourist attractions may be a counteracting positive factor. A destination that offers a large variety of interesting attractions has more pull, at an equal distance, than a location that offers only one or a few low interest attractions. This doesn't cancel the fact that travel to and from an area is an important part of the total experience, as "pass-through" communities have discovered. Demographics refers to characteristics like age, sex, marital status, number and ages of children and life stage (young single adult or retired) that have direct and obvious effects on travel patterns. For example, unmarried men and married couples with young children have vastly different spending patterns. Behaviour refers to how potential tourists act, such as length of stay, new us. Repeat visitors, and skills (novice expert). But market segmentation using behaviour variables also refers to why they behave as they do, their interests, and their values. There are many factors that affect travel by individual consumers: the reasons for travel, activities enjoyed during travel, a person's general interests and opinions about travel, and personal values.

For one person, travel may mean a tour of museums, monuments and other cultural attractions. Another person may travel to a meeting of a professional organization. A third person seeks amusement at a sporting event; another visits a park to fish. For different reasons they engage in different activities while travelling and value different types of attractions.

Information on behaviour can be difficult and expensive to collect. Some details are available from observing visitors analysing existing records, but most knowledge is likely to come from surveys or interviews. Work with a marketing professional about survey design to assure a representative sample if you try this method.

New and even established host communities must evaluate each major target market for its economic potential. Consider your product and estimate the drawing power of the attractions. Think about proximity to metropolitan areas and the quality of the transportation network. Consider the of people travelling near your area; consult Minnesota Department of Transportation records.

Use size and accessibility of the target market as criteria. There must be enough members of the target market justify the investment in reaching them. You must be able to reach the target market through a standard form of promotion. Boaters, runners, and anglers, for example, are very accessible: they belong to organizations and read specialized publications. In contrast, young single parents less accessible market because there is no common affiliation or central source of information.

Finally, select one or more of the target markets. You can concentrate on a single target market to the exclusion of all others, or you can use a strategy where promotion campaigns are developed for two or more markets simultaneously. It is likely you will change market segments during the season in the same way resort operators shift their marketing efforts from anglers (spring) to families (summer) to retired couples (fall). Most important, a community shouldn't try to be all things to all consumers. Primary destination areas like the Twin Cities, state offices of tourism, and major attractions such as Disneyland have the resources to accomplish that. You are much more likely to be successful if you narrow down the target market you want to reach.

Set Marketing Objectives

Now write down marketing objectives that clearly state what community wants to accomplish in its promotion campaign. Objectives keep energy and action focused on what's important. They help you track your success and judge when it is time to review and shift strategies. A good objective contains four elements:

- A specific action of interest such as increased visitation, sales volume, or awareness;
- A measurable outcome, expressed in dollars, a percentage or numbers for example, that indicates how much change will
- A time frame within which the action should occur; and
- An indication of the target market you are trying to reach. Some poorly stated objectives are "to increase visits," "to midweek business," and "to attract more retired couples." In contrast, some examples of well-written objectives follow:

- In the next year, increase midweek (Monday-Thursday) occupancy to 55 percent by attracting business travellers.
- The Chamber of Commerce will book 500 advance reservations from vacationers travelling the Lake Superior circle route in summer (June 1 through Labour Day).
- Increase phone and mail inquiries by 20 percent from fall magazine advertising between August 15 and October 15.
- Increase retail sales on main street during a summer festival by 25 percent over last year's.

Carry out Promotion Strategies

Many communities and private entrepreneurs mistakenly assume that marketing is just deciding on a promotion strategy.

They direct broad appeals to poorly defined markets through a variety of media. You can't afford to spend scarce promotion dollars in appealing to people who are not prospects for purchase of your product. Effective and efficient promotion decisions build from a situation analysis, identifying products, selecting target markets and setting objectives.

The message content comes directly from the product and the associated theme. It emphasizes both tangible and intangible aspects, focusing on customer benefits your product offers.

Carrying out promotion strategies involves taking your message to the consumer through a specific delivery system. Promotion is any attempt to stimulate sales by persuasive or informative communications to current or potential customers. The major types of promotion used to stimulate travel and tourism follow:

Advertising: Any paid form of nonpersonal presentation and promotion of ideas, goods, or services by an identified sponsor using mass media. Television, radio and print media some of the major Minnesota destinations are an example.

Personal Selling: An oral or written presentation to one or prospective customers on a face-to-face basis, including telephone solicitation and direct mail. Attendance at sports shows is a form of personal selling.

Sales Promotions: Activities other than advertising and personal selling that stimulate purchasing or create awareness. Sales promotions, including contests featuring free tickets or trips, may be geared toward the individual visitor, while other promotions may be directed toward organizations selling travel services. The Duluth contest to guess the date the first ship will enter the harbour in spring is an example.

Public Relations: A nonpaid presentation of ideas, goods or services generally using mass media. Unlike advertising there is no identifying sponsor. Travel feature stories written after a "fam" (familiarization) tour are a result of public relations efforts.

These promotional categories are known together as the promotional mix. Strictly speaking, the promotional mix refers to the relative amounts of efforts or dollars put into each major promotional category. To find its optimal tourism promotional mix, your community might look at towns comparable size and attracting power. However, do not copy programs-no two communities will be exactly alike.

Finally, the committee may be drawn from owners. The committee structure is used most often to guide tourism development. There are several ways to organize a tourism promotion committee. Some groups originate within the Chamber of Commerce because of shared goals. Others form freestanding community endeavour; the final plan must represent goals independent committees with community-wide representation.

The Minnesota Extension Service publication "Tourism Advertising: Some Basics" outlines a process for selecting an advertising strategy. The tools discussed include magazines, newspapers, radio, television, direct mail, and outdoor displays.

Evaluate Results

There is no secret promotional formula. Test and evaluate regularly. A community or business must continually monitor evaluate results, and experiment with various types of promotion. Even with an effective promotional mix now, the situation may change. Preferences and characteristics of travellers change: marketing efforts must respond.

Evaluate Results

The Minnesota Extension Service publication "Evaluating Tourism Advertising with Cost-Comparison Methods" describes methods such as cost per inquiry, cost per reservation, and return on investment. The importance of coding advertisements to track results cannot be overemphasized.

The Next Step

Working through the tourism development process is a community endeavour; the final plan must represent goals commonly agreed to by area residents and business owners. The committee is used most often to guide tourism development.

There are several ways to organize a tourism promotion committee. Some groups originate within the Chamber of Commerce because of shared goals. Others form freestanding independent committees with community-wide representation. Finally, the committee may be drawn from current leaders in existing tourism agencies, associations, businesses, and attractions. You know the dynamics of your community best to pull together a core group of individuals make things happen.

There must be periodic feedback between the committee and the community at large. In some locations, the tourism committee begins its task with a community-wide survey (by mail, newspaper, or phone) to solicit opinions about tourism development. The results advise the committee and can create a widespread base of public support early in the process. The other strategy is to be sure there is always an opportunity for community discussion at key decision points. The local media can play a major role in keeping the public informed.

Here are seven steps to get started (from "Developing a Tourism Organization," 1987, a Michigan State University Extension Service booklet):

1. Select a name that creates an image and identifies the group.
2. Develop a policy statement, including a statement of purpose and bylaws.
3. Develop an action program: set goals and methods of accomplishing them.
4. Set up committees and subcommittees as needed. Some of the major tasks relate to community involvement, attractions and support services, promotion, budgets, research, and information.
5. Create community awareness and support for tourism.
6. Establish lines of communication and develop a flow of information.
7. Foster a spirit of close cooperation and coordination among the various communities, agencies, and other organizations.

Where to Look for Funding

Often good community marketing plans go unrealized or even unused because financial support could not be obtained. Funding can be a difficult obstacle. Communities that have developed a steady and reliable source of marketing funds generally have the most success. Constant scrambling for marketing funds drains energy away from the original marketing objectives. Some of the basic strategies used to raise money for tourism and travel marketing are a lodging tax, local government sources, internal organizational fundraising, private businesses, foundations, and the Minnesota Office of Tourism. Adapt these standard methods to your local situation. Minnesota Statutes permit the creation of a local option lodging tax. Home rule or statutory cities and townships with elected officials may enact a tax of up to three percent on the proceeds of a lodging facility-with a possible extension to municipal campgrounds. In unorganized townships, county officials may enact a lodging tax. Cities townships can create joint districts to better reflect the local tourism region.

Of the proceeds collected, 95 percent must be used to fund marketing and promotion of the area as a tourism or convention destination. These monies may not be used for capital expenditures such as buildings, parks, and civic centres. Lodging facilities are directly affected by the tax, so any plans for a lodging tax should include early discussions with representatives of overnight accommodations. Some communities have had special legislation passed to help fund tourism programs: two options are expansion of the tax base or increases in the tax ceiling. It is normally difficult to pass special interest legislation, but such authority can prove valuable to communities where tourism is a major industry.

Many local governments recognize the importance of the tourism and travel industry to their economies; a number of provide funding to marketing programs implemented by local groups. Monies can come from the general fund, bonding sources, special assessments, or a variety of other sources. Government support can greatly assist local marketing efforts, but funding is less stable due to changing demands for government funds, the health of the local economy, and the fortunes of local politicians.

Tourism organizations typically employ some internal fundraising strategies, in addition to outside sources. Membership dues is the most common method. Set either a standard rate or variable fees based on factors such as business size or number of employees. The organization's ability to attract members then becomes critical. Assessments above and beyond dues are another alternative. Assessments are often based on percent of gross revenue or business size. These may help to fund an overall marketing program, but are also used to pay for specific promotional efforts. Tourism organizations can also sell products, services, and activities directly to the public for income.

Examples are publications, souvenirs and merchandise, tours and tour guides, and operation of attractions, special events, festivals or auctions. Major businesses operating in the community and benefitting from travel and tourism sometimes make substantial contributions to a marketing program. An important element in obtaining this support is to thoroughly identify the benefits of such a contribution, both to the marketing program and the contributor. Direct benefits-increased sales-as well as secondary benefits-general expansion of the local economy-are important. Tax benefits may be an issue. Do not overlook the potential to build goodwill in the community.

There are opportunities to obtain project-specific grants through organizations such as foundations, the Minnesota Office of Tourism and nonlocal private businesses that will fund ongoing expenses for tourism marketing. Projects that provide promotion to an expanded region or attempt to market an area with an innovative approach are more likely to attract a foundation grant. The Minnesota Office of Tourism administers a joint venture marketing program that allocates matching funds on a competitive basis for advertising, creative marketing, and new brochure development. Private businesses beyond the specific area might also sponsor an activity if there is a connection between their product and the focus of the event. For example, dog food manufacturers could be approached for national sponsorship of a sled dog race.

Travel and Tourism Resources

Tourism USA: Guidelines for Tourism Development. 1986. University of Missouri, Dept. of Recreation and Park Administration, University Extension. Prepared for the U.S. of Commerce.

- Excellent "how to" handbook with sections on) appraising potential; 2) planning for tourism; 3) assessing product and market; 4) marketing tourism; visitor services; sources of assistance. Single copies are available for $3.00 from U.S. Dept. of Commerce, 1 4th & Constitution, Room 1

865, Washington, D.C. 20030, 202-377-0140. Managing Small Resorts for Profit. 1 985. Minnesota Extension Service, University of Minnesota.

- Contains a marketing section with articles on the market planning process, brochure development, advertising, positioning and package tours. Available for $20.00 from Bud Crewdson, Small Business Development Centre, Minnesota Extension Service, 248 Classroom Office Building, University of Minnesota, St. Paul, MN 551 08, 61 2-625-31 Minnesota Office of Tourism, 250 Skyway Level, 375 Jackson Street, St. Paul, MN 551 0 1,-800-652-9141, 6 1 2-296-Contact for information on a joint venture marketing program. Marketing activities may be eligible for matching funds allocated on a competitive basis to any local, regional, or statewide nonprofit organization formed to promote tourism. Tourism Centre, Minnesota Extension Service, University of Minnesota, 240 Coffey Hall, 1420 Eckles Avenue, St. Paul, MN 55108.
- Offers educational programs and materials for the visitor industry on community tourism development and small business management. Contact your local county extension agent for copies of the extension publications listed in the folder. So Your Community Wants Tourism: Guidelines for Developing Income from Tourism in Your Community (CD-FO-0679, Available 1988) Creating a Tourism Promotional Theme Tourism Advertising: Some Basics (CD-FO-331 1) "Evaluating Tourism Advertising with Cost Comparison Methods" (CD-FO-3372) Tourism Brochures to Boost Business (CD-FO-3273).

Community Improvement Resources

Tourism development depends on citizen cooperation to accomplish community goals and improve the local environment. The Minnesota Department of Trade and Economic development administers four such programs that give residents an opportunity to develop expertise in identifying and using community resources-the Minnesota Community Improvement Program, the Governor's Design Team, Minnesota Main Street, and Minnesota Beautiful. Program coordinators can be reached at the Department of Trade and Economic Development, 900 American Centre Building, 1 50

East Kellogg Blvd., St. Paul, MN 551 01. The general office number is 612-297-3190.

The Minnesota Community Improvement Program (MCIP) is a community (or county) revitalization and recognition program. Citizens conduct a community analysis and set goals. They build broad support networks and document the improvement process so that MCIP judges can evaluate annual progress. The Minnesota Extension Service provides educational and technical support. Involvement in MCIP can build the skills and coalitions necessary to accomplish other specific tasks such as economic development, downtown revitalization and design, and beautification.

The Governor's Design Team calls on architects, landscape designers, urban planners, artists, and other professionals volunteer their time and services and virtually descend on a community for a two-to three-day intensive design consultation and work session. Communities want the team to a fresh look and new ideas in such areas a downtown revitalized town image, and development potential. Before applying for a visit, the community should focus on specific issues and areas of need. During a visit, broad-based active citizen support and involvement is expected.

Minnesota Main Street encourages revitalization of downtowns in small and midsize cities, working with assets already inherent in the downtown tradition. Rebuilding main street's image depends on improvements in organization, promotion, design, and economic restructuring, made in operation with downtown groups.

Minnesota Beautiful supports activities that help keep Minnesota a clean and quality place to live, work, and visit. Projects include recycling, landscaping, general cleanup of waste materials and unsightly areas, tree planting, and mineland reclamation. Minnesota Beautiful offers educational materials to communities undertaking these projects, and organizes an annual conference to recognize significant progress.

Cultural Tourism Promotion and Policy in Malaysia

Malaysia is experiencing a tremendous pace of tourism development. Tourism sector has been recognized by Malaysian government as a major source of revenue and catalyst to the Malaysian economic renaissance. Tourist arrivals to Malaysia for the last ten years have shown a significant rise. In the year 2004, this country attracted 15.7 million foreign tourists generating around RM29.7 billion into the company. Major tourist market for Malaysia has been the neighbouring ASEAN nations especially Singapore, Thailand, Indonesia and Brunei. Other main traditional foreign markets include China, Japan, Taiwan and India.

Coupled with the growth in tourism is a booming interest in the 'new tourism'. Cultural tourism has emerged as a potential form of alternative tourism among both international tourists as well as Malaysian domestic travellers. Cultural tourism in Malaysia attracted great publicities with the increase in the number of incoming tourists annually. Malaysia has marvelous cultural tourism resources that are readily available to be explored such as the existence of multicultural, historical buildings, colorful lifestyles and friendly atmosphere. The purpose of this paper is to give an overview of the promotion of culture and heritage in Malaysia as well as the related strategies and policies that support the measure. It also discusses several underlying issues pertaining the cultural management in Malaysia.

Table 1: Tourist arrivals and receipts to Malaysia

Year	*Arrivals (million)*	*Receipts (RM millions)*
1995	7.46	9,174.9
1996	7.14	10,354.1
1997	6.21	9,699.6
1998	5.55	8,580.4
1999	7.93	12,321.3
2000	10.22	17,335.4
2001	12.78	24,221.5
2002	13.29	25,781.1
2003	10.58	21,291.1
2004	15.70	29,651.4

Source: Tourism Malaysia, 2005

Defining Cultural Tourism

Culture in tourism is an important issue. The relationship between tourism and culture can take many forms and the outcome can be viewed as negative and positive when meeting of hosts and visitors occurs and possibly leads to the transformation of the hosts' culture. The destruction of local culture as a result of tourism is well documented. However, studies by researchers' consider this as a lopsided view of the impact of tourism. Studies have shown that tourism have lead to the strengthening of local culture. Culture is defined broadly as quoted in Meethan (2001:117), *".....as a set of practices, based on forms of knowledge, which encapsulate common values and act as general guiding principles. It is through these forms of knowledge that distinctions are created and maintained, so that, for example, one culture is marked off as different from another".*

World Tourism Organization (1985) defines cultural tourism as the movements of persons for essentially cultural motivations such as study tours, performing arts and cultural tours; travel to festivals and other related events. Essentially, cultural tourism is based on the mosaic of places, traditions, art forms, celebrations and experiences that portray ones nation and its people.

Meethan (2001:128) rightly observed that there are array of tourist activities that come under the heading of cultural tourism. However, he argues for a distinct demarcation of cultural tourism and hence a distinct profile of cultural tourists quotes;

> *"....the cultural tourists are those who go about their leisure in a more serious frame of mind. To be a cultural tourist.....is to go beyond idle leisure and to return enriched with knowledge of other places and other people even if this involves 'gazing' at or collecting in some way, the commodation essences of otherness".*

Studies of western culture by Richard (1994) described the cultural tourists were *'a high socioeconomic status, high level of educational attainment, adequate leisure time, and often having occupations related to the culture industries'.* It must be borne in mind that culture is not static but one that is dynamic and evolving. Meethan (2001: 127) draw attention to globalization of culture and also the mobilization of culture for internal and external purposes. Yamashita, Kadir and Eades (1997: 29-30) further illustrates the processes that transform culture.

Heritage tourism can be classified as a subclass of cultural tourism. Both cultural and heritage tourism become a growing segment of the tourism marketplace. Cultural tourists appear to be motivated for different reasons than do traditional tourists.

Some tourism destinations see cultural tourism as a promotion for tourism products, and this has been lamented. Millar (1989) and others suggest that heritage tourism is "about the cultural traditions, places and values that... groups throughout the world are proud to conserve." Cultural traditions such as family patterns, religious practices, folklore traditions, and social customs attract individuals interested in heritage as do monuments, museums, battlefields, historic structures, and landmarks.

Cultural Tourism in Malaysia and its Management

In Malaysia, heritage and culture has also been identified as new niche products to be developed extensively in tourism development. Cultural vibrancy is clearly manifested in the ongoing and successful "Malaysia: Truly Asia" promotional drive by the country's promotion arm, Tourism Malaysia. In this promotion, Malaysia boasts to host a wide variety of Asian ethnic groups that making it into a little Asia. Malaysia also has distinctive multicultural architectural heritage with strong Islamic, Chinese and Western influences; all of which have been portrayed in the heritage buildings.

The major heritage elements; historic building, historical sites and unique local cultures are commonly found in many historic cities throughout Malaysia. An inventory has revealed that 30,000 heritage buildings are located in 162 cities throughout Malaysia. From this figure, 69.6% are shop houses and dwellings built before World War II. The unique colonial architectural styles of buildings have played major role in the creation of historic cities such as George Town, Ipoh, Malacca, Tapping, Koala Lumpur and Kuching.

Table 2 Distributions of Pre-War Buildings in Selected States in Malaysia

States in Malaysia	*Number of Pre-War Buildings*	*Percentage (%)*
Penang	5057	24.3
Perak	3351	16.1
Johor	2323	11.2
Malacca	2177	10.5
Koala Lumpur	1763	8.4

The management of culture and heritage in Malaysia was put under the Ministry of Tourism and Culture, established on the 20th of May 1987, combining Department of Culture from the Ministry of Culture, Youths and Sports with the Malaysian Tourism Development Corporation from the Ministry of Trade and Industries. On 22nd October 1992, the ministry was renamed into Ministry of Culture, Arts and Tourism.

This ministry was later divided in Mac 2004, into two ministries, namely the Tourism Ministry and Ministry of Culture, Arts and Heritage. This separation is seen as recognition of tourism as a potential number one sector of the country and a move to appreciate the value of heritage of the country.

Agencies under this ministry are the National Archives, the National Art and Gallery, the Department of Museum and Antiquities, Malaysian Handicrafts (Kraftangan Malaysia), the National Film Development Corporation (Finas), the National Art Academy, the National Library and the Istana Budaya (the Culture Palace).

Despite the move to strengthen the ministries, the separation of the cultural elements from the Tourism Ministry can give impacts on the direction of 'cultural and heritage tourism', leaving this niche area as an no-man's land!

The Formulation of National Cultural Policy

At a national conference organized by Malaysia's Ministry of Culture, Youth and Sports in 1971, the Malaysian government formulated what was to become a national cultural policy based on the following principles:

(i) The national culture of Malaysia must henceforth be based on the cultures of the people indigenous to the region.

(ii) Elements from other cultures which are judged suitable and reasonable may be incorporated into Malaysia's national culture.

(iii) Islam will be an important element in the national culture.

In the period since its implementation, Malaysia's national culture policy has become one important point of vigorous debate and political conflict. In the years since the formulation of a National Cultural Policy, and particularly in the late 1980's, the

Malaysian government has been concerned to implement its basic principles by intervening directly and across the board in the cultural field. Not surprisingly, and perhaps because it has not been altogether clear and efficient about its task, government intervention in the cultural field has produced a response on the part of a variety of non-Malaya groups who feel that their cultural freedom has been curtailed.

For example, at a meeting of the Chinese guild and associations of Malaysia held in March, 1983, delegates passed a series of resolutions that were compiled in a joint memorandum to the Ministry of Culture, Youth and Sports.

In April 1984, a group of the best-known Indian cultural, social and religious organizations submitted a similar memorandum. Both memoranda accused the government of having formulated a cultural policy which was Malaya-centric and undemocratic, and requested that a new policy on national culture be established which was more clearly multi-ethnic and democratic.

Law and Legislations on Cultural and Heritage Properties

The legal foundations of the Malaysian cultural policy are derived from the following acts and regulations:

i) Antiquities Act 1976 (Act 168).
ii) National Art Gallery Act, 1958.
iii) Legal Deposit of Library Material Act, 1986 (Act A667).
iv) National Library Act, 1972; The National Library (Amendment) Act, 1987.
v) National Archive Act, 1966 (Act 44), (Revised 1971), (Act A85), (Revised 1993), (Act 511).
vi) Tourist Development Corporation of Malaysia Act 1972 (Act 1972).
vii) Broadcasting Act 1988 (Act 338), Broadcasting (Amendment) Act, 1997 (Act A977).
viii) Cinematography Film-Hire Duty Act 1965 (Revised 1990), (Act 434).
ix) (Perbadanan Kemajuan File Nasional Malaysia Act 1981 (Act 244), Perbadanan Kemajuan File Nasional Malaysia (Amendment) Act, 1984 (Act 589).

x) Perbadanan Kemajuan Kraftangan Malaysia Act 1979 (Act 222).

xi) Theatres & Places of Public Amusement (Federal Territory) Act 1988 (Act 182).

xii) Bernama Act, 1967 (Revised 1990), (Act 449).

xiii) Entertainment Duty Act 1953 (Revised 1973) (Act 103).

Efforts to preserve the heritage buildings in Malaysia are supported by various acts and legislations. The prominent acts have been the Town and Country Planning Act of 1976 or the 172 Act, The National Land Code (Kanun Tanah Negara), the Street, Drainage and Building Act 133, the Antiquities Act 1976, as well as local legislations such as the Malacca Enactment No. 6 (1988). Act 133 for instance stipulates that "No person shall erect any building without a prior written permission of the local authority".

This provision is supported by Section 18 of Act 172 which states "All land/building use shall comply with the local plans (structure and local plans). Any development shall obtain planning permission. And if there is no development plan prepared for the area, the owner/developer of the land shall inform their plan to the adjoining landowners (Act 172,).

To date, a guidelines on the Guidelines on the Conservation of George Town Inner City details out specific recommendations pertaining extensions, renovations, revitalizations of heritage buildings within the prescribed zones.

At present, any erection of buildings is loosely bonded by both Acts (133 and 172). Section 16 of 133 defines erections of building includes 'renews or repairs of any existing buildings in such a manner as to involve a renewal, reconstruction or erection of any portion of an outer or party wall to the extent of one storey height". Further, all building that fall within the definition of development, stipulated in Act 172 also requires planning permission. The Guidelines is in concordant with Part Vll of Act 133 that gives the State Authority to make bylaws or in respect of every purpose which is deemed by him necessary. In regards to the preservation of buildings, the State Authority, among other things, has the right to make by laws in:-

(i) The construction, paving, width and level of arcades and footways;

(ii) The construction, alteration and demolition of buildings and the methods and materials to be used in connection therewith;

(iii) The minimum timber or other building material content in any building.

Issues

The promotion of culture and heritage in Malaysia faces several underlying issues that both are related to the complexity of the society living in Malaysia. Among the issues are:-

Whose Culture?

Despite the fact that Malaysia is proud of its multiculturalism, promoted worldwide as the 'Truly Asia', the question remains on whose culture should be promoted at the forefront. As discussed above, Chinese and Indians have continuously felt that their cultures are not well represented in the tourism brochures produced by the government.

Similar sentiment was raised up during the nomination process for the listing of Penang and Melaka into the world heritage city. Malays in Penang especially feel that the listing do not benefit them and the island's Malaya history is not taken into consideration.

Some also feel that the listing of the 12000 heritage buildings where many of them are colonial buildings—is just another post colonization of the country, lamented on why we have to glorify the colonial past!

4

Strategic Management of Travel and Tourism

Travel policies aren't designed just to keep costs down. You also need to consider your team's needs, the system's ease of use, and convenient locations and schedules.

If you've been to the supermarket or the drug store lately, you've likely learned the basic rule of purchasing: Frequent customers get the best prices and the best service. American Airlines first invented a frequent shopper's program when it launched Advantage to encourage travellers to bring all their business to one supplier.

Thirty years later, even small firms and their clients can save money and make taking to the road a little easier for their travellers by applying this basic rule of purchasing. This edition of Transit Authority will outline the nine components of a corporate travel program that small and midsize firms can institute for their own employees and partners or recommend to their clients. Our goal: finding the delicate balance that keeps travel costs down and road warriors happy.

At companies with larger travel spends (where the annual travel tabs run over $100 million), managing the travel program is a serious business handled by a dedicated staff. When travelling for the firm, their employees are urged — or even ordered — to book their trips through a designated travel agency or Internet travel site, using airlines and hotels with which the firm has negotiated discounts. Travellers charge their tickets to a single charge card, drive cars from the firm's designated car-rental company, bring their meetings to preferred hotels, file their expense reports online. The best practices of their corporate travel programs can be adapted on a smaller scale by companies and firms of every size.

Optimizing travel comes down to making decisions about nine things: the corporate travel policy; the manager of the program; the type of travel agency that will serve as your intermediary to suppliers; the airlines, hotels, car-rental, charge-card and online travel-booking companies with whom you will partner; and the system you will use for tracking and reporting spending data. We'll look at and offer best practices for each piece of the puzzle, with a focus on small and midsize companies and their business customers.

Start the Journey with a Map

Whether your employees are travelling on firm business or billing every charge back to a client, they are only human. Everyone likes to fly first class — and will, unless someone sets clear limits. Every firm and company should have a travel policy outlining the basic rules, signed off on by top management and distributed to every employee who travels. Keep in mind, however, that buying travel is not like buying paper clips; flying far from home is a stressful and emotional business, and the time of executives is a valuable commodity not to be wasted. A bus may be the cheapest option for getting from Chicago to New York, but odds are good that Southwest Airlines will be the better value in terms of time and effort saved.

While travel policy should come from the top, be sure to include a broad contingency in the discussion, including at least one of the most frequent travellers and the assistants who will make the actual reservations. Many firms also consider a two-tier policy, one for road warriors, senior partners, and executives, and a second for those who travel only to an occasional conference. Keep the policy concise and clear, covering the basic goals and guidelines for each of the nine major components.

Building a Framework

Companies have two options for selecting the framework for the travel management function: whether to handle it internally or to outsource it to a travel agency. Unless your annual travel budget is over $1 million and your office is open 24/7, the best practice usually is to contract with a professional travel agency. Keep in mind, though, that while you can outsource the tasks involved in making reservations, providing customer service, collecting spending data and negotiating contracts with suppliers, you cannot outsource management functions. It's imperative, therefore, to designate an employee of your own to oversee the program, manage the relationship with the travel agency, insure best practices in pricing and execution, and negotiate some deals of your own.

Consolidating all travel through a single travel agency is the best way to collect data, provide 24-hour service to travellers on the road, and rarely cause for objection by travellers themselves. In the not-so-distant past many firms had travel agents physically sit in their buildings, but rising personnel costs make that unfeasible today, and technology makes it unnecessary; travel agency call centres provide excellent service to small firms and companies at a fair price.

Even less costly is the option of booking travel online, through dedicated small-business programs offered by the major online travel agencies: Expedia, Travelocity, Travelport, and Orbitz. All four systems produce monthly spending reports for your firm or company and can be configured so that when travellers say they need a hotel in Phoenix, for example, the Hyatt with which you have a negotiated discount will be highlighted. Shifting traveller behaviour so that they book their own trips online instead of calling Mary at the agency down the block may take some doing, however. A clear policy from top management is imperative; even then, expect about 50% compliance unless your top executives are prepared to not reimburse travellers unless they comply.

Beyond the fees you can save, letting travellers self-serve by making their own reservations invariably results in lower costs. Perhaps the biggest surprise travel managers have realized from online booking is that when travellers are offered a wide range of options on their computer screen, a surprisingly high number do the right thing and change their plans slightly to take advantage of lower-priced options. In fact, if we had to offer a single piece of advice for cutting travel costs, it would be this: Get as many travellers as you can to book their travel online as fast as you can.

Note that many small companies report that they are being inundated by offers from Southwest Airlines' SWABiz program. The savings there are real, as travellers are entering their own information directly into Southwest's computer system and saving the agency transaction fees. But, travellers will see only flights and fares for one carrier, and lose the ability to comparative shop.

The travel industry is built on discounts and market share bonuses. No matter what agency or online system you are using, opt to pay them flat fees for services rendered and have any discounts you earn flow back to your firm. The point is to underline to both the agency and the suppliers that your firm is the customer here, not the travel agency.

Trains, Planes, and Automobiles

While larger companies are often best served by pushing all their travellers to use one airline and then negotiating discounted rates, small companies generally fare better allowing travellers to just pick the airline or hotel with the lowest fare on each trip. Remember that every dollar not spent falls right to your bottom line; saving a few thousand dollars in expenses may be as valuable as ten times as much in additional sales.No matter how hard you try, though the need for some high-end travel will not go away. These are where the airlines derive their biggest profit margins. Track them and try to negotiate a discount for all first-and business-class tickets with a single major airline that offers frequent flights from your home city. Virtually every airline, hotel and car-rental company offers discounts to business customers; make it someone's formal responsibility to negotiate on your behalf and then to nudge travellers to use these vendors. Airline programs typically offer small-business programs that yield free tickets with the purchase of a given number; take advantage of them. Beware the prepaid miles programs, however, which generally cost about 53 cents per mile; firms that let travellers choose their own lowcost flights online report that they average about 22 cents a mile. When employees are travelling on client business and billing their expenses back, there is a fiduciary responsibility to travel at the same level as the client would. Many firms follow client travel policies in such cases, and sometimes use the client's travel agency as well. Be careful about how you handle negotiated discounts in such cases; KPMG and Price water house Coopers in 2004 paid $17 million and $54.5 million, respectively, to settle a class-action lawsuit that charged them with billing clients for full fares and then keeping corporate discounts they got back from travel suppliers.

Checking in with a Hotel Program

While it's possible to push your travellers to use one or two major airlines without inconveniencing them much, hotels are a different story. Location really does make a difference. Staying in a particular hotel often offers tangible and intangible benefits: saving cab fares and wear and tear, keeping you close to the action at a conference or meeting, and allowing for mingling with important contacts or potential new customers. Rather than insist that everyone always stays at a Marriott or a Holiday Inn, a best practice is to focus on the five or six cities to which your firm travels most frequently, and negotiate discounts with a hotel or two in each. If your travellers or their assistants are using a corporate Internet site, set the system up so that these properties appear first and are highlighted as your preferred properties.

Maximize your business at these properties by requiring employees to register any meetings they will be holding with the travel manager, who in turn can encourage them to use the same properties as much as possible. Managing meetings is politically sensitive, as many meeting planners receive gifts and rewards from the hotels to which they bring business. Like every purchasing decision, though, it's important to base the choice of a meeting location on what's best for the firm, not the individual doing the buying. Centralizing and managing your meeting spend is likely the biggest single remaining opportunity for travel management for smaller companies.

Other Pieces of the Puzzle

Of all the pieces of the travel framework, moving travellers to a single car-rental supplier is the easiest. The issue here, again, is cost vs. Convenience; in general, on-airport companies cost more, off-airport companies cost less. But any preferred car-rental program brings one important advantage: free insurance. With car-rental companies typically charging $9-14 a day, and the average rental lasting 2.5 days, the savings from directing your travellers to just one are compelling.

The most important piece of the travel program, though, is a single corporate charge card to which all travel expenses must be billed. This is a relatively easy step to enforce; mandate that charges not booked on the credit card will not be reimbursed. Charge cards (like the American Express or Diner's Club corporate cards, which are not "credit cards" as they must be paid off every money)-capture the data that shows what your travellers actually bought, and are the key to rebates, discounts, and enhanced services. When dealing with the data, don't allow the sheer magnitude to overwhelm you. Pick out the key items or objectives that matter most and track those. Some companies have developed a dashboard or scorecard of key travel program measurements they track quarterly: percent of compliance to travel policy for air, car, hotel; average airline cost per mile through the agency and through online booking sites; rate of online booking adoption; average hotel room rate in key cities. Those are your fundamentals. Establish the parameters for success for each key measure and work toward achieving those. When you get there, develop new measures.

Passenger Space Travel and the Wright Brothers' Vision

It is a great pleasure and a great privilege to be invited to contribute to the Centenary celebration of one of the truly world-changing inventions of the 20th century — Orville and Wilbur Wright's development of controlled, powered flight. It is also a particular pleasure to speak at the session on space tourism, of which I am confident the theme will be recognised in coming years as the most significant at this Symposium. The topic I was invited to discuss is the market demand and transportation infrastructure for space tourism, but it seems only appropriate to begin by giving some thought to the relation of this subject, passenger space travel, to the Wright brothers' achievement and vision. If the word genius has any value, then we can certainly say that Orville and Wilbur Wright were engineering geniuses, not in the popular sense of being able to solve incomprehensible mathematical problems, but in having the rare combination of different abilities that enabled them to do something important that no-one else at that time was able to do. It seems reasonable to guess that if the Wright brothers were alive today, they would be working to realise passenger space travel and the future developments to which it will lead. So we might ask: "If the Wright brothers were alive today, what would they think of progress in space travel so far?" Well, if we look at their own experience in developing air travel, and at the present situation in space travel, I think we have to conclude that they would be *shocked and appalled*.

To see the truth of this we need to remember the treatment the Wright brothers received from the U.S. Government. At the same time as they were pursuing flight as a hobby, Professor Samuel Langley, secretary of the Smithsonian Institution, was funded by the U.S. Army to develop what he called an "aerodrome". Though Langley was a fine researcher, he did *not* make the conceptual breakthroughs necessary to achieve flight. However, the Smithsonian supported Langley, even years after his death, and refused to recognise the Wrights' achievement. It even collaborated in 1914 with Glenn Curtiss in flying a modified variant of one of Langley's failed attempts at an aeroplane — whereupon they claimed that this proved that Langley was the co-inventor of flight with the Wright brothers.

Orville and Wilbur could not accept such dishonesty — and so the Smithsonian refused to recognise their invention. It was not until *44 years* after the Wright brothers' first flight, 1947, that the government-funded Smithsonian finally acknowledged what everyone else in the world already knew — that the Wright Brothers alone invented flight.

This may have been the most shameful episode in the Smithsonian's history. So it would be comforting to believe that its shockingly dishonest mistreatment of the Wright brothers — who contributed perhaps more to U.S. technological prowess and prestige than anyone else in the 20th century — was a unique aberration. However, we have to face the fact that such self-serving behaviour is not anomalous; it is typical of governments everywhere, including particularly "democratic" ones, as they act to protect the interests of economically powerful groups within the economy against others, notably newcomers and the general public. It is indeed quite similar to the British government's decades-long refusal to award the "Longitude Prize" to John Harrison, the genius inventor of the chronometer. The defining feature of governments is that they employ force to achieve their purposes, and controlling this force to work for the public good, instead of for the benefit of the people comprising the government, is the central problem that humans face in trying to create and maintain free and fair societies.

In this context it is relevant to refer to the work of another American genius, Professor James Buchanan, who received the Novel Prize in 1986 for his work on the economic analysis of governments' behaviour and how to control it. The basic assumption of the field of economics concerns human psychology — it that humans are intelligent animals who use their brains to improve their situation. Adam Smith, the father of economics, analysed the implications of assuming that people act in their own self-interest in the case of business people and their customers; however, although he also noted that government officials "...have generally an interest to deceive and even oppress the public", he did not analyse the implications of this in detail. Buchanan and the colleagues with whom he pioneered the field of Public Choice economics analysed its implications for the behaviour of politicians and bureaucrats, and for the formal constraints needed on government. Niskanen extended this work, showing that in order to constrain government organisations, or "bureaus", to act in the public interest, their activities need to be the subject of close scrutiny not by politicians but by large numbers of the general public.

It is widely recognised that the USA has an exemplary Constitution, designed both to ensure the provision of the services that only government can provide, and also to protect the people from government's inexorable tendency to become tyrannical. However, governments become more tyrannical the larger they grow, and the U.S. government is surely no exception to this, despite the Constitution. In order to appreciate this we do not need to consider anything controversial such as foreign policy; we need only consider the case of Prohibition when the U.S. government imposed a disastrous law invasive of private liberty and against the wishes of an enormous number of its own population — or the fact that the U.S. government today keeps a larger proportion of the national population imprisoned than any other government in the world. So the shockingly dishonest mistreatment of two of the nation's greatest geniuses, whom we are celebrating at this symposium, by a government organisation should not be thought of as an aberration, but as typical. Every government system is different in innumerable details, and the 44 years that it took the U.S. government to finally admit what everyone else in the world already knew can perhaps be seen as the "cycle time" of the U.S. Federal government system in correcting an error.

This digression brings us directly back to our main topic — since it is now 42 years since Alan Shepard performed the first space flight by a U.S. Citizen. Of course Shepard was a government employee — it's as if the U.S. Army-funded Langley had succeeded in developing controlled, powered flight. It is therefore *extremely striking* that no private US citizen has yet been permitted to travel to space, but only a tiny number of government employees and related invites selected by the U.S. Government's 45-year old monopoly space agency, Nasa. In addition, despite having spent an astonishing $1 trillion of taxpayers' money on nominally civilian space activities (that is, nearly $1,000/second for 40 years, measured in 2003$), the U.S. Government *has not reduced the cost of travelling to space at all.*

So if we were to ask the Wright brothers what they thought of space flight today, perhaps in such terms as: "Don't you think our space agencies are doing a wonderful job?" they would not be impressed — they would surely laugh bitterly: "Are you joking? What did you expect? You left it to the U.S. Government. *Look how they treated us!*

The U.S. Government's 45-year old monopoly space agency, Nasa currently has a travelling exhibition called "Starship 2040" which includes a mock-up of a small module which it suggests might be feasible for tourism by 2040 — which would be *79 years* after Alan Shepard. Based on this we can perhaps guess what would have happened if Langley had indeed invented flight: at the rate of development of space travel proposed by the U.S. Government, passenger air travel would have started in 1982. In fact, by that date private passenger air travel, as initiated by the Wright brothers, already exceeded 1/2 billion people/year, or 1.5 million passengers/day! Fortunately, 44 years seems to be a better estimate than Nasa's estimate of 79 years. For it is surely not unrealistic to hope to see private suborbital space flights – that is, short trips of just a few minutes like that made by Alan Shepard himself – starting by 2005. If they do start then, it seems likely to be with little or no help from government space agencies, which continue to spend $20 billion/year of taxpayers' money on non-science space activities of little economic value, as discussed in Aviation pioneered by the Wright brothers contrasts sharply with space flight pioneered by governments, most notably in providing transportation services to the general public whereas space agencies provide no such services to the public, for whom their activities are largely incomprehensible. In terms of cost-performance the results are predictably disastrous: despite Nasa's use of $1 trillion of taxpayers' money, the first private U.S. Citizen to pay for a space flight, Dennis Tito, had to fly on the 1,657th Soyuz rocket— essentially the same vehicle that carried Yuri Gagarin 40 years earlier in 1961! Tito also faced public abuse from the then Nasa administrator. If that $1 trillion had been used as productively as the cumulative investment in the civil aviation industry launched by the Wright brothers, we would have a nearly $1 trillion/year space travel industry today. This failure of "space" to follow in the economically successful footsteps of "aero" represents a massive hiatus in "aerospace" development in the U.S.A. Due largely to the influence of the cold war. As a consequence, the U.S. Government decided to compete with the Soviet Union on its own terms in space, and established a monopoly agency which quickly developed self-serving habits, such as holding invitation-only press events (paid for by taxpayers), which are extremely effective in minimising critical media scrutiny. If the Wright brothers were developing passenger space travel today – well, obviously they would develop services that the public want to buy. Government space agencies periodically pay for surveys of public support for their budgets; but what they have never done – except finally, grudgingly, in just the last two years, with a tiny budget, and with minimal publicity – is ask the public what they want, and specifically whether they would like to travel to space.

Passenger Demand

In a paper presented at the 1986 IAF Congress, a colleague and I wrote: "Great interest must therefore attach to any detailed market surveys that are performed to determine the likely level of demand for space tourism services of various kinds". At that time the idea of space tourism was not considered a serious topic within the space industry, and the proposal was met with silence – which is the first point to be made about passenger demand for space travel.

Lack of Data

Surely the most striking feature of the data on the demand for passenger space travel is *how very little data there is*. In view of the fact that Nasa is required by U.S. Federal law "to encourage to the maximum extent possible the fullest commercial use of space", and other government agencies such as Esa, Nasda and the BNSC have similar responsibilities, it is clearly wrong for them to ignore a potentially major new market for space transportation. Such a decision might be acceptable if the agencies were achieving great success in their preferred activities, but the economic performance of the non-science activities in which they have collectively invested $1 trillion is disastrous: the resulting commercial turnover is about 1/50 of what ordinary companies would have achieved with the same investment.

However, this behaviour is in close agreement with Niskanen's analysis of the economic behaviour of bureaucratic organisations, in which, as he explains succinctly, individual officials "have no incentive to know or seek to know the public good, nor to work for the public good". It is particularly striking that space agencies continue to rigidly ignore the passenger market even in the early years of the 21st century while the space industry is shrinking drastically for lack of demand: U.S. aerospace employment has fallen to its lowest level for 5 years, and both the European monopoly launch supplier, Arianespace, and the remaining European monopoly manufacturer of large satellites, EADS, are cutting staff by a further 30%.

Prior to the first market research data published in 1994, "guesstimates" had been published by Ehricke, Citron and the author. As part of a Nasa study of future launch markets, some more detailed "guesstimates" were also published in 1994. In view of the growing evidence that tourism is the only activity capable of growing large enough to develop space economically, it seems clear that having relied on government monopoly organisations for access to space has greatly delayed its realisation. Indeed, in view of the growing interest in suborbital space travel services, which could easily have started during the 1970s, this delay caused by space agencies has reached decades already.

Worldwide Demand

The second very striking feature of the data on the demand for passenger space travel is that it is hugely positive, across all categories— age, sex, income-level and country — everywhere and every time that people have been surveyed. In 1993 I was finally able to use a small budget to perform the first ever market research on the subject, as a Science & Technology Agency Fellow in Japan; with a number of colleagues I distributed a pamphlet and questionnaire to 3030 people selected quasi-randomly from all age-groups, and roughly nationwide. As Figure 1 shows, a substantial majority of the general population, both men and women, said they wished to travel to space: the youngest were the most keen, but even many older people also said they would like to buy such a service.

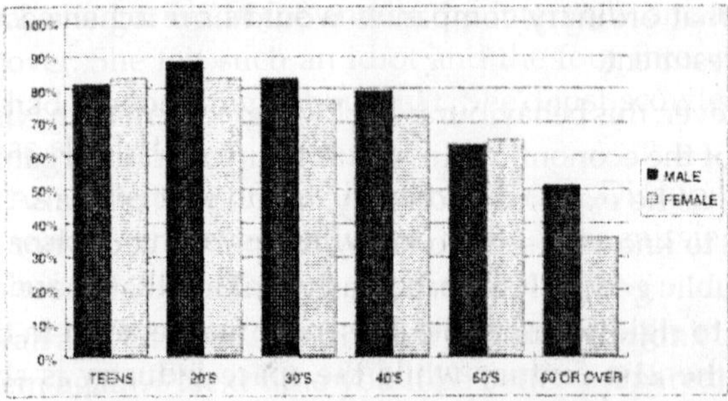

Figure 1: Wish to travel to space by age-group, Japan

Figure 2 shows the response to the same questionnaire delivered by telephone in the U.S.A. The main difference is that U.S. women are somewhat less enthusiastic than men, which is presumably due to the military connection and more "macho/ techno" image of space flight in the U.S.A. than in Japan.

In response to the question "How many months' salary would you pay for a space flight?", some 70% of those wishing to travel to space in Japan, North America and Germany said they would pay several months' salary, and in each country a few percent said they would pay even 1 year's salary or more. Bekey usefully surveyed various different studies as of 1998, as Crouch did in 2001. More recently Kelly Space & Technology Inc and Futron Inc, in studying potential markets for reusable launch vehicles for Nasa, surveyed the potential demand for space tourism — using Nasa funds for this purpose for the first time. Both studies concluded that passenger travel offers the most promising market for space transportation.

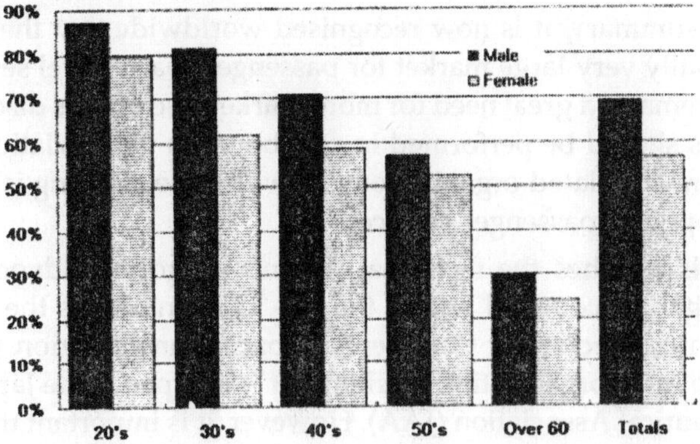

Figure 2: Wish to travel to space by age-group

The great popularity of passenger space travel makes the lack of data even less excusable. It is indicative of space agencies' failure to follow aviation's successful lead, as well as their failure to do work that has economic value. There are many striking examples of space agencies refusing to act appropriately, even after having paid for and published research stating these facts. For example, in the U.S.A. the Nasa administrator refused for more than three years to make its report "General Public Space Travel and Tourism" available through its website, and even today it is not directly findable — only indirectly through a link to another site. In Japan, the director of planning at the government's National Aerospace Laboratory (NAL), even after having paid $4,000 for a survey in the U.S.A., and having coauthored four papers including statements such as "the demand apparently has the potential to grow to many times the most optimistic projections for existing commercial space activities", stopped all work on the subject, while continuing to spend hundreds of millions of dollars/ year on activities with little economic value, for six years — until it was decided to merge the NAL with other research organisations.

These examples are sadly typical of space industry officials who feel no pressure to contribute to economic growth. At a time when commercial demand for space transportation (i.e. satellite launch) has been shrinking progressively, and the U.S. and Japanese economies are in their worst crises for 50 years *due precisely to the lack of investment in commercially promising new businesses*, this deeply irresponsible attitude has been disastrous for taxpayers.

In summary, it is now recognised worldwide that there is a potentially very large market for passenger space travel services. There remains a great need for more market research, as discussed in. This should be performed in collaboration with aviation and other travel-related organisations, of which the thinking is based on supplying passenger services.

This matches the facts that the most vigorous advocate of passenger space travel within the U.S. Government is the FAA's Associate Director for Commercial Space Transportation (AST), and the main organisation working for it in Japan is the Japanese Aeronautical Association (JAA). However, it is important that the need for more market research on space tourism should not be used as an excuse for further delaying work towards its realisation; it should rather be widened to include research on a range of related matters. These include the planning of many aspects of passenger space flight services as seen from the point of view of passengers, including vehicle specifications, passenger cabin interior design, orbital accommodation facilities and thence to the entire range of infrastructure needed.

Transportation Infrastructure

In trying to envisage the details of the future development of passenger space travel services, and what vehicles and other infrastructure will be needed, the historical development of passenger air travel offers a useful precedent. In combination with elements of the hotel industry and the cruise-liner industry, civil aviation seems to offer a fairly complete model for passenger space travel services. For the regulatory aspects, in addition to aviation and other safety regulations there will be a need for traffic rules, police services, specialised pilot services (as on difficult-to-navigate waterways), and possibly an equivalent of coastguard services. However, what we may expect to see a few decades in the future depends both on what is technically possible, and on how much is invested in coming years to realise passenger space travel.

Technical Possibilities

Very similar to the situation concerning demand, there is strikingly little information on the technical possibilities for passenger space travel, but all the information that does exist is positive. The lack of data is due to government space agencies — never having commisioned a feasibility study of a dedicated passenger launch vehicle in more than 40 years.

In order to understand the potential it is perhaps useful first to dispel the remains of a very widespread myth — that in order to provide space travel services a vehicle like the U.S. Government's "space shuttle" is needed. From this it is commonly concluded that, since that vehicle costs about $100 million/passenger/flight, space tourism is therefore a fantasy, or at least conceivable only in the far future after several more decades of government-funded space technology. The most important point to note is that the "space shuttle" was designed to military specifications; its hypothetical cost/passenger is therefore of no more relevance to space tourism than the cost of carrying passengers in a bomber aeroplane would have to commercial air travel. Hence the only relevant data are those relating specifically to dedicated passenger vehicle design studies. Over the past decade or more, a number of such studies have been published based on varying degrees of effort. However, they show considerable consensus about the cost of developing a fully reusable passenger-carrying launch vehicle capable of repeated flights to and from low Earth orbit, with most estimates clustered around $10 billion.

Designs of single-stage, vertical takeoff and landing (VTOL) rockets include Pacific American Launch Systems' " Phoenix", a passenger-carrying variant of the German " Beta", and the " Kankoh-maru" designed as part of the Japanese Rocket Society's (JRS) space tourism research program started in 1993. Designs of two-stage horizontal takeoff and landing (HTOL) vehicles include the "Spacecab", "Spacebus" and precursor vehicles proposed by Bristol Spaceplanes Ltd., several designs studied by Penn and Lindley at the Aerospace Corporation, and a recent study done at Boeing. Development and operating costs for several configurations are usefully tabulated by Bekey in. The estimated development costs in these studies range from a few billion dollars to about $16 billion.

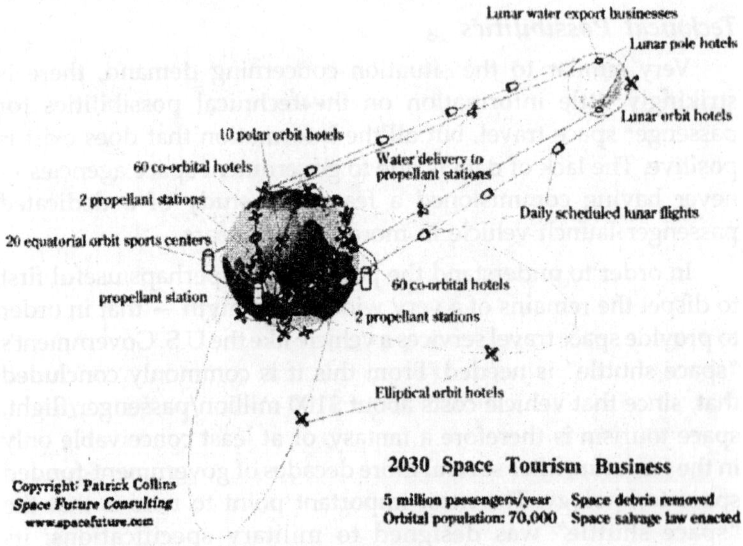

Figure 3: Transportation infrastructure required for space tourism

What is perhaps most striking about these figures is that even the largest is less than one year of G7 space agencies' current spending on non-science activities — which have little economic value in terms of generating commercial space revenues. Thus such an investment could be funded by using about 5% of space agencies' annual budgets over a decade, which would clearly not be a significant burden to taxpayers. Indeed, if planned government space projects' funding were reduced by 5%, and their timetables extended a little, the vast majority of the general public would not even be aware of the change — but at the end of the period, space activities would enter a new era with the start of lowcost, reliable access to orbit.

If the actual cost of developing the transportation infrastructure required for passenger space travel was even ten times higher, this would be only of the same order of magnitude as the international space station (ISS), which has little measurable economic value (particularly since its future depends on an unreliable transportation system). Consequently developing a passenger vehicle would be greatly preferable. How best to achieve the desired result organisationally is a different issue discussed further below. The estimated timetable to reach initial passenger service is about 10 years, if the resources were provided without interruptions. In that case the transportation infrastructure in 2030 might look like Figure 3. First published in 1999, this scenario has lost 4 years at time of writing, but it could probably still be achieved if sufficient investment was started in the near future. Its value would be some $1 trillion greater than continuing government space activities as they are today, as discussed further in.

The range of on-orbit infrastructure would be determined primarily by the requirements of daily life of members of the general public living in a zero-gravity environment. This would have great economic value through the flowering of new business opportunities in every sector of economic activity, in contrast to the minimal effect of traditional space agency activities. Hence Figure 3 can be seen as a step on the way towards the $1 trillion/year scale of activity which might be expected from the scale of public investment made to date. In the present depressed state of the world economy, including particularly the aerospace industry, such activity is economically very desirable. Furthermore, it is the *only way* of achieving commensurate economic benefit for taxpayers from the public investment in developing space capabilities to date.

Actual Progress

How much progress we will actually make towards the future illustrated in Figure 3 depends of course on how much is invested in achieving passenger space travel, how soon it is invested, and how effectively it is invested. This particularly includes achieving efficient, complementary roles for both government organisations and private companies. Unfortunately it is currently unclear how much space agencies are capable of contributing to this very desirable outcome, due to their inappropriate organisational structures. This problem can be seen from the orders of magnitude difference in cost between G7 space agencies' procedures, and what can be taken as a proxy for commercial "best practice" today. This was put into sharp focus recently when it was stated that the

Russian company NPO-Energia builds Soyuz crew vehicles for $12 million, Progress cargo craft for a little more than $6 million, and Soyuz launch vehicles for about $16 million. By contrast, Nasa estimates the cost of developing a 4-to-6-person "orbital space plane" (OSP) to be launched on an existing expendable rocket by 2010 at $13 billion or more. Even after allowing for the fact that the OSP is intended to be reusable, and ignoring the higher cost of U.S. expendable rockets, it is clear that its cost/flight would not approach that of Soyuz in even 1,000 flights. When the difference in reliability between the two systems Soyuz having made nearly 2,000 flights, including hundreds of successful manned flights are taken into account, it is clear that Nasa's technical capabilities are of little economic value. Indeed, at the time of writing, the latest news is that Nasas proposed Orbital Space Plane may actually be a non-reusable capsule, which closes the circle: Nasa is now proposing to use $13 billion of taxpayers money to redevelop an Apollo capsule 40 years after the original.

Some people might conclude, puzzled, that the US space industry cannot compete with 50 year old Russian technology! But this is not so. Even despite the Soyuz's advantages of having low labour costs and development costs written off long ago, if given a free hand US companies can get at least close to the same costs, as can be seen from a single example. HMX Inc proposed its reusable XV cargo carrier in 2000 for Nasas Alternate Access to Space program (AAS). Total program costs for four XV launches carrying 300 lb payloads were estimated at $145 million.

If produced, the first flight would have been in 2003; this would have been invaluable after the loss of the space shuttle Columbia, and would save US taxpayers billions of dollars. However, the AAS program was imposed on Nasa by the Office of Management and Budget (OMB) and the Congress in an attempt to get value for money for U.S. taxpayers; consequently, out of $62.7 million that Congress provided for the AAS program in 2003, Nasa brazenly redirected $40 million to its favoured OSP program, and announced that AAS will not continue in 2004 !

Why is AAS resisted by Nasa in favour of OSP? The answer is plainly because it is not in the short-term economic interest of Nasa and its client companies to permit such a simple lowcost solution to their requirements. Unfortunately, as Niskanen also explains, nor would it be in the short-term interest of the politicians who nominally "oversee" Nasa and its budget. One might paraphrase Winston Churchills famous description of Russia as a riddle wrapped in a mystery inside an enigma by saying that G7 space agency cost estimates are a scandal wrapped in a sham inside a farce.

In truth, Nasa's own cost estimates in this case are economically meaningless. Quite apart from being undependable and prone to balloon, they refer to the development of a service for which there is no demand except from Nasa itself, devised in a "sui generis" manner and hence under no pressure to be an economically competitive or "best-practice" result, and following no agreed standard so that the resulting service cannot be judged. An aviation expert involved in the JRS space tourism study programme accurately described the difference between civil aviation and space industry practice in vehicle development by saying that the latter are like children making model aeroplanes: they make up rules as they go along, deciding what is acceptable (to themselves) on an "ad hoc" basis rather than following agreed rules derived from accumulated experience, and designed to achieve a target level of performance.

That is, after more than 40 years, governments' role in space activities is still at the same stage as the early days of aviation when government aircraft development projects suffered repeated disasters from which the fundamental lesson was learned that the three roles of customer, manufacturer and safety regulator must be performed by independent organisations. If they are not, the conflicts of interest that arise between political and commercial objectives ensure failure. This is well illustrated in the book " Slide Rule", which describes the simultaneous development of the successful, company-developed R100 and the disastrous, government-developed R101 airship projects. As a result of experience, governments (reluctantly) corrected their role in aviation from (disastrously) developing aircraft directly, to (successfully) supporting the development of commercial aviation. U.S. government actions such as the 1925 Airmail Act privatising the air mail, and the 1926 Air Commerce Act giving the Department of Commerce responsibility to promote aviation, were in much the same vein.

In order to make progress in this situation, the single most important step for the space industry is to collaborate with the civil aviation industry, as discussed in. As Antunano has described, the "aviation approach", its fundamental way of thinking, is the opposite of space agencies: the objective of aviation authorities is to enable as many people as possible to enjoy the services they wish. Consequently instead of government defining rules for selecting candidates for space flight, passengers select themselves, and it is necessary only to advise them of possible risks.

However, space agencies currently have no plans to even study the feasibility of passenger travel services, let alone initiate the fundamental rethinking needed to generate economic value for taxpayers in this way from their massive investment in space technology development. The huge cost to taxpayers' of permitting the present economically wasteful situation to continue, that is the cost of governments' continuing failure to amend their mistaken approach to space development contrary to what they did successfully in aviation is discussed next.

Economic Cost of Delay

As described in Section 3.1 above, the development of passenger space travel services is economically very desirable. As a corollary, delaying this development represents a very large economic cost to taxpayers, which can be considered as comprising four components, namely the direct cost of $1 trillion to date plus $20 billion/year spent on non-science space activities with little economic value, and the economic, social and macroeconomic costs of the lost potential value of new economic activities, as discussed further in. In the following we consider the economic cost of not benefiting from the commercial space activities that could have been generated.

In addition to space agencies' investment of $1 trillion over recent decades, G7 governments have spent some $2 trillion on nuclear power and ten times this on economically unproductive military activities. Using these funds for political purposes instead of for taxpayers' economic benefit hinders the innovation which is vital for the continuation of economic growth. These three fields also employ a very significant fraction of all engineers; employing these highly skilled people in economically unprofitable work greatly reduces the economic value of technological progress –

to the point that it becomes a threat to the stability of the economic system.

Each individual decision to use taxpayers' money for purposes other than to create wealth by developing services for which there is potential demand, is made in the belief that there will always be another year's budget from the "golden goose" of government. Collectively, however, these economically damaging decisions have nearly killed the golden goose, by gradually choking off the possibilities for growth. These cumulative wasteful actions have contributed greatly to the present situation of spiralling government debts, collapsing corporate profits, and ever-rising unemployment – in the USA as well as in Japan, and elsewhere. Indeed, this cost has now reached such a scale that it is causing serious dislocation of not only the US economy but the world economy as a whole, which is in serious distress due to excess capacity in many older industries and lack of new industries, leading to the highest level of unemployment for decades in almost every country today. G7 space agencies have contributed their share to this problem, by adding to taxpayers' debt burden by $20 billion/year while refusing, year after year after year, even to study the possibility of developing a new service that the public are known to want to buy. The potential being wasted in this way is illustrated in the following fictional analogy:

> *"After the invention of the camera, government established the National Camera Science & Applications Administration (NACSAA) which grew rapidly to employ many thousands of researchers developing camera technology. Highly trained "cameranauts" used the resulting government cameras, which cost many millions each, to take photographs of specially chosen subjects "for the benefit of the people". NACSAA prepared voluminous educational materials describing NACSAA's history and activities, and urged members of the general public to take more interest in camera technology. The possibility of developing cheaper cameras as consumer products was said by the leaders of NACSAA and the "camera industry" to require decades more government-funded technology development. Surveys showing a widespread wish among ordinary people to use cameras and own photographs themselves were publicly criticised as "unpatriotic", and said*

to show lack of respect for NACSAA history and for NACSAA's "cameranaut heroes". However, in response, NACSAA started a Photographic Commercialisation Initiative (PCI) which provided a range of new services to the public, including discount sales of government photographs, rental of government cameras to selected members of the public who underwent training at NACSAA in "non-cameranautic photography", and a travelling exhibition to widen access to NACSAA photographs and NACSAA history....."

It is clear that, in such a hypothetical situation, the existence of NACSAA and its political and economic interest group would have created enormous resistance to the development of a genuinely commercial, consumer-oriented camera and photographic industry. This would have imposed a very large economic cost on the public due to not having the benefits of the innovations that have in reality arisen in the absence of NACSAA's repressive influence.

In order to appreciate the scale of this "invisible cost", we need only consider the century-long, true "gale of creative destruction" that has in fact been brought about successively by the invention, development and commercialisation of cinematography, colour photography, instant photography, photocopiers, fax systems, television, video, highspeed photography, Schlieren photography, X-ray photography, holography, IMAX, cineplexes, laser discs, laser printing, disposable cameras, video-conferences, digital cameras, digital film standards, Internet graphic protocols, computer graphics, data compression algorithms, DVDs, colour faxes, mobile-phone cameras, video email, and many other actual developments in imaging technology, many of which have already gone through several generations of technology.

All of this astounding creativity, which has had enormous economic value and created millions of well-paid jobs, is driven by *demand from the general public,* from the "mere consumers" whom NACSAA — and government space agencies — spurn. The growth of passenger space travel, which is finally being grudgingly recognised as the only activity which can energise the stagnating space industry, through the power of consumer demand, can surely be expected to generate at least as great a profusion of innovative and profitable new activities as photography. That is, Figure 3 barely scratches the surface of what will be done by private citizens once they have access to space.

It is important to recognise also that the cost of not benefiting from innovation would have been invisible to those living in the world of NACSAA, and the existence of such a cost would have been vociferously denied by the leaders and political supporters of NACSAA, who would have been eloquent in their praise of its wealth of accumulated experience, the excellence of its staff, the importance of its historic achievement, and so on. Like the hypothetical NACSAA, G7 space agencies' use of US$1 trillion over 45 years – *without having improved on the access to space provided by the Soyuz launch vehicle* – represents an extreme miscalculation of taxpayers' money. The fact that, during the first four decades of their history, the agencies never even investigated whether the taxpayers for whom they supposedly work would like to visit space, further illustrates how far space agencies are from being "servants of the people": *They do not even want to know what the public wants*– precisely as Niskanen describes.

In the Wright brothers' centenary year it is time to face the fact that, as presently constituted, government space agencies are not only not capable of developing space economically, they are actively preventing it from happening. They do this by spending hugely on activities that have minimal economic value, while confusing the public about what is worth doing in space, and obscuring the truth about the enormous economic potential of developing passenger space travel. Unlike government expenditure on nuclear power and military activities, the development of space technology has created capabilities which have the potential to contribute greatly to economic growth by supplying a wealth of popular new consumer services. It is therefore economically very desirable to redirect government space activities so as to achieve greater economic benefit from the technological capabilities developed to date by supplying passenger space travel services.

Conclusions-Where Next?

Once the need to change the present situation is acknowledged, we must face the question how to realise the productive and profitable institutional and political reform that is required, which is discussed elsewhere, including in. Fundamentally it is necessary to follow the Wright brothers' lead, and provide services which the public want to buy. In order to do this economic policy-makers must be made aware of the enormous cost of the present disfunctionality of government space funding; the value of the goal of passenger space travel must be recognised officially; the public must be educated about its feasibility (undoing space agencies' cumulative influence in spreading the false idea that only statistically unusual people can survive the "rigours of space flight"); and detailed collaboration must be established with aviation organisations, of which the spontaneous inclination is to develop popular passenger services. This collaboration must be carried out in such a way as to aid the private sector, as airmail contracts did in the early days of flight. The development of suborbital passenger vehicles and related services should also be encouraged.

However, these changes will not be easy to achieve, due to the continuing influence of those with vested interests in preserving the status quo. Unfortunately, as Public Choice economics explains, governments are very slow to change, and frequently do so only in the face of crisis. We must hope that the government of a country with the required capabilities will take the initiative before the condition of the world economy deteriorates much further; the benefits of doing so are potentially very large. At a time when overproduction in older industries and lack of new ones is reaching crisis level, it is alarming that there is a faction within government arguing that this situation is unavoidable; that war is a means of "economic stimulus" (as well as social control); and that rich countries should take control of the world's "dwindling resources" to maintain their living standards far above the average. Such narrow-minded blindness is tragically mistaken; in truth the future is a cornucopia — there is almost no limit to the potential availability to humans of any known resource. The false belief in a "closed world" rests ultimately on meaningless cost estimates made by G7 space agencies. We can be sure that the Wright brothers would not have been taken in for a moment.

Among other components of the present unusually severe recession, civil aviation is suffering down-sizing, bankruptcies and overall shrinkage within the richer countries. The failure of space to contribute to the economy in any way commensurately to the massive public investment which it has received is because it has systematically put short-term political and corporate interests ahead of the wishes of the general public. The result is sadly predictable: unlike aviation, the space industry supplies almost no services that the public want to buy.

In order to achieve the limitless possibilities for peaceful, plentiful growth that can only be realised through passenger space travel opening space to economic development, the public must learn the hard lesson of the Wright brothers' own harsh experience at the hands of government— and design institutions and rules that ensure that governments' investment in space benefits the general public. Above all, this requires that the goal of space investment is changed to follow aviation's lead and ensure successful development of commercial passenger travel services. The contrast between the histories of aviation and space is key: space must learn from aviation that the only road to real growth is to supply services that the public want to buy. This must be recognised as the most valuable goal of space development. It is so simple and obvious that the only possible resistance is from those with vested interests in preserving existing arrangements. Space agencies' continuing silence on the matter testifies to their recognition that they cannot justify their long-standing negative stance in open debate; they're "hunkered down", hoping the golden goose will continue to lay. In recent years the most economically important new products have been personal computers and mobile telephones (together with the internet protocols which link them all together), of which sales revenues have reached hundreds of $ billions/year.

Both the worldwide boom in sales and the still-continuing rapid technological improvements seen in these two industries were unpredicted, indeed seemed almost unthinkable, even just a few years before they began. Both arose and continue because *they provide products and services that most of the general public wish to buy*. There can be little doubt that the development of passenger space travel has the potential to create an economic boom that will grow far larger than either of these two, and continue far longer. This is because these new services are not only known to be extremely popular among the general population – giving the potential to emulate the "Lindbergh Boom" in aviation – but they also involve opening access to new territory, which has itself been the stimulus for major booms in history. This probability is a further reason why governments mired in a global recession should urgently study the possibility in depth.

It was the Wright brothers' vision and achievement to give the human race access to the sky, thereby fulfilling millenia of dreams. The true continuation of their vision is unquestionably to give humans access beyond the sky, which is collectively our ultimate dream. It is now clear that this requires reorganising governments' role in space development to follow the hugely successful model of civil aviation that the Wright brothers pioneered, rather than continuing the economically unsuccessful model of government monopoly space agencies.

As described in Section 1, for reasons clearly explained in the field of Public Choice economics, government space agencies are not capable of putting the economic interest of the general public ahead of their own contrary interests. The centenary of the Wright brothers' world-changing first flight, which is also the 42nd anniversary of the first space flight (but only the second anniversary of the first private passenger space flight), is high time for governments to face this, and take urgent steps to ensure the further flowering of the Wright brothers' vision, to the immense benefit of us all.

5

Tourism Market

Goals

This discussion paper has three key goals:

- For tourism operators and planners to better understand Market Segmentation;
- To provide an indication of trends in the market, with special focus on emerging segments; and
- To provide a useful backdrop of information for the Product Club Advisory Board to assist in the development of new or enhanced product lines.

Market Segmentation

Market segmentation can be defined as the process through which people (both tourism providers and consumers) with similar needs, wants and characteristics are grouped together so that a tourism business/organization can use greater precision in serving and communicating with these groups (marketing). There are associated benefits of segmentation (e.g. identifying partnerships to promote networking and guiding research and development) but the bottom line is that it enables better marketing decisions, and promotes more viable operations. In more general terms, segmentation comes down to ties that connect two or more individuals (or businesses) together; it could be their age, their love of certain music, the magazines they read, or what their son or daughter is doing in school. The possibilities are endless.

Approaching Segmentation

Market segmentation can be approached from two broad directions: supply side (e.g. grouping similar products together) or the demand side (e.g. demographics and behavioural patterns of tourists). The objective is consistent: trying to reach out to potential customers in a more cost effective manner. The levels of segmentation can be broad (e.g. businesses offering an 'outdoor' experience) or narrow (e.g. a segment of the population in a set geographical boundary, who have a certain medical condition, with children, in a particular income bracket).

The approach to segmentation is important however. There is debate about 'Product Push' versus 'Market Pull'. The former is designing a product and packaging it and hoping that there is a market for it, while the latter attempts to find a niche market, identifying the needs and wants of individuals within that market, and designing a product to meet those needs. Generally it is more effective to undertake the market pull approach, but at the same time it is important to understand the strengths of a region's product. This is especially important when it comes to developing partnerships and products that fit with local community and cultural values. A mixed approach-market pull and 'manipulated or value-added' product push-is likely to be valuable when developing new product lines.

The following comments focus on the three main bases for market segmentation: product related, demographic and behavioural. Generally the more defined a market segment, the easier it is to reach out to individuals. Whichever approach is used, the segments (or niche markets) should be at least one of two things-*Focused* or *Targetable*-preferably both.

Focused: the stronger the ties that link people together the better; not just age and income but expectations, passions, habits, affiliations etc. The niche market does not have to be small to be focused, but usually the larger the market the weaker the ties.

Targetable: The easier it is to reach people in a niche market, the better. If they are all receiving the same newsletter or visit the same location on a regular basis, the better. An example of a focused market is 'ringers' (i.e. those who ring birds for counting and monitoring purposes) within the bird-watching segment. This niche is also targetable because it has its own specific newsletters, associations and conferences. An example of a niche market that is not particularly focused but is targetable is the 'David Thompson' segment. (This idea arose at a recent TASK meeting-to have a retreat inviting only those called David Thompson!). It is not focused as the only connection is the name; individuals are likely to have disparate interests and passions. With today's technology, however, it is a targetable audience.

Product Related Segmentation

- Without listing all the subgroups, typical product-related segmentation may be along the lines of the following,
- Adventure Operators/Organizers *(from family adventures and motorcycle tours to* hunting and bird-watching),
- Attractions *(from museums and theme parks to sports clubs and festivals),*
- Transportation and Services *(from train and van tours to restaurants and gas stations).*

Another product-related segmentation strategy is based on seasons, for example grouping Winter or Fall activities. The Product Clubs of the Canadian Tourism Commission (CTC) are diverse, from focusing on Greek or Aboriginal businesses to particular styles of accommodations, such as 'charming inns'. For those with an outdoor theme the product segmentation is often similar to the above, or even broader. One promotes the four choices of:

- Land Travel
- Water
- Winter
- Mixed Activities.

The use of technology, and more specifically websites, can be very beneficial for segmentation and steering potential customers to their particular vacation interests. Websites can quickly lead consumers to the same tourism package/business via different 'routes'. For instance, a cat skiing operator can be reached via 'Adventure Seekers', or 'Winter Activities'. The use of technology should also be utilized in segmenting the market into further subgroups.

For many years there has been a movement from mass production (and marketing) to customized production (e.g. with a computer manufacturer, customers can choose online their preferred specifications and have it 'built to order'). So too, with the tourism product. Given the consumers' limited time (and tendency to book last minute vacations), they may choose a vacation with a variety of outdoor activities, even offered by different operators. The message here is not to offer consumers what the operators *think* they want, but to provide a wide array of choices, ask them what they want and then organize it for them.

Nature-Based Tourism

The Kootenay region as a whole can largely be viewed as a nature-based tourism product given the plethora of national and regional parks, small communities, lake systems, mountain ranges and truly outstanding natural beauty. Cultural and heritage tourism will continue to play a strong role, but the major draw will be the natural surroundings. Segmentation has already occurred with the creation and naming of the new Product Club. *Explorers of the Western Canadian Wilderness Product Club.* Aside from the geographical identifier, there are two key words: *Explorers* and *Wilderness.* These conjure up an image of unspoilt natural beauty and outdoor activities – it is a nature-based tourism product. The nature-based tourism industry has grown so much in recent years that it now contains four broad sub-markets or segments:

Eco-Tourism: Travel for a learning experience about natural environments, using tourism products and services that are sustainable and sensitive to its surroundings. It should be noted that one recent local project 3 identified a regionally useful definition of Ecotourism within the nature-based tourism segment: "Ecotourism is responsible travel to natural areas which conserves the environment and improves the welfare of local people".

Adventure Travel: Personal accomplishment though thrills of dominating dangerous environments.

Wilderness Travel: Personal recreation through travel in natural environments which are devoid of human interference.

Car Camping: Family travel, providing a safe interface between wild and civilized. All of these descriptions or definitions are open to interpretation. At one end of the spectrum for 'wilderness travel', for example, may be a tourist on a mountain-bike traversing a logging road though a planted forest. Others may believe that wilderness is nonexistent in South-East BC because there are few mountain ridges where there is absolutely no visual human intrusion. This is an important aspect with regards to marketing (and product development) as it is important that the region does not attempt to 'sell' something it does not have. It is equally important not to put off potential visitors because they perceive that the area as too wild and rugged. When undertaking product enhancement or development it should be recognised that these four subgroups are at different stages of the typical life cycle. Broadly speaking, wilderness travel is likely nearing the peak of its business life cycle. This is because true wilderness areas are diminishing and only a limited number of tourist activities can take place in wilderness settings before the product can no longer be categorized as wilderness.

Car-camping too, on a global scale, is either approaching the peak of its life cycle or even started the downward slide. One component of 'vehicle camping' is still on the rise, however, and that is RV travel. Nearly one in twelve (or seven million) vehicle owning households in the USA own an RV, exhibiting nearly an 8% increase in the last four years. There is expected to be a further 15% increase over the next decade. Baby boomers are fuelling this growth and many have yet to reach the prime purchasing age of RV ownership. The rising cost of gasoline and the continuing weakness of the Canadian dollar might provide opportunities for South Eastern BC to offer alternatives to the 'Alaskan experience'.

Both eco-tourism and adventure travel are likely to have greater growth potential and are still on the upward curve of the life cycle. Eco-tourism was recently identified in a series of local community consultations as "the greatest opportunity for tourism growth in the region". 4 Sustainable tourism should not be confused with eco tourism. The latter is a sub sector of sustainable tourism and is a more narrowly defined segment within nature-based activities. Sustainable principles, on the other hand, can apply to all types of tourism activities.

Examples of Segmentation of Outdoor and Learning Travellers

Outdoor travellers and learning travellers are reviewed in more detail given the nature-based local tourism product and the, as-yet-untapped, potential of learning vacations.

Outdoor Segment

Even though a large part of the local tourism product is based on the outdoor experience and natural beauty, this does not mean that all tourists regularly participate in outdoor activities. The graph below provides a picture of the outdoor segmentation of the US market. As seen, a large component of the segment is categorized as 'outdoor inactives' (36%).

There are many market segments that overlap. The pie chart above provides the segmentation split for outdoors travellers. Another market segment, the 'Learning Traveller' was identified as an emerging market. The learning Traveller may overlap with a number of above segments of the outdoor traveller, some being naturalists, some resort lovers, etc.

Outdoor-Wilderness Segment: There are many different ways that markets can be segmented, and an equally diverse number of descriptors that could be attached to each segment. With respect to outdoor wilderness travellers, the Adventures of the Northern Wilderness Product Club identified three main sub sectors for wilderness travel to the Yukon. Its research consisted of 800 telephone interviews and mail surveys to California, Vancouver, Calgary, Chicago, and Ontario. The identified segments were:

- Earthly Explorers: (24% *of respondents*) *like to keep it simple, lower budgets, into nature and roughing it, prefer to keep to one activity rather than trying them* all;
- Adventure Collectors: (*18% of respondents*) *like to sample lots of different* activities, looking for higher quality, with fun, shorter trips;
- Pampers Consumer Boomers: (*14% of respondents*) *Smaller segment but market expected to rise; looking for high quality, want to relax, but also* experience activities in a non-threatening way.

There was a fourth segment identified (*'No Thrills'*), but this sub-market prefer to stay closer to home for their wilderness trips and are not looking for any risk or adventure. Although this was noted as a weak market for the Yukon given distance and remoteness, it may hold some opportunities for the Kootenay region. In terms of product development and target marketing it would be beneficial for the Kootenay region to focus more on the Adventure Collectors and Pampered Consumer Boomers given their ability to pay, interest in winter, and the relatively more desirable (compared with the Yukon) climate offered in the local region, especially in the shoulder seasons.

Learning Traveller Segment: Learning travellers are often referred to as 'educated travellers' not because the trips they take have educational components but because they themselves have higher overall education levels than the population at large. *Elderhostel Canada* (since 2000 it has been renamed *Routes to Learning Canada–RTC*) has been the single largest provider of learning travel programs in Canada for 20 years. The North American Elderhosteller is on average 68 years old, and 90% have post secondary education (in a time when post secondary education was less accessible). Nearly 1 in 5 report having 7 or more years of post-secondary education. 7 The segments for learning travellers are:

Explorers are those looking for learning programs that offer opportunities to explore a new part of the world and learn about local area history, customs and cultures;

- *Activity-Oriented* are those seeking outdoor experiences and are interested in the natural environment;
- *Content-Committed are people who look for a specific subject of interest (e.g.* lepidoptery – the study of moths and butterflies);
- *Convenience-Oriented look for programs that are within a six-hour driving radius of* home.

Of the four segments, the last one is the one that would fit least well with the location and tourism product in the Kootenay Region. 'Activity-oriented' individuals and 'explorers', however, mesh perfectly with the strengths of the local tourism product, and the direction of the new product club.

Demand-Based Segmentation

Demographics

Understanding demographics is imperative to product development and segmentation, especially with regard to understanding trends in the market place. Demography (the study of age, sex, education, family status, life cycle etc.) is an excellent tool for product developers and marketers. According to the well respected demographer, David Foot, demographics accounts for "two-thirds of everything", (markets, social problems, demand for services etc.).

The subject therefore plays a key-role in decisionmaking regarding demand for tourism products.

Age in particular is an important example. The baby-boom generation is of prime importance due to its size (roughly 1/3 of the Canadian population – proportionally the largest of all the industrialized nations) and characteristics. It is well educated with above average income. The front end is also approaching (within 10 years) retirement age and will therefore have the money and the time to travel.

The 'echo' generation (children of the boomers) are also creating peak demands on certain products and services. Born between 1980 and 1995, the front end is into their twenties and taking part in independent, adventure travel. They are also much more technologically advanced and have been brought up in a generation with strong concerns for the environment Other sub sectors and age cohorts also need to be understood to more effectively communicate with them.

Lifecycle Segments: A recent and comprehensive travel motivations survey was undertaken for both Canadian and US travellers. The data was used to provide a series of reports and one 9 focused on demographic analysis of the various tourism market segments. The life cycle segments were as follows:

- Youth Market (18-35, no children under 20 living at home);
- Family Market (with children under 20 living at home);
- Mature Market (36-65 – no children); and
- Seniors Market (over 65, no children living at home).

Each one of these is broken down into sub categories, as shown in the pie chart below. The two largest segments are the Family Market and the Mature Market – accounting for over two thirds of the entire travel market. This, again, reflects the boomer bulge in the population. The single largest segment, at nearly one quarter of all travellers, is Mainstream Young Families (children under 12 living at home). A quick overview of the characteristics of the various segment follows:

Youth Market: (20% of the travel market): lower than average incomes, high energy approach to travel (extreme sports), high participation rate in activities, especially likely to seek out personal indulgence travel, use the internet as a research and booking tool.

Family Market: (33% of the travel market): above average education and income, most affluent of the four markets. Tends to be shorter-haul travellers (with children); important domestic market; greater focus on recuperative vacation experiences; less likely than average to take day and overnight tours; less than likely than typical American traveller to visit Canada.

Mature Market: (32% of the travel market): relatively well educated and affluent; slightly more than average likely to seek out exploratory vacation activities; more than likely to have gone on natural sightseeing vacations & visited cultural attractions; above average users of travel packages.

Seniors Market: Smallest of the four markets (15%): lower than average education and income levels; American seniors more likely than the average traveller to visit Canada, and most likely of all the markets to seek out exploratory vacation experiences, much less likely to view vacations as opportunities for relaxation. Above average participation in natural sightseeing (although generally less active in outdoor activities) and above average in cultural and heritage attractions; more likely than average to take guided tours; rely more on printed material and television for travel opportunities and information.

Although currently smallest, special attention should be paid to the seniors market, as its members look for exploratory experiences and prefer value-added components such as guided services. Although currently not a wealthy segment, the baby boomers are approaching retirement with higher income and education levels.

As can be seen, the largest sub-markets are mainstream young families, mainstream mature couples and mainstream youth. All the affluent segments are very important to the tourism sector as they tend to be better educated, well travelled, have the means to travel and are often looking for new experiences. The affluent sub-markets account for over one-quarter of all travellers.

Behavioural Segmentation

People's '*activities, interests* and *opinions* (AIO's) also play a key role in decisionmaking and travel habits. These behavioural characteristics (also known as psychographics), when used in conjunction with demographics, provide a much stronger marketing tool for tourism businesses and planners. By understanding people's AIO's and their subsequent motivations, certain subgroups can be targeted more effectively, as well as reflected in new product lines.

Another TAMS report (Emergent Vacation Interests) 10 focussed on emergent themes in tourism and indicated which demographic sub market was likely to drive which emergent theme. A more detailed description of the report's findings (relevant to The Product Club) is outlined in the *Tourism Trends Discussion Paper.* Suffice to say the key emergent themes (in order of anticipated net change) were as follows:

- Intimacy & Romance,
- Experiencing Different Cultures,
- Natural Wonders,
- Fine Cuisine and being pampered,
- Escaping winter weather,
- Adventure and Excitement,
- Experiencing Unspoiled Nature,
- Historic sites,
- Hands on Learning,
- Hobby or sport.

Any product development should try and incorporate one or more of these themes if it is going to meet future markets. Selecting a couple that are most relevant to The Product Club-*experiencing unspoiled nature* and *adventure and excitement,* the predominant sub-market driving both experiences is mainstream mature singles. Other important sub-markets that show great interest in these vacations are the young mainstream and mainstream young family markets.

The affluent family market is also a key driver. According to some travel writers 11, one of "the hottest trends in travel in 2002 was the family vacation", especially for affluent families.

This may have arisen, in part, from the events of Sept, promoting a desire not to stray too far from loved-ones. With regard to transportation segmentation there is now even an airline designed exclusively for family travel: FamilyAir based in Los Angeles.

What the Sub-markets will be Looking for

As noted, the largest sub-market is the mainstream young family market, accounting for 23% of North American Travellers. This group is looking for a number of outdoor activities, four out of the top five (in terms of anticipated net increases) of which are offered in the region. These are:

- horseback riding (12% expected increase);
- downhill skiing (11%);
- white-water rafting (10%); and
- kayaking or canoeing (10%).

The one not offered regionally (in the top five of emergent activities) is whale watching.

Other notable outdoor experiences that are gaining in popularity within this single largest market segment are snowmobiling on organized trails (8%) and recreational biking (7%). Although smaller than mainstream markets the affluent segments require special attention due to their larger discretionary spending.

In each sub-market the level of affluence varied. For example with affluent young couples, two-thirds of the market have household incomes between $40K and $80K with a third having $80K plus. With the affluent mature and senior couples 100% had income in excess of $80K.

There are a number of common threads. Intimacy and romance was top of the list of emergent themes in three of the five affluent markets and top of the list of two of the three largest markets. Natural wonders, different cultures, hands-on learning, being pampered and adventure vacations were all repetitive emergent themes.

The growing demand for exploratory and learning travel was highlighted with a recent travel write-up of a Scottish whiskey school (a 3-day learning experience). One individual was there after being involved in a climbing accident: "as he lay on his back looking at the stars [he] realized that he had always loved the night sky but knew nothing about it. He promised himself that, if he lived, he would never be so negligent with his passions." [Incidentally at least two of the individuals on the ccurse (in their 30's) went because they had received it as a gift].

In the near future, increased numbers will have greater awareness of the fragility of life and there is likely to be an increased push in making memorable vacations. The Vancouver office of the Canadian Institute for the Blind, for example, has one new client walking through its doors every ten minutes. This is expected to double, to one person every five minutes, within the next fifteen years.

Activity-Related Accommodation

Nearly all (19 out of 20) activity-related accommodation types were more likely to be stayed in over the subsequent two years (at 2000) compared with the previous two years. Again this confirms the importance of experiential vacations.

Especially promising increases were expected in the bed and breakfast market. Less common activity-based accommodations (in other words niche markets, stayed-in by less than 10% of travellers) showed great potential relative to their market size. These included health spas, learning experiences, working farms, and wilderness lodges, which all suggest that more exotic forms of vacation are on the increase. Of particular note is the 'staying at a wilderness lodge that you can drive to by car', showing a twofold (anticipated) increase. This study was conducted prior to September 11, and the increased fear of flying (and cost) may contribute to enlarging this segment still further. The increased interest in activity-related accommodation types amongst American and Canadian travellers.

Conclusions

A number of conclusions can be drawn from the data above, especially with respect to creating or enhancing product lines. These are:

- Market Segmentation is crucial. No business can be everything to everyone and those that can differentiate their markets will be in a much stronger position.
- Segmentation should not based purely on similar product attributes; a 'market pull' approach should be adopted where planners/operators first understand the needs/desires of individual market segments and then design packages/products to meet those needs.

- There is no right or wrong way to segment the products or market but segments, or niche markets, should be both focused and targetable.
- Developing and implementing new product lines is only half the battle; other real work comes in trying to reach the target market-identifying accessible (and focused) markets first and then designing packages and products that will draw tourists in.
- The Product Club should not expend significant effort and dollars on undertaking primary research into market segmentation. Significant analysis of the market place already exists.
- The Product Club should primarily focus on its strength: delivering a nature-based tourism product. Within this, there should be a mix of different activities and experiences offered, from themes promoting intimacy and romance to learning vacations.
- The Product Club should not solely focus on one lifestyle segment, e.g. the needs of current baby-boomers, because these will be replaced by a much smaller ("bust" population) in the years ahead. A mix is required and planning for future changes is important.
- The lines of segmentation are becoming more blurred as people mix activities.
- Special attention should be paid to emergent themes among segments. These include learning, intimacy and romance, heritage and historical trips, adventure and excitement, experiencing unspoiled nature, being pampered, health and spa retreats, bed and breakfasts related to activities, and lodges that can be driven to, among others.

The Application of Benefit Segmentation in Tourism Promotion

A basic starting point for tourism marketing efforts is a formal or informal marketing plan. In such a plan target market analysis or market segmentation is usually the first step and the most important part. An excellent market segmentation is half success of a marketing strategy. Promotion is particularly important in the tourism marketing strategy. A recurring problem in the tourism promotional area is "at whom should the promotional effort be aimed" and "what should be said to the prospective tourist". Market segmentation may give these questions good answers. Many people have proposed guidelines for dealing with the problem of identifying tourism target markets. They have attempted to position tourism products in the mind of the prospective tourists, or split up the market based on latent or overt psychological desires., price trip purpose, use type, or other characteristics of tourist in geography, socioeconomics and demography. However, some researchers have found with respect to the inability of demographics to explain important differences in travel and vacation behaviour. What is proposed here is a benefit segmentation approach which can combine many different ways of looking at the tourist and the travel market and actually simultaneously reduce marketing and promotional costs while increasing tourist demand. In other words, clever segmentation strategy can improve marketing and promotional efficiency for the tourism marketer. In addition, a tentative procedure will be rendered to help one to conduct a benefit segmentation research.

Tourism Marketing

In 1985 the American Marketing Association defines marketing as the performance of business activities that direct the flow of goods and services from the producer to the consumer or user. However, tourism industry is unlike many other industries in many ways: unseen before selling, intangibility, paying time and money before actually using, direct or indirect reservation in advance, far away from customers, combination of resources from a variety of businesses, cannot be stored, limited supply in the short term, instability of demand, and high elasticity of demand. The objective of marketing is to reflect the present marketing plan assessment, create the right image for the tourism product, and satisfy consumers. The most widely accepted method for this has been the development of marketing programs based on the 4 p's (product, place, price, and promotion). Within tourism generally price and place to visit is very difficult to be manipulated by tourist agencies in the short run. However, the product itself (various attractions in tourism industry) and promotion of that product (mass communications, direct mail, brochures, etc.), are much more controllable. The product itself can be improved to better match market desires but product calibration decisions involve longterm consequences since substantial developments require extensive time for planning and actual implementation.

The tourism industry can be differentiated from many tangible product businesses by the consumers' perception of risk when they buy intangible services. Promotion can reduce consumers' perception of risk. In addition, some features of tourism business, such as seasonal demand, price sensitive, selling without viewing the product, low brand loyalty, severe competition, and high substitution have made promotion play important role in tourism marketing. Promotion decisions involve the determination of copy appeals, media strategy, and production costs, and are easily controlled in the short run. Proper execution of the promotion task requires a thorough understanding of the levels and types of market heterogeneity faced by the tourism marketer. That is, a marketer needs to know his/her markets and their desires. Segmentation research can help with this task of identifying markets and can lead to more effective promotional strategies.

Market Segmentation on Benefits Sought

Generally speaking, market segmentation is based on four assumptions: (1) Tourists can be grouped into different but homogeneous market segments; (2) People in different market segment have different tourism needs and preferences; (3) A specific destination or tourist experience will appeal to some segments of the market more than others; (4) Tourism suppliers can improve their marketing efforts by market segments. Many ways exist to segment a market. The marketing literature is replete with examples of ways to group consumers based on geography, purchase behaviour, socioeconomic and demographic factors, use type, price, and various cognitive measures.

A method that has the highest usage in recreation or tourism is "benefit segmentation". It also uses a behavioural approach to segmentation but is the hardest to identify. This approach groups consumers according to benefits desired from a particular product category. It seeks to identify that part of the market that derives specific benefits from the product/service. The variables that a supplier has that are benefit based include recreational facilities and equipment, length of stay, transportation mode, experience preferences, and benefit expectations. With benefit-based segmentation, a supplier must determine what benefits potential customers are seeking from their tourist experiences. Groups are then formed of people who assign a similar amount of importance to the same product benefits. It is based primarily on cluster analytic method and has enjoyed widespread application. Once this is done, those benefits are presented to this market segment to encourage additional business.

The Procedure of Benefit Segmentation

The general approach of benefit segmentation consists of collecting data from various tourists by using survey instruments designed and applying appropriate statistical procedures to analyze these data. In brief, this approach includes two major phases: segment creation and segment testing.

Phase 1: Segment Creation

The first step is developing a set of attributes (benefits) which exhaustively describes the range of attributes available from and desired in the product. This list of attributes may include redundancies which are either real or perceived as real by the consumer. These benefits, for example, may be like scenery, cost of vacation, social activity, friendliness of people, cleanliness of environment, quality of shopping, quality of sporting opportunities, cultural opportunities, quality of accommodations, quality of entertainment, and so on. In practice it is usually developed from previous studies (content analysis of related literature), from judgment of a jury of experts, from perception testing of the relevant sample in the field (perhaps through focus groups), and pilot study of the instrument. This step is conducted to assure the list of attributes is clarity, concise, relevance, and validation, Engel, et. al.,., furnish a more thorough discussion of product attributes and their measurement.

The next step is eliciting subjects' assessments of the relative importance of each of the various attributes by Likert scale. For instances, "1" is very important and "5" is less important. In this way, an importance vector is created for each individual. Practically speaking, random sampling from a population of tourists is an impossible task. Generally, we can try to obtain a representative sample through randomizing time and location of questionnaire distribution. Cluster analysis.usually factor analysis of the importance vectors, is then employed in identifying groups of individuals in a benefit segment which is the package of benefits that they all are looking for when choosing a product or a service.

Phase II: Segment Testing

Segment testing directly describes the market structure. Each segment is described using several groups of variables such as principal benefits sought, general activities (lifestyle), interests, trip purpose, alternate destination favoured, different media habits and strengths, and opinions in travelling. These also include demographic and socioeconomic variables such as age, income, and size of family. Sometimes the discriminant analysis will be taken to test if demographic or psychographic variables are significant difference across each benefit segment. A summary of the overall profile of each benefit segment will be presented. Ultimately, promotional strategies are proposed for each of the segments which management wishes to reach.

Initially, each segment is described in terms of the unique, differential benefits sought by its members. This analysis is usually enhanced by a comparison of segments on their lifestyle and personality traits. Schewe and Calantone provide an example of this kind of comparison in a travel context. Also, demographic and socioeconomic statistics (SES) comparisons are made between groups to facilitate media purchases that efficiently reach target segments.

Next, purchase behaviour of each segment is evaluated. The assumption is that people tend to choose products which most closely fit their "ideal" in terms of benefits sought. Each group is identified by the benefits it seeks and the attractions (or brands) it prefers. From this point marketing strategy development draws on the manger's understanding of the situation. Key variables have been identified which make a segmenta i.e. market position) unique.

Managerial Implications

Sometimes the benefits that customers seek determine their purchasing behaviour much more precisely than do geographical, demographic, or psychographic factors.. The tourism marketer can develop demographic profiles of those groups identified in the benefit segmentation in order to promote to those segments.

This and other valuable information in such research have provided marketer for designing promotional appeals to its consumers and potential consumers, brochures, package tours, direct selling, point-of-purchase materials, or other media, to the product in the study, and training of branch office personnel. When introducing a new product/brand, the manager can develop copy appeals based on benefits of the new product/brand matching the desired benefits of an identified target segment. This can be especially effective where a new product or brand possesses more of a desired benefit, a differential advantage, than an existing product or brand. Alternatively an existing product/brand might be repositioned with new appeals to better appeal to a particular benefit segment. Each of these strategies, as well as others, depends on the strength each existing product has in its position and each segment's demand for the product's benefits.

Also important is the stability of the segments over time. People change, the environment changes, enough promotion to segments will in and of itself change the market. Just people's need for variety causes segmentation schemes to change over time. Thus, all segmentation schemes have time limits on their usefulness. In addition, this kind study provided the impetus for further marketing studies in the travel and tourism industry.

Conclusion

Benefit is one of key factors in tourist's decision process. People pay to buy a service or product because they can gain some kinds of benefits from this' service or product. Therefore, the tourism marketer should understand purchase behaviour based on the-benefits the consumers seek. Choosing target segments and promotional themes are crucial to marketing any product or service. Benefit segmentation provides an excellent technique for effective and efficient marketing.

The wealth of information provided by the benefit segmentation technique can be directly translated into marketing and promotional strategy. No technique can eliminate the need for good managerial judgment and knowledgeability concerning products and markets. However, it is hoped that the above discussion of benefit segmentation with research recommendations, furnishes a convincing argument for its usefulness in tourism promotion.

The International, Local and Social Efforts Involved

India expects a tourist inflow of around 10 million in 2010. The country's tourism sector was growing steadily with 3.92 million tourist inflow in 2005 and 4.43 million in 2006, a confidence is being generated that the inflow would touch the eight million mark in 2009.

There is considerable government presence in the travel and tourism industry. Each state has a tourism corporation, which typically runs a chain of hotels/motels and operates package tours, while the central government runs the India Tourism Development Corporation. Divestment of these state-run tourism corporations have either already taken place or are in process.

Incoming foreign tourist arrivals have shown a 6% compounded annual growth rate over the last 10 years. The government has realised the potential and has advanced several incentives to promote infrastructure growth in the tourism sector. Current investments are likely to see hotel room capacity increase by 20% over the next three years, with several international hotel chains entering the hotel industry. With specialised types of tourism becoming a craze throughout the world, India is coming up with Dubai-type shopping tourism facilities at several places besides focusing on health tourism. At least four such destinations would come up soon and another is likely in West Bengal. Aurangabad near Ajanta-Ellora in Maharashtra is one of the leading shopping tourism destinations coming up amongst others like Noida in Uttar Pradesh with world class facilities, Shilpagram near Hyderabad, permanent art and crafts fair at Bhubaneswar.

Tourism in Aurangabad

The incredible India campaign has given a brand new dimension to the marketing of India as a country. Aurangabad and particularly Ajanta-Ellora have enjoyed a steady stream of local and international visitors from a long time, even before any specific promotion or campaign was done for it. The tourists are classified as " Budget Tourists" and " Star Tourists". They can choose the type of vacation they want to enjoy in this part of the country. It also enables the government and other bodies to subsequently divide their efforts on them The centre organizes exhibitions and trade shows especially in the Aurangabad region. These give an excellent platform for rural and ethnic culture of the region to be displayed before the international tourists. Various handicrafts, local crafts, food etc. are exhibited. Over the past 5 + years, Aurangabad has seen a regular flow of both national and international tourists. Acknowledged as one of the fastest growing tier-II city, Aurangabad offers a range of site seeing, shopping and experiencing opportunities.

But amongst all, the most visited and most revered, still remain the beautiful Ajanta Ellora caves. In addition, the city has seen the development of relevant education providing institutes, courses – vocational, developmental etc. to provide world class atmosphere and service to the customers. The contributions of such entities were indeed exemplary.

Mentioning the infrastructure actors, the presence of three five star hotels in a tier–II city speaks a lot. Good quality roads, renovation of squares, bus stands, and railway stations, restoration works have been the focus to give a world class experience to the tourists. Promoting the place as a 'must see' on the list of the international Buddhist traveller has indeed been a national effort, but in line with that the contributions of local authorities can be seen in their adaptation of every heritage signage, symbol and story in their day to day activities.

The JBIC Project

An entire project named 'Ajanta – Ellora Conservation and tourism development project' is dedicated to the conservation of Ajanta – Ellora site. MTDC (Maharashtra tourism Development Corporation) an undertaking of Maharashtra state conceived the Ajanta – Ellora Conservation and tourism development project and prepared in 1991 a master plan from Tata Consultancy Services, on the basis of which the Government of India requested the Government of Japan to consider grant of financial assistance for the project.

The Government of Japan got the plan assessed from the Overseas Economic Cooperation Fund (OECF) now Japan Bank for International Cooperation (JBIC) and offered loan assistance for the implementation of the master plan as phase –I of the project. The government went into agreement for the loan in 1992. A Joint Venture of Pacific Consultants International (PCI) and Tata

Consultancy Services (TCS) were appointed in November as consultants for planning and overseeing the implementation of the works under the loan. The objectives of the project are:

1. To conserve and preserve monuments and natural resources in the Ajanta-Ellora region.
2. To improve infrastructure in order to accommodate the increasing number of tourists to the region and enhance their experience by providing improved facilities and services.

The first phase consisted of building up essential infrastructure facilities. The consultants, then as was stipulated in Terms of Reference drafted a proposal for Phase –II. It was presented by the Ministry of Tourism for consideration of OECF in the Interministrial Meeting in 1998.

Phase –I and Extended Phase –I Expenditure

The project cost was estimated at Yen 4,406 million which is equal to Rs.817.1 million at the exchange of Rs. 1 = Yen 5.39. The support from JBIC was Yen 3,745 (Rs. 498.8 million) which was 85% of the total project cost.

Ajanta-Ellora Conservation and Tourism Development Project

Phase-II

The second phase of the Ajanta-Ellora Conservation and tourism development project with the Japanese Bank of International Cooperation (JBIC) sanctioning a soft loan of Rs. 300 crores became effective from July 31, 2003. The loan clearance was announces after JBIC held a series of talks with the central department of tourism and culture and MTDC in Delhi. The first phase of Ajanta– Ellora heritage circuit up gradation scheme won appreciation not only from Japanese government but also UNESCO. The second phase envisaged taking forward the conservation and a development scheme initiated in the first phase.

The second was targeted to be completed in 5 years time and was meant to generate additional employment in Ajanta-Ellora region. The plans envisaged restoration and repair of entire cave circuit of Maharashtra i.e. between Mumbai and Aurangabad. The work carried out at these places includes structural reinforcement, chemical conservation of the paintings and artifacts, preservation of percolation within the caves, upgrading the environment, training conservation staff and improving visitor management system.

A Brief Account of the Work Being Done

Monument Conservation

It included the conservation and repair of he cave belt. Project packages of ASI (chemical branch) for chemical conservation of monuments., survey and maintenance/operation of equipments and purchase of equipments for conservation laboratory at Aurangabad and detailed documentation of heritage monuments.

The package included:

1. Protection of rock mass,
2. Prevention of water seepage in the caves,
3. Slope stability of caves and adjoining hills,
4. conservation, preservation and protection of sensitive paintings,
5. Surface water management,
6. Landscaping the adjoining region,
7. Visitor management,
8. Restoration of essential/structural elements and investigate/exploration of surroundings.

Aurangabad Airport (Executing Agency – Airport Authority of India)

The major work included to facilitate domestic and international flights to land in Aurangabad and the airport facilities to be upgraded. The development was aimed to significantly boost the international tourist traffic. The package included:

1. Construction of new passenger terminal building and ancillary support facilities.
2. construction of new apron 500 x 400 and construction of taxi track.

Afforestation (Executing Agency – Forest Department, Maharashtra) The central idea was to enhance the greenery adjoining the classic plains surrounding the caves. This was aimed to improve vegetation cover which will prevent soil erosion subsequently reduce pollution vicinity of the caves. The package included:

1. Major afforestation activity in adjoining areas of the caves.
2. Information and maintenance, erection of fire tower, fire line cutting every year, fire fighting equipments, display card on trees.
3. Tourist facilities, camping and accommodation facilities, establishment of nature trails and watch towers.

Road (Executing Agency – Public Works Department, Maharashtra State)

A number of roads were selected for repair and up gradation. All the roads lead to tourist destinations and it was considered that these improvements will lead to reduction in time and commuting costs. Also the towns and villages in the vicinity of these roads will also benefit.

Water Supply (Executing Agency – Maharashtra Jeevan Pradhikaran)

Water supply and sanitation was the main focus. The aim was to provide essential facilities to tourists visiting the caves.

Tourism and Marketing and Visitor Management System (MTDC) Development of Ajanta Tourist Complex: which included construction of visitor information centre, arrival area, interpretation centre, site museum, virtual reality hall, cave replicas, restaurants, plazas and service areas.

Development of Ellora Tourist Complex: which included construction of visitor centre, arrival area, interpretation centre, site museum, virtual reality hall, restaurants, plazas, and service areas.

Public Awareness Activities

For promotion of Maharashtra and Buddhist circuits along with Ajanta-Ellora region using press, print, audio visual and electronic media.

Human Resource Development

Training of staff for maintenance and operation of tourism destinations, visitor management systems, and tourism planning and environment conservation was the main focus.

Computerization of tourist information: A new system to be set up for computerization of tourist information.

Conservation of State Archeological Monuments

A number of sites, monuments and gates in the Aurangabad city and its vicinity were chosen for repair and conservation and also beatification so that it would act as an additional tourist attraction in line with the caves.

Development of Lonar crater: Lonar is the lake formed by an meteorite. Hence the focus was to promote it as a "must see" site. Roads, fencing, restoration, clearing of prosopsis plants, creation of visitor information centres etc. were undertaken. Additional sub projects at the vicinity of the caves: These included restoration and maintenance of various cave belts and regions. Development of access roads, signage, power and water infrastructure at these tourist places were on the list.

Micro Credit for Low Income Tourist Service Providers

This is the first of its kind in tourism sector in India and aimed at organizing and training service providers at tourist sites who are otherwise considered as nuisance by tourists and planners alike but are essential part of Indian tourism scenario. Along with the development of infrastructure in Aurangabad there is a need to cater to small necessities of tourists which are met by mushrooming hawkers whose service to tourists leave much to desire.

The micro financing sub projects aimed at organizing, training, and financing this low income segment. Women entrepreneurs will be given preference and suitable NGOs ha been identified to training, disburse and monitor the micro credit funding credit and recovery. The beneficiaries include of the scheme small restaurant owners, tea shops, kiosks, guides, photographers, hawkers, fruit vendors and taxi operators. This would make them more presentable as well as increase their entrepreneurial skills and abilities. The loan amount of the will be chanelised through rural banks.

Marketing the Shopping District

Aurangabad has an exclusive set up of mini markets and lanes dedicated to selling ancient craft. The areas near Panchakki,

Ajanta – Ellora, Paithan, Daulatabad and the Aurangabad city have their own shops, which sell exclusive speciality items. Aurangabad has seen the thriving of many retail, government owned privately held outlets that offer a variety of regional handicrafts, clothes, jewellery, food etc.

This has immensely contributed to local employment generation. The marketing of Ajanta as a shopping destination is also a driving factor that made customers come to buy region specific products like Himroo shawls, jewellery etc. A best example is 'Paithani Saree' which is handmade and known to have originated at Paithan which is a 30 minutes drive from Aurangabad. On the way to Ajanta-Ellora there are number of government owned and also privately owned shops which sell Paithani sarees, Kurtas, Scarves handkerchiefs etc. All of these have a contributing effect on the marketing of India.

The shopping markets that have evolved in the form of mini shopping districts around the place/site made the shopping experience more relevant to the heritage promotion of Ajanta and Ellora. Even the five star hotels that are running successfully here have exclusive galleries dedicated to the handicrafts made in this region. Here the international traveller gets a glance at the Indian culture. This is a good place for shopping for the tourist who does not want to be bothered by local vendors and sellers.

Rural Tourism-" Atithi Devo Bhava!"

This is the central idea behind all the tourism activities done by the government. The tourists are given the taste of the Indian hospitality and treated as 'God' just the way it is written is scriptures and taught to every Indian.

The authorities have very strategically promoted the theme of 'Rural Tourism'. The focus is on promoting rural culture and enabling employment generation. Tourism is considered to be the major revenue generator in these regions. Typically the allied and dependant areas like restaurants, tourist guides, handicraft shops have been considered to be the focus areas for revamping and enhancement. An active platform is given to boost the generation of income in rural households. Tourists can now stay at the very homes of rural citizens. The government has started the ' Bed and Breakfast scheme' where they can stay at a local household and get an exclusive experience of the ethnic and rural flavour of India. The housewives get a chance to earn as they provide Indian food and shelter to these travellers. While staying with these local families these tourists get a chance to enjoy the day to day life of an Indian village. As this region is extensively dependant on tourism, here the government is also helping them out to get a more professional way to carry on their business.

Along with the handicrafts that are widely sold, special promotion is given to the Indian wear like sarees, kurtas etc. Also women are given a chance to set up their units where they can put mehndi on the hands of the tourists. An entire package of rural site seeing, staying with a local family and enjoying Indian flavours, traditions and handicrafts is being successfully sold to the tourists. India is internationally known to be a diverse yet very vibrant and colourful country. Marketing it as an 'rural experience' that is a must have for every tourist has many varied dimensions to it. The basic beneficiary is rural India and also the international tourist in many ways. On one hand it gives a good platform for rural India to showcase its culture and also earn from it. And for tourist, it is a very different and exclusive experience. The incredible India campaign has given a real boost to the inflow of international tourists. The global and local authorities are striving hard to maintain the eco friendly zone which they have recently declared around the caves.

Ajanta-Ellora Festival

A large crowd is pulled annually by the Ajanta Ellora festival, formerly known as Ellora festival, which sees a lot of national, state, local and international involvement. It is one of the best ways to study the marketing mix involved in promoting the site as a tourist attraction. Local students from institutes like hotel institutes, tourism courses etc. are invited to join the organizers and delegated various tasks to be a part of this mega event. It has been one of the drivers of tourism has been the Ajanta –Ellora festival that was started as a cultural event by the authorities. Many well known Indian artistes perform on this occasion. Of all the 4 P's the most used, necessary and exemplary were the heritage place itself, people involved, products/services offered and the simplified processes in making Ajanta to top the traveller's list.

6

Growth of Global Tourism

Globalization Process: Challenge for Tourism Countries with SME Structures

Tourism is one of the world economy's growth sectors. Despite crisis-induced slumps the long term growth trend appears to be stable. Tourism is a beneficiary of the irreversible process of globalization and indeed is an accelerating factor for this process. The trend to a division of labour on a worldwide basis has been particularly favourable to tourism, resulting in increased productivity and prosperity in a great many countries. We owe these welcome developments to the introduction of a market economy and democracy in many of the emerging and transitional economies, a process that has been encouraged by the OECD.

Tourism is today one of the most internationalised sectors of the world economy. The world tourism market has been extended a lot, adding considerably to the potential for further growth and at the same time bringing about greater competition between tourism countries.

This raises the question whether or not tourism will be able to survive and prosper in such a competitive world economy in countries where the structure in this sector is based mainly on small-to-medium-sized enterprises (SMEs), and if so how.

It is for this reason that the overriding objective of the conference in Gwangju, Korea, is to devise new concepts that can help to make tourism countries in which small businesses dominate more competitive. These efforts require a good analytical understanding of tourism market structures.

Demand-driven Phenomenon: Importance of Visitors' Spending

Tourism is a creation of the modern industrial economy and the leisure society to which it has given rise. It is a sector that can only be defined in terms of demand. The key unit of measurement is the visitor. Whether travelling for business or pleasure the visitor spends money and creates demand for tourism products and services. In each case the decision to travel precedes the act or acts of consumption. There is no tourism industry as such. The supply side structures of tourism are volatile. They only make their appearance once the potential visitor has made the decision to travel and become an actual visitor, consuming a variety of goods and services. Visitors from the home country as well as from abroad pay money for individual goods and services, for reasons and motives that vary considerably. These products and services are produced by many different sectors of the economy and by companies both small and large. In this context it makes a great difference whether or not the goods and services consumed are selected by the individual tourists themselves, or on the contrary are put together by professional tour operators.

Macroeconomic Approach: Typical Tourism Related Industries

Thanks to a concept initiated and developed in the 1980s by the OECD Tourism Committee, the so-called Tourism Satellite Account (TSA), it is possible today to track the spending of visitors and see which specific sectors of the national economy benefit from this spending and to what extent. This makes it possible to measure the extent to which tourism contributes to value added and employment in a given country or region. This complex and time-consuming approach has also made it possible at the macro-level, with the help of a theoretical-statistical construct, to achieve a better understanding of the heterogeneity of production in tourism. Industries which obtain the lion's share of their earnings from the spending of visitors can now be identified as "characteristic branches of tourism, or collectively as the "tourism industry". In addition to identifying these specific tourism-dependent sectors of the economy we can now determine the extent to which the spending of tourists also benefits other industries which are connected or non specific to tourism. The core sectors of the tourism industry are the passenger transport segments, the hotel and catering segments and the leisure, culture and sports segments. It is clear, however, that economic sectors that do not have any formal relationship with tourism, such as the retail trade, the construction industry, or the banking and insurance sector, also benefit a lot from the spending of visitors.

Microeconomic Approach: Tourism Systems and Service Chains

Visitors of course do not see tourism as a statistical construct. For them the journey to and from, and the time spent in the destination, all add up to a single experience. Given this holistic perception of the potential customer we need to adopt a system-oriented view of tourism market structures. The increased value of tourism as an experience has forced suppliers to develop packaged services, and to do everything they can to create a more magical atmosphere, in short to orchestrate and dramatise the whole tourism experience. It is increasingly worthwhile therefore to view the production of tourism goods and services in the context of service chains or networks, made up of a variety of companies and sectors. It follows therefore that tourism product systems must be of a complex nature.

Dual Industrial Structure: The Rise of a New International Travel Industry

The field of tourism has developed a dual economic structure over the years. Whereas in the target countries or destinations SMEs continue to offer such tourism services as accommodation, catering and leisure time activities, an international travel and tourism industry has gradually emerged in the source countries as part of the globalization process.

This new tourism industry is based on many innovations. In civil aviation charter flights were invented as a way of dealing with seasonal peaks in demand. Hotel chains that sprouted from family firms, including the Hilton and Marriott empires, grew out of a desire to satisfy the needs of business travellers, initially those travelling from the USA. The rent-a-car sector, which is today a giant industry, allows visitors to have the same mobility abroad as they do at home. Credit cards have made international money transfers much easier while at the same time reducing the risks involved in foreign exchange operations.

The international travel and tourism industry consists mainly of big companies that organise tours to various destinations on an industrial basis. They offer standardised products, and develop global strategies that enable them to make the best use of the local potential anywhere on the planet.

The available statistics seem to indicate that the number of big tourism companies is relatively small, in all of the more developed tourism countries.

Even so, this handful of majors generally accounts for more than half of total turnover in this sector. Sixty to ninety percent of all companies in the hotel sector, a leading branch of tourism, and also in the travel agency sector, are micro companies, i.e. firms that employ between one and nine persons.

Thanks to standardisation the bigger tourism companies are in a position to offer their clients more attractive services at very competitive prices. They are able to develop new tourism markets and offer new products. This helps them to increase the "customer value" and to reduce their production costs. Many visitors do not want standardised products however. They prefer to tailor the holiday experience to their own specific needs and tastes. They insist on personalised services. Thanks to the multi-optional supply of products and services they are able to offer, destinations are in a position to adapt relatively quickly to the ever changing requirements of the individual tourist.

Dominant Market Structure: Imperfect Competition

Truly perfect competition should be the rule in a world tourism market which has been extensively liberalised, with prices being dictated by the market.

But the fact that the availability and distribution of resources varies greatly from one place to another creates a situation of monopolistic competition in tourism markets. The different natural, cultural and civilisation-related attractions that exist in each country make it possible to differentiate destinations on a geographical basis. Each tourism country, region and place is thus unique and unmistakably individual.

Global Tourism Growth: A Challenge for SMEs

Tourism companies profit from this uniqueness of destinations. Thanks to the customer's increased willingness to pay for these special attractions, tourism companies can set prices that are higher than the market costs. "Value based pricing" allows a wide range of pricing policy measures. Differentiation is the market strategy of destinations. It brings individual SMEs a rent in the form of "brand value". Differentiation strategies work because of the need for variety. This "love of variety" also helps to explain the exchange of tourists between the countries of the industrialised world. The monopoly rent of the SMEs in destinations is returned to the visitors in the form of an increased variety of products and services. Competition in tourism is therefore primarily competition between destinations, and only secondarily competition between individual service providers. Visitors begin by choosing a destination. Only then do they choose the combination of products and services they wish to consume. It is the availability of attractions and the relative importance of each that to a great extent determine a destination's tourism potential.

SME Problem in Developed Countries: Cluster Advantages and Size Problems

Tourism-dependent SMEs benefit greatly from the host destination, which are in almost all cases unique, difficult-to-imitate competitive systems. They can also be described as "clusters". Most tourism destinations have emerged after a long process of specialisation. Companies compete within very narrow confines. They have the benefit of competitive experience, they take advantage of existing test markets, and they can count on reliable suppliers. However these competitive advantages are no longer enough to resolve all the problems of tourism-dependent SMEs. In the industrialised world, where productivity in this labour intensive industry is lower than in less developed countries, SMEs in tourism suffer from the cost disease. They have to increase their prices to compensate for their relative lack of productivity, which in turn harms their ability to compete in the world market. Furthermore the size disadvantage of SMEs reduces their profitability. Bigger companies are able to produce at less cost thanks to economies of scale. Their products and services are more attractive thanks to reduced costs and offer more customer benefits. The bigger firms attract more visitors and produce at lower cost.

Integration and Cooperation: A Necessity for Destination Oriented SMEs

Generally speaking, SMEs in destinations never produce with the most efficient structures. This is one of the drawbacks that result from monopolistic competition, despite its various advantages.

Most producers reduce the quantity and set their prices higher than the costs. It is for this reason that individual tourism is expensive in destinations, with a structure dominated by small businesses. It is also a fact that each service in the chain of services has to be paid for separately, and the cumulative final price is high.

There are few service packages on offer within destinations. The fragmented small business sector that dominates tourism in the destinations often finds it difficult to remain competitive in the international market, as in the factor markets. Subject as they are to fluctuations in demand the capacity of these small firms is often under-utilised and their earning power is limited. They do not have sufficient cash flow.

Global Tourism Growth: A Challenge for SMEs

The way forward for tourism-dependent SMEs is to take far greater advantage of the potential for internal growth. Additional rooms in hotels, more seats in restaurants, these are some of the ways small firms can reduce their average costs. SMEs that make the effort can gravitate towards the optimal size. External growth is also urgently needed however, to overcome the disadvantages that go with insufficient size. At the vertical level of the destination production and marketing need to be increasingly based on partnerships, which would enable SMEs to better position themselves in the markets.

Horizontal cooperation is also necessary to increase production and lower costs. Cooperation should only be considered however if it is cheaper than producing in house or buying in the market. The OECD's Centre for Entrepreneurship, SMEs and Local Development is reviewing the organisation and functioning of global value chains for various industries as a way for SMEs to participate more fully in global growth and become more productive.

In the case of tourism, one of the five industries covered in this project, the hotel sector, a leading sector of the tourism industry, consists on the one hand of internationally active hotel chains that are continuing to expand, and on the other of small local hotels. In the worldwide competition to attract visitors with the greatest purchasing power, independent family-run hotels in the SME category are increasingly forced to cooperate at the level of marketing or themselves to become part of a hotel chain of some kind.

State Incentives for Tourism Dependant SMEs

Another question that needs to be asked is whether or not the further development, and indeed the economic survival of tourism-dependent SMEs require any specific state incentives. Tourism policy is basically concerned with the creation of more favourable framework conditions for destinations. It does not specifically address the problems of SMEs.

Support for infrastructures or for marketing efforts does not take company size into consideration. Opportunities are always seized however, in the context of tourism policy, to help overcome the disadvantages that go with insufficient size.

Few measures exist that are specifically aimed at tourism-dependent SMEs. Such measures include state assistance to promote urgently needed efforts in the area of cooperation, as a way of reducing high transaction and organisation costs. It can make sense in this context to promote cooperation projects in order to update existing products and services through innovation. A number of governments do in fact promote innovation and cooperation today.

The differentiation strategy of destinations does not only bring advantages to SMEs however. The development of umbrella brands is difficult and expensive. These promotion efforts have to be borne by the SMEs themselves. Furthermore, brands have to be maintained in quality through constant investment in product improvements and quality assurance systems. For these reasons virtually all governments promote market communication, or destination marketing by their national tourism office. Finally, it should not be forgotten that the multi optional nature of the products and services on offer in destinations is expensive, since a great variety of infrastructures, goods and services has to be provided.

This is why many governments also support tourism-dependent infrastructures. This includes rejuvenation of the accommodation sector and the creation of new companies. There is a real need for policy action in the tourism sector. However, the granting of credits can result in certain market distortions at the expense of SMEs.

The Evolution of Space Tourism from Novelty to Opportunity

At a space business forum in June 2008, Dr. George C. Nield, Associate Administrator for Commercial Space Transportation at the Federal Aviation Administration (FAA), addressed the future of commercial space travel: 'There is tangible work underway by a number of companies aiming for space, partly because of their dreams, but primarily because they are confident it can be done by the private sector and it can be done at a profit.'

Indeed, private companies and entrepreneurs are currently aiming to make this dream a reality. While the current economic downturn will likely slow industry progress, space tourism, currently in its infancy, is poised to become a significant part of the hospitality industry.

Unlike the space race of the 1950s and 1960s between the United States and the former Soviet Union, the current rivalry is not defined on a national level, but by a collection of first-mover entrepreneurs that are working to define the industry and position it for longterm profitability. The race includes and depends on technology firms focused on developing the safest, most reliable, and most economical spacecraft, as well as service firms, or space lines, that will ultimately market and provide space travel experiences to willing "Novanauts."

In this race to send private citizens into space, the first team to cross the finish line will not necessarily win international bragging rights, but can expect to benefit from establishing a name within the space travel industry. Companies that hope to have any chance at success must first establish credibility and demonstrate reliability and safety to a population that may be skeptical of the prospect of commercial space travel.

Specialty firms have announced intentions to develop the technology and/or market commercial space travel to the masses, with some currently collecting deposits for future suborbital flights and, in one instance, lunar missions. Billionaire Charles Simonyi joined a team of astronauts for his second paid visit to the International Space Station on March 25, 2009. While this experience may currently be available to the world's wealthiest individuals, opportunities for the average earthling to experience space travel are on the horizon.

"Space-like" experiences such as the Zero G Jet are currently available, while true space flight opportunities are in development. This article will explore the latest advancements in space tourism and will consider opportunities for this fledging industry. The impact of the current global economic conditions on the evolution of space travel is also considered. We further investigate who the current major players are, review the existing space tourism studies published by industry experts, and provide our expectations for the future of this industry.

Commercial Space Travel: Types of Experiences, Major Players, and Offerings

No longer an exclusive endeavour of the government, space travel is being pursued for commercial gains – enabled by the FAA's Commercial Space Launch Amendments Act of 2004[2] (CSLAA) and further influenced by the $10 million Ansari X Prize. Within the past decade, private citizens have paid large sums to be among the first to experience a variety of space and space-like experiences, including parabolic flights simulating weightlessness, suborbital flights, and higher-altitude weeklong orbital flights to the International Space Station.

The prices associated with these experiences have ranged from roundly $5,000 per person for a parabolic flight to roundly $20 million for a trip to the International Space Station. The following figure provides definitions for space-like and space flight experiences.

Private investors, companies, and the industry as a whole are currently working towards making space travel possible from a variety of "Spaceports," which would be located around the globe. Locations noted during our research include, but are not limited to, the United States (California, Florida, New Mexico, Texas, and Oklahoma), Kazakhstan, French Guiana, Russia, Sweden, Australia, Singapore, and the United Arab Emirates.

As more spaceports are developed, commercial space travel providers anticipate providing point-to-point global travel. Other projects under way include the development of orbital space facilities that would serve as "space hotels."

Ultimately the goal of the industry is to provide a profitable means of offering suborbital, orbital, and possibly lunar-and-beyond expeditions. The development pace of the more complex service offerings (orbital point-to-point flights, space hotels, lunar expeditions, etc.) will be greatly influenced by the initial success of the commercial space tourism industry's first movers, offering suborbital experiences.

Parabolic Flights and Beyond

Established in 1993, Zero G was the first company to market a simulated space experience, offering tickets for parabolic flights based in major tourist destinations in the United States. Zero G offers passengers the sensation of weightlessness without travelling to space. The company's specially fitted jumbo jets perform parabolic manoeuvres to recreate the sensation of Martian and lunar gravity, as well as total weightlessness.

The Las Vegas-based company has flown over 100 flights and currently offers tickets for roundly $5,000 per person, as well as charter flights for groups. In January 2008, Zero G was acquired by Space Adventures, Ltd.

To date, Space Adventures is the only private company to have sent citizens into space – including the "first space tourist," Dennis Tito. Space Adventures sent Tito into orbit for nearly eight days in 2001 via the Russian Soyuz shuttle for a reported $20 million. According to a 2007 article from FOX news, Space Adventures has sold almost $200 million in tourist space flights since 2001. The company is looking to expand its offerings and is currently taking reservations aboard the "first private expedition to the moon" for $100 million per seat.

Others forging their way into commercial space travel include Sir Richard Branson's Virgin Galactic. Virgin Galactic has teamed with X-Prize winner, Scaled Composites, to shuttle private citizens on suborbital flights beginning in 2010. Tickets are currently priced at $200,000, and the company has collected a reported US$30 million as of January 2008.

Other companies collecting money for reservations for suborbital flights include Rocketplane for $250,000 per person and XCOR for roundly $95,000. Another player that has received media attention is Bigelow Aerospace. Currently the sole manufacturer for several of NASA's key expandable space station modules, the company is developing a family of modules to serve as the first commercial space habitats. Bigelow plans to launch the first "orbital resort" in the near future but currently has no target timeframe for the launch.

A similar initiative is being pursued by Galactic Suite, a Spanish Company with plans to package pre-space training on a remote island, with space travel to the orbital resort by 2012. A 2007 press release indicated a roundly €3 million per person price for this experience.

With the space tourism industry in its infancy, each prospective operator and space technology development firm is working to set the standards for safety, comfort, and the overall Novanaut experience. One thing can be concluded from our research of existing space tourism companies: Multiple organizations and individuals believe that there is a future for us in space travel. The following figures provide details on a selection of players in the space travel industry as of the time of our research.

Understanding the Market Potential

As Space Tourism has yet to establish itself as a viable industry, there is little tangible evidence to conclude that a substantial market exists. However, an in-depth market study was conducted to forecast potential demand and revenues for space tourism activities through 2021 by Futron, a U.S.-based firm specializing in technology management consulting. In 2006, Futron revisited an extensive market study they conducted in 2002, adjusting for the year, ticket prices, and updated population wealth statistics.

The original study was based on a pool representative of those able to purchase such a luxury experience – surveying 450 wealthy individuals to determine their interest in space tourism and willingness to take part in such flights at a number of price points.

Such luxury travellers are estimated as 3% of the total international tourist arrivals worldwide, yet account for 25% of total international travel expenditures – totalling US$180 billion in 2006.

Considering the world population of people wealthy enough to afford space flights, as well as their fitness and interest levels, Futron used a 40-year maturity model to forecast demand and potential annual revenue from suborbital services in 2021 to reach 13,000 passengers and an estimated US$676 million – taking into account declining ticket prices due to economies of scale and applying the Fisher-Pry S-Curve to the potential demand pool. The original study also estimated orbital flights to generate $300 million per year, generating a $1-billion industry by 2021.

While Futron's updated forecasts for 2006 are down from 2002's estimate of 15,000, the study concludes "despite a delayed introduction of commercial passenger suborbital flights, and an increase in initial ticket prices over earlier expectations, demand for suborbital space tourism remains strong." In addition, one should note that the FAA's Office of Commercial Space Transportation has set no specific health or fitness requirements for passengers, suggesting a wider range of acceptability. In addition, the updated study does not take into account any changes in "the public's perception of, or level of interest in, suborbital space tourism," which is likely to have changed since the Ansari X Prize was awarded and companies like Virgin Galactic announced their plans. Although the Futron study cannot provide us with certainties for the future of commercial space travel, the report does give us a sense of potential revenues and scale of the primary demographic. As of the summer of 2008, over 250 people had put deposits down or paid the full price for Virgin Galactic's suborbital flight tickets, while another 600 had signed up to buy tickets once flights begin. As with any new innovation, these individuals will lead the way for the industry's expansion, eventually creating economies of scale, lowering ticket prices, and increasing accessibility to a wider demographic.

Impact of the Current Economy and Future Trends for the Space Tourism Industry

Is there enough demand to warrant longterm success of the commercial space travel industry? Only time will tell. With the current economic recession, technological advances and the launch of regularly scheduled suborbital (and beyond) flights are likely to be delayed.

However, when we consider the forecasts from the Futron study and the inclinations of a large population towards adventure tourism and activities generally perceived as higher risk, or extreme (i.e., skydiving, scuba diving, rock climbing, etc.), the authors foresee the progression of commercial space travel as a viable industry in the long term. While information is limited on the payoff and functionality of each company's plan and proposed operating models, longterm success will rely on basic critical factors such as safety, reliability, service differentiation, and value. As spaceports are built and ticket prices lowered as a result of economies of scale, we predict point-to-point space travel to spur demand and a sustainable source of business. As demonstrated by the cruise industry, combining a destination with the travel experience may justify this mode of travel for some and support repeat purchases, avoiding the possibility of becoming a once-in-a-lifetime experience. In this case, destinations may include "hotels" in space or locations across the globe that can be reached quickly and conveniently.

We also predict that existing and new luxury brands will partner with space technology developers to offer upscale service and accommodations for affluent travellers in the first space hotels and hotels located proximate to space training and launching sites. We expect to see tourism centres (hotel accommodations, entertainment, and restaurants) to be developed adjacent to spaceport locations to house guests during space training. These supportive developments will be especially necessary in remote Spaceport locations.

As the first space flights are expected to be affordable to only the wealthiest individuals, who are accustomed to the finest accommodations, we expect that these hotels will be in the luxury segment.

For some, the dream of space travel could be a reality within the next decade. The innovators in the space tourism industry will do much to define the future experiences of prospective Novanauts, setting the standards for safety, creating realistic expectations of the in-flight experience, and developing packages and experiences that will represent the most value for the target market.

The start of the second space race is currently under way, with possibilities that are truly out of this world!

7

Human Resources in Tourism

Overview and Objectives

Tourism sector industries generate a large number of highly diversified jobs in different branches of activities such as hotels, restaurants, travel agencies, tour operators, leisure activities and passenger transport. Human resources are a key element in ensuring the quality and content of tourism products. There is a growing need for skilled manpower able to meet the needs of a changing environment and to maintain the competitiveness of tourism enterprises. In a competitive labour market, the tourism sector suffers from a relatively poor image and finds it difficult to retain employees on a longterm basis.

In the light of these changes and challenges, strategies for managing and promoting human resources have a central role to play in a sustainable development approach to tourism. The understanding of labour markets in the tourism sector remains inadequate.

The effects of the new practices introduced by certain governments and the industry to improve skills and enhance the competitiveness of the sector in the labour market have not been widely shared and assessed. The pursuit of strategies to promote the skills needed in a globalizing tourism industry must be continued. Lastly, in a context of liberalisation and globalization of tourism services, the possibility of harmonising the differing regulatory approaches to the labour market in the tourism sector should be discussed in depth with all actors on national and international labour markets.

The conference on "Partnership in Vietnam's tourism human resources development" was the second annual conference held by the Vietnam Human Resources Development in Tourism Project at the Furama Resort, Danang.

The conference on "Partnership in Vietnam's tourism human resources development" was the second annual conference held by the Vietnam Human Resources Development in Tourism Project at the Furama Resort, Danang. It took place on 30th November 2006 and followed the conference on "Vietnam tourism human resources development and regional integration", held in Hanoi during December 2005.

Among the 150 participants (international and local) were representatives from Vietnam National Administration of Tourism, the National Steering Committee for Tourism, representatives from ministries, the Delegation of the European Commission to Vietnam, the Secretariat and National Tourism Organisations of ASEAN, provincial tourism departments, representatives from hotel and travel enterprises, tourism training institutions, etc. By attending the conference, regional tourism representatives viewed the activities of Vietnam's tourism human resources development at first hand, and Vietnam's tourism administrators and experts gained further insights into regional practice.

After the introduction by Mr. Jozef W.M. van Doorn, the Co-Director of the Project, presenting the Project's outputs to date, Mr. Jaap Funnekotter, Chairman of the conference, reviewed outcomes from last year's conference. Conference 2006 followed the same format as last year's edition in order to create continuity, so speakers from both public and private sectors presented their experience of partnership in tourism human resources development.

After the presentations, there was a panel discussion on the topic: "Has any synergy between the educational institutes and the hotel and tourism enterprises taken place in the last year?" along with some further discussion of best practices.

Attending the Gala Dinner, participants were introduced to a training DVD on housekeeping according to the Vietnam Tourism Occupational Skill standards (VTOS). This is one of 14 videos that will be developed by the Project as support for training. It is designed to be used in conjunction with the Project's Trainer

Development Programme training manuals, or for entry-level staff training within enterprises.

The second day of the conference was spent on a field trip to My Son and Hoi An, two of the World Cultural Heritage sites.

UNWTO Summit Discusses New Reforms for Human Resources in Tourism

According to the January 2009 issue of the UNWTO World Tourism Barometer, in 2008, international tourist arrivals worldwide increased by 2%. The Middle East registered the best performance among all world regions with 11% growth in international tourist arrivals in 2008 over the previous year. Based on passenger traffic data from worldwide airports for the first two months of 2009, it appears that of all the world regions, the Middle East is the least affected the global crisis thus far. It was the only region with a positive traffic growth of 3.1%.

The Summit has demonstrated the complexity of labour markets in the region and constantly returned to the fact that the rapid growth of tourism in the region brings with it issues of labour supply gaps and skills shortage. The Qatar Summit identified a range of human resource challenges for tourism.

Tourism employment comes in the shape of a broad spectrum of roles and varied tasks, across all sectors benefiting in particular women, the young and the unemployed. Tourism is well known as a generator of employment, so a well-trained tourism labour force will both anticipate and remedy such economic crisis.

Longer-term challenges include the poor image and lack of understanding of tourism jobs, and the fact that availability of labour and skills is highly variable across the region.

The Summit addressed these issues into four key pillars of reform:

> *The first one is the need to change the mindset of both governments and communities towards employment in tourism, as well as the need for the industry to change its view of human resources to one that values peoples, their skills and knowledge, develops them and treats them as valued resources.*

The second pillar means the necessary understanding of labour markets. With the Tourism Satellite Account (TSA) methodology, it is now easier to understand and measure labour markets, diagnose the problems and act. Governments will be able to plan for future labour and training needs.

Re-engineering education and training, the third pillar of reform, will demand national standard setting in partnership with industry and the development of articulated and legible pathways to allow students to gain qualifications, and ensuring that programmes are creatively packaged, innovative and utilize edge technology for lifelong learning.

The final pillar of reform relates to the work and leadership of both the UNWTO and Qatar in addressing these challenges and engaging stakeholders to craft new strategies. The solutions demand the forging of effective partnerships and working together to implement the recommendations of the Summit, as well as the findings of the Bali conference and the ILO's Decent Work Agenda.

Professor Chris Cooper, summit moderator, commented:

> *"The message of this summit is clear-tourism is a people-centred industry, the sector must invest in the education, training and development of the labour force to secure the future." Alongside the Qatar Summit, the 32nd meeting of the United Nations World Tourism Organisation commission for the Middle East took place on April 22nd and 23rd.*

Dr. Taleb Rifai, Secretary General of the UNWTO, presented to the members of the Commission a snapshot analysis of the current economic downturn's impact on tourism in the Middle East and North Africa. Country briefs and response measures were also discussed in a regional perspective. The Secretary General presented the research programme: "Tourism towards 2030", as well as regional training programmes and possible adjustments in the light of the global economic downturn. This meeting of the UNWTO commission for the Middle East reviewed the preparations for the eighteenth session of the General Assembly of UNWTO, that will take place in October 2009.

On the occasion of the conclusive press conference, Mr. Ahmed Al Nuaimi, Chairman of Qatar Tourism and Exhibitions Authority, declared, "I am really pleased Qatar Tourism and Exhibitions Authority hosted this UNWTO conference. With 250 participants, we shared different experiences and had very fruitful discussions that enabled us to create a roadmap with four pillars of reform. Tourism is a key economic pillar and we need to ensure the future of the region."

Tourism Human Resources in Shortage, Weak

Weakness in Foreign Languages

According to statistics of the Vietnam National Administration of Tourism (VNAT), the total number of workers in the tourism sector is around 850,000 at present, including 250,000 workers who directly serve tourists. However, only around 50% of them are trained.

The tourism sector needs an additional around 35,000 trained workers each year but training centres can provide only about one-third of the volume.

Besides weakness in terms of professional knowledge and skills, the largest disadvantage of Vietnamese tourism workers is foreign languages. Besides English, the major foreign language, Vietnamese tourism workers are also weak in other languages like Japanese, Chinese and Korean.

Specifically, the number of Korean travellers coming to Vietnam is increasing fast (ranking second after Chinese) but Vietnam currently has only 50 tour guides who can speak Korean. For the Japanese market, the third potential market of Vietnam, just 8% of tour guides speaking Japanese can fluently speak this language.

English: Below Standards

As part of a programme to raise the quality of the tourism human resources of Vietnam, the Test of English for International Communication (TOEIC) Vietnam has currently made a survey to test the English ability of some occupations in the tourism sector.

Based on the need of using English in each position, TOEIC Vietnam performed nearly 400 surveys of the need for English skills of nearly 200 hotels of three-to five-star standard and travel agents throughout the country. The major subjects of those surveys are directors, human resource managers and direct managers like team leaders who clearly understand the need for English of their staffs.

Random surveys of 1,000 workers at tourism companies reveal that the English skills of most of them are low and below the standards required by their employers. The survey also points out that hotels of higher standard have high percentages of staffs that don't meet standards in English.

According to Doan Hong Nam, director of the TOEIC Vietnam, the standards that we apply to evaluate the English skills of tourism workers is to ensure the minimum quality of service so the survey results show that the English skills of surveyed tourism workers is even lower than the low standards.

This is not only a hindrance for the development of the tourism sector but others as more and more foreign tourists are coming to Vietnam to seek business opportunities. Mr. Nam said that Vietnam needed to quickly improve the quality of the current tourism services by issuing common standards for foreign languages for each position in the tourism sector. This is a necessary foundation for the training tasks of training centres and tourism firms.

Philippines: DoT holds 1st Tourism Human Resources Congress Today

In line with the Department of Tourism's (DoT) "Gandang Pilipinas, Galingng Pilipino" GP2 campaign which aims to further develop tourism services, DoT Secretary Roberto "Obet" M. Pagdanganan will lead the launch of the 1st Tourism Human Resources Congress today at The Peninsula Manila Hotel.

Pagdanganan said the activity, which will be held until tomorrow (June 18), will further enhance the industry's manpower resources enabling them to meet the international standard of tourism service.

"In order to cope with the global challenges in the tourism industry, we must arm ourselves with the changes in the international market. Quality services and products are fast becoming a norm in the new global economy. We must make precedence by introducing speed, innovation and customization," he added. The Tourism Industry Board Foundation, Inc. (TIBFI) organizer of the event, is a non-stock, nonprofit institution composed of representatives from the government (which include the DoT as founding member), private and labour sectors.

The foundation aims to provide manpower development, ensuring an adequate supply of trained workers who will match the skills of the labour force with the manpower requirements of the tourism industry.

TIBFI invited distinguished guest speakers including World Tourism Organization (WTO) representative Professor Chris Cooper to talk about the TedQual Programs, which focuses on quality service assurance and the WTO products and services standard.

Human resources directors and heads of various tourism subsectors, associations, industries and government agencies (TESDA, CHED, Government Training Institutions), tour guides and the academe including state colleges and universities are invited to participate in the two-day assembly. Registration fee is R1,500.

Tourism Human Resources

The Tourism Industry

* Tourism is the largest earner of foreign exchange in Antigua & Barbuda.
* It is estimated to be the largest employer when all enterprises providing direct and indirect services to the sector are combined.

Tourism and The Labour Force

* Though there are no definitive statistics on the labour force involved in tourism in Antigua & Barbuda, a recently produced Antigua & Barbuda Tourism Strategic Plan (2005-2009) stated that surveys suggest that approximately 8,000 workers or 26% of the total labour force could be employed in the accommodation sector: hotels, guests houses, apts., villas, with other sectors of the industry creating a further 3,000 jobs.
* Therefore, the total number of workers employed in the tourism sector is 11,000 representing 40% of the total labour force.
* When compared to statistics which indicate that globally tourism accounts for 8.3% of the total work force, Antigua & Barbuda can clearly be considered one of the, if not the most tourism dependent countries in the world.

Tourism Human Resource Audit

- A tourism human resource audit should be conducted to give true and reliable data relating to the tourism work force.
- Such data must of necessity address the issues of:
  - male/female ratio.
  - age-group.
  - percentages employed in various sectors, for e.g. accommodation, F&B, yachting, adventure, etc.
  - education.
- It is important to note that the paucity of reliable data is a regional problem and unfortunately the experience of many economic sector areas, the tourist industry being no exception.
  - As recently as February 2006, CTO in recognition of this situation include the improvement of data collection as one of its Key Focus Areas.

Assessing Training and Education Needs

- In a 1998 study conducted by the CTO within its member countries, the focus was on assessing training and education needs for the tourist industry in the new millennium.
- The study was designed to provide data about the nature and level of skills deficiencies in the industry so as to inform Caribbean Governments and regional training agencies where their training priorities should lie and how their training $$ should be spent.
- It was intended that the study would provide a launching pad for tourism training in this millennium as well as to represent a benchmark for future studies.
- The information provided on HRD in the Caribbean region as a whole (through this study), is quite applicable to the Antigua & Barbuda situation.

Highlights of the Study

- Industry Profile:
  - Majority of the responding organizations were from the Accommodation sector, with F&B and

Transportation sectors running a far second and third behind, respectively.

* Events and Conferences and Attractions provided least number of respondents. Reflection of the level of development of these two sectors in the Region.
* ¼ less than 5 yrs. Old/¼ over 20 yrs. Old
* Majority of the work force permanent full-time staff with more males than females (56% to 44%). Over 70% under 40 yrs.

- Recruitment and Retention of Staff:
  * Local and regional tourism training institutions are not a preferred source of employees.
  * Most organizations recruit their staff from secondary/primary schools and from university, depending on the level of staff.
  * Many also hire from their competitors or from among relatives and friends.
  * Generally, managerial and professional vacancies are difficult to fill.
  * Also difficult to recruit skilled/semiskilled persons in the accommodation, F&B and adventure sectors.
  * Unskilled positions generally easier to fill.
- Industry Training and Development.
  * Only 1/3 of the establishments in the survey had a full-time trainer on staff.
  * Training done primarily in customer relations and technical skills.
  * Of 1/3 of the respondents providing information on training budget, 2/3 spent less than US$5,000 for a year.
  * On the job-training is the preferred training strategy for all levels of staff.
  * External trainers and local tourism training institutions used but to a much lesser extent.
  * Local and regional tourism training institutions are not perceived by the industry as important or effective in satisfying its training needs.

Training Needs Identified

- General and technical training deficiencies identified at different staff levels.
- General training needs:
    * Interpersonal skills deficiencies found at all staff level.
    * Marketing and management deficiencies at managerial level.
    * Computer literacy and foreign language deficiencies (also found).
- Technical training needs: these were linked to deficiencies within the various tourism sectors; accommodation, food & beverage, transportation, travel trade, adventure and tourism services.

Accommodation

Technical Skills:

* Culinary.
* Maintenance.
* Housekeeping.
* F & B Service e.g. Bartending, Waiting.
* Front Desk.
* Tour Guiding.
* Customer Service.
* Other, e.g. Safety & Security, Tourism Awareness, Computer.

Food & Beverage

Technical Skills:

* Culinary.
* Food & Beverage Services e.g. Bartending, Waiting.
* Customer Service.
* Other e.g. Inventory Control, Maintenance, Cashing, Sanitation.

Transportation

Technical Skills:

* Ticketing.

* Customer Service.
* Tour Guiding.
* Maintenance.
* Other e.g. Customer Procedures.

Travel Trade

Technical Skills.

* Ticketing.
* Tour Guiding.
* Other e.g. Customer Service, Maintenance, Computer, Marketing.

Adventure

Technical Skills.

* Tour Guiding.
* Watersports e.g. Boating, Sailing, Scuba Diving, Fishing.
* Maintenance.
* Culinary.
* Other e.g. Customer Service, Golf, Housekeeping, First Aid, Piloting, Food & Beverage Service.

Tourism Services

Technical Skills:

* Statistical Analysis.
* Property Management.
* Environmental Protection and Conservation.
* Public Relations.

Attractions

Technical Skills:

* Tour Guiding.
* Customer Service.
* Other e.g. Ticketing, Heritage Conservation/Preservation, Museum Management, wildlife Management, Environmental Protection, Marine Biology, Heritage Studies.

Meeting Technical Training Needs

The Antigua and Barbuda Hospitality Training Institute.

Antigua & Barbuda Hospitality Training Institute.

* Mission To provide training and education with a commitment to excellence; to equip persons to work in the Tourism and Hospitality Industry with a high degree of professionalism.

One Year Certificate Programme

* Food and Beverage Service.
* Training at Skills level.
* Basic Cookery.
* Knowledge & Skill in basic Cookery techniques.
* Housekeeping.
* Training at skills level.

2 *Year Diploma Programme*

- Culinary Arts.
  * In depth practical and supervisory level training.
- Reception and Sales.
  * Broad base training in Front Office Operations.
- Hospitality Management.
  * Knowledge and skill to embark on supervisory or junior management level.

Accreditation

- 2 Year Diploma Programmes.
  * Hospitality Management.
  * Culinary Arts.
- University of the West Indies.
- Monroe College.

In-House Training Courses

* Butchery Techniques.
* Caribbean Cuisine.
* Art and Science of Service.

Collaboration with Tourist Operators

- Federation of Tour Operators.
  * Food Hygiene & Safety Seminar.
- Antigua Hotels and Tourist Association.
  * Internship for students.
  * Membership on Board & Sub committees.
  * Partnership with Trans Caribbean Marketing & US meat Export Federation.

Regional Collaboration through Caribbean Tourism Organization

* Core Curriculum.
* Certified Hospitality Educator.
* Dynamic Supervisory Management Programme.
* Quality Assurance and Articulation.
* Human Resources Conference.
* Promotional material on careers in Tourism.

Sources of Funding

* Consolidated funds of Antigua & Barbuda Government.
* European Commission.
* Organization of American States.
* First Caribbean International Bank.

Annual Government Funding Allocation

* ABHTI Estimates 2006 $1.8 Mil 21%.
* ASC (Antigua State College) $5.7 Mil 65%.
* ABICE $1.2 Mil 14%.
* ABIIT unknown-
* Total $8.7 Mil 100% Revenue (2005) ABHTI $122,000 ASC $60,000.

Conclusion

* Tourism is a high-touch, high-tech, high-involvement industry where it is the people who make the difference.
* The ability for the industry to succeed and the future performance of the industry and related activities will depend largely on the skills, qualities and knowledge of

its employees. Indeed the challenges facing the industry can only be met successfully by a welleducated, well-trained, bright, energetic, multilingual and entrepreneurial work force.

* A high-quality tourism work force can only be achieved through high standards of tourism education and training which in turn will impact our destination's ability (the ability of our twin-island state) to compete successfully in this global competitive industry.

Special Symposium on APU's Tourism Human Resource Development Project

A Special Symposium on APU's Tourism Human Resource Development Project titled, "Creating the Future of Regional Tourism-Fostering Talent for the Next Generation" was held at Beppu B-con Plaza on Friday, March 10. The Special Symposium was held for people who will have major roles in the future of the tourism and service industry including the accommodation sector.

APU's "Tourism Human Resource Development Project" was commissioned by the Ministry of Economy, Trade and Industry as part of its "AY2005 Power Supply Regional Service Human Resource Development Business." Mr. TOYODA Masakazu, Director-General of the Commerce and Information Policy Bureau of the Ministry of Economy, Trade and Industry Mr. TOYOTA Masakazu commenced the first-half of the Symposium with a keynote address on "Promoting the Hospitality Industry." Afterwards, the President of the All Japan Ryokan Association, Mr. Kohara Kenji gave a presentation on "Creating a Tourism-Orientation Nation."

A panel discussion on the theme of "Creating the Future of Tourism in Kyushu-Regions and Business/Developing Human Resources" took place in the second-half of the Symposium. The participants listened attentively to the animated exchange of ideas.

Human Resources in Tourism: Still Waiting for Change

People, we are frequently told, are a critical dimension within the successful delivery of tourism services. "The story of successful tourism enterprises is one that is largely about people—how they are recruited, how they are managed, how they are trained and educated, how they are valued and rewarded, and how they are supported through a process of continuous learning and career development" points to recognition of this philosophy in the mission statements of hotel companies within which a far higher proportion of respondents include reference to human resources than is the case within manufacturing companies.

This contemporary manta or reflection of the "'soft' rhetoric of people as an organisations's greatest asset" (Bolton & Houlihan, 2007) may have had equal veracity at various points during the development of tourism over the past century, but the practical implications of the claim, in terms of the role that people play, will have been interpreted in different ways at varying points over this timeframe.

In particular, there is an apparent paradox in the dramatic evolution of the global tourism sector over the past half century and, within it, the manner and conditions in which people deliver tourism services which have remained timeless in many respects but also subject to significant change.

During this time, debate about labour intensity, the number and cost of people required to work in many areas of tourism, has sat alongside discussion of the skills necessary to deliver quality tourism services, remuneration and working conditions and the role that technology plays in both supporting and changing this delivery.

Inevitably, the nature of such analysis has shifted over time. In particular, the profile of many workers, but by no means all of those in tourism's work force, and the role that they play in the labour markets of developed countries, has been subject to change. At the same time, tourism work must be set alongside major economic and labour market restructuring in post-industrial societies so that direct comparison between tourism and traditional heavy manufacturing work in shipyards, mines and steel works, which formed an important element of the early industrial sociology in the emerging service sectors, is less relevant.

Rather, tourism work now sits alongside and is compared to other activities within the dominant service economy of developed countries, and the analytical paradigm for such comparison should consider employment opportunities in the sector in a rather different light. Whether such comparison leads to a positive assessment of work in tourism is a matter that we shall consider in this paper.

In the light of external change, in developed countries, certain aspects of human resource management in tourism demonstrate evolution over time, by responding across the breadth of the contextual environment within which tourism is located, notably in sociocultural, marketrelated and technological terms. Such change is clearly evident within some of the large tourism companies in transport, entertainment and accommodation.

At the same time, the headlines of change do not reflect reality across the totality of the tourism sector. There is a real contrast between major multinational tourism companies and smaller operators within some subsectors of tourism (particularly accommodation and restaurants) which contain areas of work where many things have not changed over the past 20 years—productivity remains stubbornly low, working conditions are poor and remuneration levels are well below national averages in many countries.

In some areas of tourism, businesses have been unable to cope with the pressures of external change-induced competition so that, for example, work opportunities in traditional travel agents have declined in many countries.

By contrast to the developed world, in poorer countries, the picture is rather more homogeneous whereby much work in low labour cost economies, including that of the tourism sector, has an appearance of timelessness so that change, if any, has been at the margins of the overall employment experience.

This paper seeks to make a partial assessment of the impact of external change on the human resource environment within tourism over the past 20 years, with particular focus on work and employment themes within the sector. In addressing a topic as broad as this, there is a real danger of uncritical generalisation within a highly heterogeneous sector such as tourism.

There is real and ongoing debate with regard to definitional issues in the tourism sector and this has presented some challenges in the context of this paper. Discussion here seeks to embrace an inclusive interpretation of tourism with illustrations of human resource practices across various subsectors. This challenge is illustrated by highlighting features such as the diversity within tourism with its various subsectors (accommodation, food service, transport, facilitation, heritage); the size of operations; the location of these operations; business arrangements that are in place to deliver services within tourism; and the economic context within which operations do their business.

Published empirical and conceptual analysis of human resource issues in tourism has focused disproportionately on the hospitality subsector and, inevitably, evidence here is substantially drawn from hotels and restaurants to the possible neglect of major areas of employment such as transport.

This is a challenge faced by others in considering human resource themes in tourism in this way. Our assessment is further complicated as a result of ambiguity in understandings of what the term, human resources and its management, encompasses. This ambiguity includes the consequences of changes that have taken place at a functional level as the traditionally accepted concept of personnel management has given way to a broader functional application in human resource management, operating as part of a company's wider business and strategic environment.

Human resource themes are also applicable at both the levels of the firm and in a macronational or regional context. This paper adopts conscious selectivity in focusing on human resources in the specific context of the work place and considers whether and how the employment environment has altered over the past 20 years.

Attempting a retrospect, with regards to a theme such as human resources in tourism, presents a challenge in determining an appropriate benchmark against which to measure possible change. Notionally, a 20-year yardstick is used, taking us back to the mid-1980s. At the same time, it is important not to ignore the insights from earlier times and to consider these in a contemporary context. Conceptually, the most useful and comprehensive framework against which to judge change is that provided by Wood's (1992, 1997) consideration of work in the hotels and catering subsector of tourism.

While Wood's discussion purposefully does not address the breadth of what is taken to be tourism here, it provides a valuable insight into research and analysis across the largest of tourism's subsectors, but one that is both the best studied and most problematic. Wood's assessment of the evidence discussed in his book, much of it drawn from the 1970s, 1980s and early 1990s, is that Hospitality work is largely exploitative, degrading, poorly paid, unpleasant, insecure and taken as a last resort or because it can be tolerated in the light of wider social and economic commitments and constraints.

Our concern here is to consider whether the context of and practice in contemporary tourism is such as to allow work in the sector to have moved significantly beyond the bleakness of this assessment and, if it has, to consider the extent to which wider contextual change has imposed itself on the management of human resource within tourism.

Therefore, this paper is concerned with assessing the nature and extent of contextual change on the management of human resources across the international tourism sector. This is a very broad aspiration, given the scope and scale of tourism as an economic activity, consisting of widely differing subsectors and located across virtually all communities, countries and cultures. The themes and contexts addressed here, therefore, must necessarily be selective, and include dimensions that appear to have broad salience across major tourism destinations, both established and more recently emerging.

The paper commences with a brief look back to the nature of work in tourism as depicted in early research into the sector, substantially the sources which led Wood to his bleak assessment. The paper then focuses on a number of themes which allow us to evaluate the extent of change and its impact—undertaking an assessment of the practice of the management of human resources in contemporary tourism; followed by consideration of the consequences of global and social forces on perceptions of work and careers; the impact of ICT on work and employment in tourism; changing interpretations of skills within tourism; and, finally, the increasingly diverse nature of the tourism work force in developed countries.

The paper concludes with an assessment of whether change, within these selected areas, outweighs the dead hand of the status quo that may appear to pervade tourism employment in other respects.

Where we have Come From

Recorded and formal accounts of what was and is involved with work in tourism, beyond passing fragmentary evidence, are relatively recent. One of the first in-depth pictures of aspects of tourism work comes from the 1930s and the writing of George Orwell (1933). His description of the work of the plongeur within the working hierarchy of Paris hotels is as perceptive as it is moving and, in many ways, provides a benchmark against which much subsequent sociological discussion of working conditions in the tourism and, particularly, the hospitality industry can be assessed.

Orwell's approach is to describe his own experiences of working in Paris hotels and his relationship with colleagues and superiors from the perspective of the foreigner and the 'down and out'. Orwell's objective is to expose the extremes of social deprivation during the depression of the 1930s and, as such, is one of extreme pessimism. He considers the work of the plongeur in its social context.

When one comes to think of it, is strange that thousands of people in a great, modern city should spend their waking hours swabbing dishes in hot dens underground.

The question I am raising is why this life goes on—what purpose it serves, and who wants it to continue, and why I am not taking a more rebellious attitude. I am trying to consider the social significance of the plongeur's life. I think I should start by saying that the plongeur is one of the slaves of the modern worldy he is no freer than if he were bought and sold. His work is servile and without art; he is paid just enough to keep him alive; his only holiday is the sack.

Orwell was looking at society through eyes that would have sat comfortably alongside that of other social commentators of the time, such as Seebohm Rowntree, a major contributor to understanding of poverty in Britain during the first half of the twentieth century. Rowntree prepared three assessments of social conditions in York and these progressively analysed the causes of poverty at the respective times, gathering increasing optimism as greater levels of state engagement with work, health and related social matters impacted upon British society and the work place.

Rowntree and Orwell shared a faith in the capacity of the state to improve the lives of the poor and were part of a movement that spawned detailed analysis of social conditions through initiatives such as the Mass Observation project. This included the domain of work.

Political change since the early 1980s has, perhaps, weakened the basis of such faith, notably through the impact of "Thatcherism" in the UK and elsewhere.

Therefore, contemporary commentators question the basis for optimism in assessing the conditions of work to which may service workers, including those in tourism, are exposed. For example, Orwell's disenfranchised and marginalised world of the plongeur has resonance in more contemporary studies.

Toynbee (2003), walking in the footsteps of Orwell, describes life in low-wage Britain, including her experiences in sectors of hospitality, and this world is not dramatically different from that of 1930s Paris within which Orwell talks about work as a "sort of delirium" within which "we were going as though we had only five minutes to lively. It was now that the tempo of the shift moved from hard and fast work to a controlled frenzy of washing up. Conversation came to an end. We were, I suppose, cheaper than industrial dishwashing machines but we imitated them quite well.

The tough reality that is presented in early descriptions, building from the influence of Orwell's analysis and, subsequently, reflected in Toynbee, can also be seen in other more recent studies of the industry (primarily but not exclusively, hospitality), many of which focus on problematic aspects of tourism work in a comparative social context. There is, therefore, little evidence, notwithstanding exceptional best practice examples by some organisations from across the industry, that working conditions in tourism have improved significantly from the time of Wood's pessimistic assessment.

Returning to Orwell, however, also brings us to his depiction of the craft and professionalism of hospitality work, set so starkly alongside the grim "below stairs" experience out of which the waiter seamlessly moves.

It is an instructive sight to see a waiter going into a hotel dining-roomy. As he passes through the door a sudden change comes over him. The set of his shoulders alters; all the dirt and hurry and irritation have dropped in an instant. He glides across the carpet with a solemn priestlike air. And you cannot help thinking, as you see him bow and smile, with the benign smile of the trained waiter, that the customer (is) put to shame by having such an aristocrat serve him.

There is another side of the coin which perhaps depicts tourism work in a rather more positive light and one which highlights what Riley et al. describe as "the obvious contrast of glamour on the one hand and low menial status on the other". One example of the glamour, that is equally precise and from the same period as Orwell, is represented by the accounts written, between 1937 and 1942, in five books by Ludwig Bemelmans.

However, in contrast to Orwell, Bemelmans is the supreme optimist and describes hotel work from the point of view of someone climbing to a senior position in a luxury New York hotel.

In a similar vein, Le Sueur's (1998) account of managing a hotel in Tibet presents an upbeat and very positive perspective on work at this level within the industry. The airline sector was also, historically, held up as the glamorous side of work in tourism, particularly in the 1950s and 1960s, and was widely depicted as one of the "blue ribbon" sectors for employment within personal services. During the 30-year period up to airline deregulation in the United States (1979) and Europe (early 1990s), it is fair to say that employment in the airline sector, especially with major national flag carriers, had many of the security of tenure attributes of public sector work and its attendant benefits combined with high levels of trade union participation while, at the same time, offering perceived glamour and a "fun" image. Calder describes this in terms of "A job in aviation—glamorous, secure, well-paid employment".

This perspective of airline work has been critically assessed by, among others, Bolton and Boyd (2003), Tyler and Taylor (1998) and Williams (2003) and further debunked as a result of high profile disclosures relating to work in some new model lowcost airlines as well as post-2001 changes within the aviation industry.

However, vestiges of status and glamour remain current in the airlines of many developing countries. Other areas of tourism work, while not well covered in the research literature, also point to clear ambiguities with respect to the working environment of tour guides and tour operator representatives.

Riley's application of internal labour market models to tourism provides a useful analytical framework in seeking to understand and explain the lack of significant change with respect to working conditions and remuneration in many areas of tourism work.

Riley and Szivas describe tourism as a sector "where easily acquired, transferable skills coexist and engender weak internal labour markets in organisations that economically are bound to a rate of throughput." Riley (1996) points to the features of employment in these conditions in terms of recruitment, training and professional status and, unsurprisingly, notes that many areas of tourism work typify weak internal labour market characteristics.

Alongside this assessment sits trends within most developed countries and within economic regions such as the European Union which point to erosion of elements of labour market strength and a general weakening of work place conditions. This has been driven by both economic and labour relations changes, notably in countries such as Spain and the United Kingdom but also, to a lesser extent, in bastions of strong labour markets such as France and Germany.

As we shall see, access to low cost sources of migrant labour in many European countries has further acted to weaken labour market conditions within businesses in the tourism sector, despite the introduction of national minimum wage levels in countries such as Ireland and the UK.

An assessment of progress or otherwise, with respect to the overall working conditions and remuneration levels of tourism employees, does not provide clearcut answers.

There has been progress in some countries and within many, particularly, larger, organisations where case examples of high quality working lives and opportunity can be found to match that within most other sectors of the economy. However, much tourism work remains menial and undervalued and the plethora of smaller organisations also point to working environments where practices remain Dickensian and show little change from Wood's let alone Orwell's depiction.

Reflections on the Role of Human Resources in Tourism

The underlying premise of Failte Ireland's ground breaking strategic plan for human resource development in Irish tourism is predicated upon the argument that "good HRM practices will be adopted because they deliver bottom line profitability". This primarily economic justification for investment in HRD has underpinned much of the history of this field, whether in the guise of personnel management, strategic human resource management, high commitment management or the management of human capital, among other iterations.

This, in turn, is manifested in a range of good practices, adopted by companies recognised for their leadership in the management of people within the tourism sector. Failte Ireland (2005a, 2005b) identify a number of good practice themes, based on a study of excellence in the tourism sector in Ireland and other countries.

Bolton and Houlihan (2007), in their powerful plea to reintroduce a human dimension to our consideration of HRM, note that these dimensions are uni-dimensional in their focus on employer benefits so that they ignore any notion of reciprocity. They effectively encapsulate this oneway street in their assessment of the HRM contract in terms of its humanity.

Bolton and Houlihan's case is, on the face of it, simple. Arguments in favour of work place flexibility among other forms of accommodation and change in the work place are generally, business and employer driven. Notwithstanding blandishments that advocate recognition of employee lifestyle requirements and work-life balance, some of which is enshrined in legislation addressing matters such as paternity leave, the overwhelming evidence is that reciprocity with regard to flexibility and accommodation in the work place is relatively rare, both for remunerated employees and among volunteer workers in tourism and heritage organisations.

Bolton and Houlihan point to imbalance in the expectations of contemporary industrial relations within tourism. As a weak labour market sector, tourism in most developed countries has never been highly unionised and what strength trade unions may have offered in seeking greater reciprocity in the human resource contract has been eroded further in recent years.

High profile disputes in international tourism companies have taken place in recent years, primarily in larger organisations located in transport related subsectors. Examples of these include disputes in Irish Ferries, Gate Gourmet.

Unions have succeeded in achieving partial amelioration of employer plans, but in no sense can these be taken as indicative of change in a general labour market process which is designed to weaken the position of employees within the sector.

Indeed, in the wider context of services, especially in smaller businesses, Korczynski argues that if trade unions "are to have meaning for frontline workers, their strategies must be informed by the daily work experiences of these workers" and that strategies that are derived from such experiences are likely to appear contrary to traditional union practice.

He notes the failure of trade unions to adapt to the needs of the contemporary service economy but, in the context of most businesses in tourism, this does not really represent change from past experience within which trade unions were of but marginal relevance within the sector. There are specific contexts within which trade unions can operate effectively in tourism.

"Traditional" airlines are one example as are hotels in Dublin, Ireland where Piso (2003) reports structural factors in the local labour market as being supportive of union participation. Perhaps the main barrier to unionisation in tourism's private sector is the attitude of management. Royle (2000), in considering work in the McDonalds fast food chain across a number of European countries, identifies the strategies employed by the company to ensure that unions cannot operate effectively.

Within tourism businesses, a process of organisational delayering and the reduction in specialist human resource staff means that many human resource responsibilities have substantially been devolved to front line managers.

Brewster and Larsen (1992) suggest that there are a number of reasons why many human resource activities have been devolved to line managers, and these are cost reduction, to provide a more comprehensive approach to HR Management, and to place the responsibility with the people who are most responsible for it.

Renwick's (2003) study established that line managers are now responsible for a larger number of employees than ever before, which in turn means that there are more issues in this area for them to manage. Storey (1992, 1995, 2001) suggests that if the work force is so critical to organisational success, the responsibility for human resource activities rests with all line managers and should not be left to HR specialists.

While larger organisations have undoubtedly invested in providing frontline managers with the new HR skills necessary for the responsibilities identified, there is little evidence that the majority of smaller tourism businesses have done much to meet this need. As a result, it is arguable that the quality of human resource management has deteriorated.

Approaches to human resource management that are suitable for a complex sector such as tourism remain contentious. The evidence is that larger organisations have become more professional in their application of key HR principles within the work place, but that such professionalism frequently remains absent in smaller businesses. The notion of reciprocity, which we introduced with regard to work place flexibility, can also be largely absent when organisations implement wider HR policies and practices.

People management may be recognised as a concern for all those in positions of responsibility in organisations, but there is little evidence that those charged with this responsibility have a full comprehension of what this strategic role means in practice.

This failure or neglect is not just one that is of concern at the level of the tourism firm but reflects a charge that can equally be directed at tourism development policies and practices at a community, regional or national level.

Liu and Wall are rightly critical of this neglect when they state that "tourism's human resource issues are poorly conceptualised and the many studies of tourism development approaches, both theoretical and practical, provide no consolidation of useful recommendations to situate the human dimension as an integral part of a comprehensive planning framework for tourism".

There is little evidence that this recent criticism has any less validity today than it might have done in the mid-1980s, and this is a real indictment of the large number of master plans and similar documents for tourism that have been funded by international agencies during this time.

A Global Industry, A Global Work Force

The tourism sector offers many and varied opportunities for working lives across its diverse subsectors and at different levels throughout the world. The industry's heterogeneity, geographical spread and stochastic demand cycle provides both opportunity and challenge in terms of mapping these against the aspirations and expectations of those attracted into the tourism industry, either as new entrants to the labour force or in the context of change opportunities within their working lives.

In most developed countries, traditional models of one sector working lives, built on the notion of a logical and progressive career "ladder" represents a reality which will face fewer and fewer entrants to the jobs market in the future. For some people, this is not a concern or a fear but provides the basis for challenge and opportunity, the ability to take control of aspects of their lives and to respond to changes within the external environment in a positive manner. Unlike their grandparents, today's school leavers and college graduates are more likely to think of their working lives in terms of finite segments rather than sustained and permanent careers, viewing the future in terms of what have been called "boundaryless careers" or "fragmented futures". Sennett, in recognising this phenomenon from a somewhat different perspective, notes that "flexible capitalism has blocked the straight roadway of career, inverting employees suddenly from one kind of work into another".

The trend data in many countries also point clearly to people being more mobile in their working lives and spending less time in the same job. For example, with respect to the UK, Macauley highlights evidence that "in 1996, half of all employees had been working for the same firm for 5 years or less. This had fallen to 4 years by 2001". The same source, points to the decreasing proportion of both full-and part-time employees who had been in their current job for at least 12 months during the same timeframe.

Similarly, the same UK labour market has seen a significant increase in the proportion of people in nonpermanent jobs. McOrmond (2004) reports on changes between 1993 and 2003 which point to increasing temporary engagement by, in particular, those aged below 24 years and those aged over 50 years.

Notably, the intermediate group, both male and female, saw a decrease in temporary employment over the same time period. Given the importance of younger workers to the tourism sector, this trend is evidence of this process of fragmentation and its likely impact within the industry and has stimulated response through, for example, recruitment from new labour markets.

Notwithstanding the trend indicated here, temporary employment in the UK, by wider European standards, remains quite low at about 7% of the total work force compared to a figure of 32% in Spain, 20% in Portugal and almost 18% in Finland. The temporary employment of female workers is consistently higher than then of males throughout the European Union. The structure of tourism is particularly conducive to supporting vocational mobility, particularly because of stochastic demand within the sector. However, the working environment in many sectors of tourism is such that labour turnover is higher than in other sectors of the economy.

Weir (2003) reports labour turnover in the UK and notes that the hotel and restaurant industries display the highest job separation rates of major sectors. High labour turnover is a reflection of the work environment within tourism and also of economic prosperity and opportunity combined with changing demographic structures and increased educational opportunity in developed countries. In the Irish Republic, for example, a centralised recruitment service for craft-level courses in tourism has seen demand move from a situation of very significant under-supply of training places in the late 1980s to one today where many courses are significantly under subscribed and some have been withdrawn.

Bauman's (2005, 2006) concept of liquidity is equally effective in explaining movement from one dimension of life to another and between relationships, whether in personal or working terms. Liquidity also points to blurring in the distinctions between working and nonworking lives, or as Hochschild puts it "family life had become like 'work' and work had become more like 'home'".

Adler (2004) reinforces this notion in his discussion of how the initiation of new work place practices, based on interdependence, can spread over into the home and change domestic behaviour in terms of a weakening of traditional gender roles. Fluid movement between working life segments allow individuals frequent mobility between different sectors of the economy, periods of study within models of lifelong learning and episodes that consist of travel or volunteering sabbaticals.

Vocational mobility is greatly facilitated by recognition of the underpinning "generic" skills set which much education and working experience provides today and which permits ease of both formal (qualifications driven) and informal (experience driven) transition, particularly within the tourism sector's weak labour market conditions.

Fragmentation or fluidity may be a relatively new phenomenon in the context of many sectors of the economy, but the reality of such employment models, generally employer rather than employee driven, is well established in many areas of tourism. Writing more than a decade ago, Riley infers that, in moving towards a future of "rising insecurity of job tenure, more unsocial hours working, more uneven workflow, a greater sense of immediacy in tasks", production industries are, essentially, playing what might be called "catch down" with a range of low skills service industries, including tourism.

Fragmentation or fluidity have long been features of work in these sectors, as noted by Orwell (1933) and are driven by, among other things, employer management of stochastic demand and growing responsiveness to customer demand or whims. What is new, however, is that work place mobility and job change are increasingly employee driven, with workers unwilling to make longterm commitments to one organization or work place. Unlike the disapproval that fragmentation or liquidity in working lives may have attracted in the past, today such mobility is less likely to be seen in terms of a lack of commitment or disloyalty to an employer nor does it necessarily create a sense of fear and insecurity for those moving between various working phases.

Perceptions of working lives held by younger people today are focused more on short-term wealth accumulation or debt reduction and much less on job status, security or permanence of employment than was the case with previous generations. Therefore, within the timescale allotted to work in a particular company or sector, commitment may be strong despite the transitory nature of the employment relationship.

Alongside the flexibility which characterises working relationships within the contemporary global work force, vestiges of the past remain within the labour market.

Major cities undergoing post-industrial transformation can face the paradox of high residual, longterm unemployment, mainly within the former work force of heavy industries such as automobile manufacturing alongside a large number of unfilled vacancies in contemporary tourism businesses, most of which can only be filled from student or migrant worker labour pools.

Sennett (2006) talks about the "spectre of uselessness" which haunts post-industrial society, in his terms the result of automation and technology substitution in the industrial work place but equally relevant where communities have witnessed growth in service, notably tourism, work and parts of the work force have not been enabled to buy into this new model of employment. At the heart of the causes of this uselessness is Bauman's notion that "the impetuous growth of new knowledge and no less rapid ageing of the old combine to produce human ignorance on a massive scale, and continuously replenish, perhaps even beef up, its supplies".

At its simplest, leading businesses have already recognised the changing nature of the employment relationship and have responded by a reconfiguration of operations and service delivery at certain levels within the traditional quality spectrum. As a leader within this process, McDonalds early on accepted that they would offer, at best, transitory job opportunities for many school and college students as well as others in the work force.

Therefore, they ensured that processes can be learnt very quickly by able people who are productive within a short period of time. Both parties know very well that there will not be a longterm commitment to the working relationship but that, while it lasts, both sides seek to maximise respective benefits.

For McDonalds and similar operators, this involves streamlining and simplifying processes and relying on the energy and enthusiasm of their workers for the delivery of their services. McDonalds have recently taken acknowledgement of the transitory nature of employer–worker relationships a step further with their announcement of the McPassport, providing opportunity for their employees working anywhere within the European Union to transfer to positions in McDonalds' shops across boundaries elsewhere in the EU, for short or longer periods of time, thus facilitating lifestyle and educational opportunity.

Other tourism businesses have recognised the value of this approach. In major cities in the UK and elsewhere perhaps half of all tourism workers are notionally full-time students. As a result, the tourism industry is configured to depend upon this source of labour and education providers have also had to adjust their delivery models accordingly. For businesses, there has been some modification of both product and technical skills demands with a greater focus on "generic skills" of communication, personality (aesthetic and emotional labour) as well as greater use of technology. Traditional training, as offered through tourism colleges in the form of formal courses and qualifications, plays a lesser role in meeting industry needs within this new model of tourism employment.

The decline in relevance of and demand for technical courses in tourism also increases the marginalisation of those with low qualifications in contemporary society (the traditional recruitment pool for such courses) who, as a result, may be further economically and socially excluded. In their place, the flexible student labour market offers employers many perceived advantages which traditional training routes do not.

Likewise, many tourism businesses in rural areas have turned to short-term labour pools of students and others from abroad, in Ireland/UK to learn English (from countries such as Spain or Germany) or for their year out (from New Zealand or Australia) as ready made, articulate and, in some cases, lower cost alternatives to local labour.

"Lifestyle"—attractive employment in Donegal, West Cork or Kerry in Ireland can be offered seasonally to workers from elsewhere in Europe at lower cost and difficulty than would be involved in drawing on local labour markets. Training required and offered is minimal and there is hassle-free disengagement at the end of the tourist season. An extension of this employment culture is reflected in the increasing use of other flexible labour strategies within tourism. Shackleton (1998) points to the contribution of targeted part-time labour in the development of 'superservice' in food retailing.

Likewise, agency staff, in some areas of tourism employment, are of increasing importance, particularly in urban locations. Hotel housekeeping and banqueting are the main work areas where agencies provide a "just in time" model for businesses which allows for rapid response to variable demand and eliminates surplus staffing on an employer's books. This also creates an environment where longer-term employment relationships and structured longitudinal training models have little relevance. These expedient models of employment are most prevalent within the systematised, middle quality rankings and "fast" delivery sectors of the tourism sector. The concept of a career within this sector for all but a minority in positions of managerial responsibility is of limited and decreasing value.

The role of education and training in the context of transitory working lives, both within the external college environment and in industry itself, is to support mobility, mid-life entry and re-entry to the sector and development in relation to new technologies and products. This represents a fast-moving, ever-changing and challenging model of lifelong learning which, in the future, will play an important role in support of the "popular" sector of the tourism industry.

"Fragmented" and transitory employment relationships and practices may still leave problems for those "high end" businesses which remain locked within traditional skills paradigms and which employ craft personnel in the conventional mode. For them, the concept of the traditional, longitudinal career within a chosen craft area has relevance and career management in this sense requires active participation by employees themselves, their employers but also by those responsible for maintaining, managing and enhancing quality within tourism. At the same time, paying for and marketing the outcomes of such skills necessitates premium pricing and careful management of the price–value relationship.

The working lives projected for today's young people bear little relationship to the linear career models aspired by their grandparents and will be characterised by change, short-term goals and ongoing renewal.

Those planning for human resource development in tourism may need to more responsive to the challenges and opportunities presented by fragmented learning and working lives and recognise, as Adler and Adler (2004) do, the diversity of motivations and interests that workers typically bring into their employment relationships with tourism sector employers. Change, with regard to this theme, has moved employee aspirations for reciprocity in the utilisation of flexibility up the agenda so that notions of work place flexibility, as introduced by Atkinson (1984) and others, can no longer be seen solely in terms of approaches that are designed to benefit organisational needs.

The response to global trends in tourism, by educational and training providers, has been mixed. Baum (2000) points to the institutional and cultural barriers to change within most educational systems, factors that mitigate against the adoption of common tourism programmes and qualifications across national boundaries, notwithstanding the intentions of initiatives such as the Bologna agreement in Europe. The range of national case studies that address educational and training themes in tourism and the wider economy also points to the intransigence of diversity.

At the same time, there has been a growth in programmes in tourism education offered to a worldwide audience online and demand for education in this field through overseas study in Australia, Hong Kong, the UK, the USA and elsewhere remains high. However, such provision is largely structured upon demand from students from developing countries seeking to acquire skills and knowledge as imparted by academic and professional experts in the developed world.

This is a questionable model of knowledge transfer and one that Botterill and Baum (2006) describe as neo-colonial in impact. It is similar to the underpinning assumptions behind the growth of tourism education in many developing countries over the past 20 years, assumptions that see European and North American models delivery put uncritically in place in the colleges and universities of recipient countries.

The Impact of ICT on Work and Employment in Tourism

There is little questioning of the impact of technological development on all aspects of working and living in developed countries and, to an increasing extent, within the developing world as well. The impact of such change on the work place and beyond is well documented.

These assessments highlight the importance of changes in the work place linked to a wide range of issues, including perceptions of time and work intensity within the work place; organisational fragmentation; flexibility and enabling the recognition of work-life balance issues in the work place; the polarisation of skills and the decline in demand for less skilled workers; disparities in remuneration linked to use/non-use of ICT in the work place; outsourced working; home and teleworking; social inclusion, ICT and the work place; ICT and knowledge management; and technology substitution among a much wider range of concerns. These changes in the work place mirror wider adoption and use of technology within society and, in many respects, feed off familiarity with and expectations of technology that stem from everyday life. A comprehensive assessment of the impact of ICT and wider technology on the work place and working lives in tourism and beyond has the potential to be a subject for separate analysis in its own right. Here, we touch on a number of key themes and issues drawn from this discussion.

What is true, with regard to ICT in a general sense, is equally valid as an assessment of change within services and tourism and, in particular, within the context of work and employment and the changing role that people play as a result of such change. It is not an understatement to argue that ICT and wider technological change have revolutionised aspects of tourism operations (particularly distribution) while leaving others virtually untouched (food preparation and service in many smaller operations).

In terms of employment in tourism and the past 20 years, technology has had a direct effect on both the elimination of work areas and on the creation of others. Some destinations, dependent on airline and other transport stopovers for their tourism business, have been bypassed by advances in transport technology so that the work associated with this industry may no longer exist. For example, Gander in Newfoundland, Canada, a major refuelling stop for trans-Atlantic flights until the early 1980s now no longer serves this purpose and work associated with the sector has ceased to exist.

Similarly, changes in technology mean that the work of hotel telephonists has faded and, in many cases, disappeared with the advent of automated telephones in bedrooms and guest mobile phones. The technology challenge, particularly the consumer option to purchase and manage the booking of tourism products direct with suppliers such as airlines and hotels via the Internet, has reduced the need for and changed the role of travel agents, check-in staff and others involved in work in the sector in developed countries.

Such change is dependent on the availability and quality of the technology and, in many developing countries, the role of the travel intermediary remains important in the absence of Internet or, at least, Broadband connectivity. A final example of changing or diminishing role is that of the tour guide whose work can, in part, be superseded by flexible, electronic alternatives at tourism sites, allowing choice of language and giving visitors a selection of perspectives on events and the site environment.

However, ICT in particular has also created new forms of work in tourism, notably through the application of ICT and its use in distribution and management of key functions such as yield. The advent of specialist Internet travel companies such as Expedia is clear evidence of this change, but the growth of specialist electronic distribution is complemented by website communications, marketing and booking options within virtually all "traditional" tourism companies so that the boundaries between them and e-companies has narrowed greatly. These developments have created demand for technology specialists in the tourism sector and also for new marketing and management skills in a more general sense, allowing companies to maximise the benefits they derive from ebusiness.

ICT has also changed the role of management information within the sector, allowing far greater depth and access to key information about guests and their behaviour. At the same time, it has revolutionised the management of pricing and yield so that human intervention is far less frequent than it would have been in the past.

Technology has also changed the nature of work and skills required for many employees, not least in tourism. Many areas of work have been moved from relatively skilled levels to the routine or lesser skilled. A good example of such change is in the area of hotel front office where enhanced reservations and guest management systems have reduced the training and technical skills requirements of such work by up to 90% in terms of the time required to acquire full competency. As we shall see, the technical demands of such work have been more than compensated for by the wider bundling of skills requirements within such work.

Moving Beyond Technical Skills

Tourism work has, historically, been calibrated in terms of its technical skills demands. This is most evident in the approach adopted by the International Labour Organization (1979) in their Taylorian breakdown of hospitality work into individual, measurable micro-tasks that, in turn, can be rebuilt into a training curriculum and assessment instrument.

On the basis of this, tourism and related service work has traditionally and widely been characterised as low skills although this stereotype is challenged in the context of hospitality by a number of authors on the basis that this represents both a technical and western-centric perception of work and skills.

In developed countries, the merging of family and working life has particular pertinence here in that many of the technical and interpersonal skills demanded of employees in tourism have close parallels with those learnt during socialisation in the home. Baum's (2006a) notion of social distance between the experience and behaviour of the tourist and employee is also of relevance here in that, in developed countries, there is considerable role crossover between the two in terms of transfer of experiences between the contexts. In less developed countries, such crossover is less likely.

Grugulis, Warhurst, and Keep (2006) talk about the evolution of what we understand to be a skill over time. In terms of tourism work, perhaps the first manifestation of change from a dominantly technical focus can be found in Hochschild's (1983) seminal study, which was one of the first to take our understanding of such work beyond the technical and professional domain, focusing on "the relational rather than the task-based aspect of work".

Hochschild's work inspired recognition of what Westwood (2004) notes are commonly referred to as 'soft skills' and, in doing so, highlights less tangible dimensions in the bundling of skills and work in tourism. Hochschild argues that service employees are required to manage their emotions for the benefit of customers and are, in part, paid to do this. Likewise, Seymour (2000) considers the contribution that this notion of emotional labour makes to work in fast food and traditional areas of service work and concludes that both areas demand considerable emotional elements in addition to overt technical skills.

Bryman defines emotional labour as relating to Employment situations in which workers as part of their work roles need to convey emotions and preferably to appear as though those emotions are deeply heldy (emotions) that are supposed to make the recipient of the emotional labour feel good about the worker and the organization for which he or she works.

Sandiford and Seymour (2002) take this definition a step further in talking about the management of emotions for financial reward. This link between human emotion and commercialisation has not been without detractcrs such as Wouters (1989) and Newton, Handy, and Fineman (1995). The expectations of emotional labour add significantly to the skills demands of work in tourism.

There are few areas of frontline or boundary spanning work in tourism that do not have a very evident and, in some cases, all important emotional dimension.

In many respects, as Bryman notes with respect to Disney, employees are expected to give the appearance of enjoying their work as much as visitors are enjoying their time in the theme park. Maintaining this emotional facade in working conditions that are, often, anything but conducive to such behaviour takes its toll and requires skills and the outcome of extensive training in order to be maintained.

Blythman (2005) discusses the problems that such demands present in the context of supermarket work. After several hours at a time, any urge to be cheery or pleasant was overtaken by an all pervasive, mindnumbing blankness.

I began to feel spaced out, as though dulled by drugs. Any energy I might feel at the start of a shift soon ebbed away. Even if you wanted to try to be pleasant with people, after only so long it was impossible to keep it up.

The demands that emotional engagement in the work place entails have not traditionally been recognised within skills hierarchies and have either been neglected or put to one side as of lower value and status than "real" productive activities.

Bolton (2004) argues a strong case for the recognition of the skills dimensions within emotion work. She argues that emotional inputs are inherently skilled elements within the work routines, control processes and socially constructed demands that typify much service work. On this basis, Bolton argues that "emotion work is indeed skilled work which contains recognisable elements of discretionary content, task variety and employee control". Ritzer (2005) extends this notion of emotional involvement in his discussion of "simulated people". Obvious examples are Ronald McDonald and the characters to be found in Disney theme parks but Ritzer notes that "Far more important, however, is the fact that most of the people we encounter in the new means of consumption are simulations, even if they are not wearing costumes".

Ritzer argues that employers prescribe how workers look, what they say and how they behave in a more general sense with the result that "these positions can be filled by a wide range of individuals. There is little or no room for creativity or individuality".

Work with a strong emotional labour component is, however, not exclusively about theatre. Williams (2003) highlights the safety and regulatory context which trumps any considerations of service and emotional engagement with passengers in the work of airline attendants.

Safetyrelated skills may be considered to be technical in nature and this illustrates that, while some areas of tourism work may focus almost exclusively on soft or ephemeral skills, the roles of government regulation and passenger concern are such that emotional engagement must always take second place to the hard skills demands of safety in the work place.

To the requirements of emotional labour in tourism can be added the skills demands of what Warhurst, Nickson, Witz, and Cullen (2000) describe as aesthetic labour, the skills required to look, sound and behave in a manner that is compatible with the requirements of the job and with the expectations of your customers.

In many cases, aesthetic labour involves staff demonstrating the ability to respond to fashion and trend imperatives in the consumer marketplace in a way that can be socially exclusive of many groups and cultures within society. Aesthetic labour is about appearance but can also be underpinned by cultural cache, the ability of frontline staff to understand and engage culturally with their customers on terms dictated by the latter.

Thus, service staff in some tourism contexts (luxury hotels, premium airline cabins, fitness centres, oneto-one personal training or other sports tuition) need to be able to make informed conversation with their guests or clients about politics, music, sport and almost any other imaginable topic, often from an international perspective. This requirement presupposes a certain level of prior education and cultural exposure as well as a commitment to remain up-to-date in these areas, what Nickson and Warhurst describe as the "gentrification of skill demand".

This implies a very significant change in the profiling of tourism skills in that work which has traditionally provided opportunity for those at the economic margins of developed country societies is, in part, now demanding a skills set that lies within the competencies of those with good general education and a more "middle class" cultural profile. This skills set is, therefore, beyond the reach of traditional recruitment pools for many tourism jobs.

Warhurst etal's interpretation of the commodified aesthetics of labour clearly builds upon Tyler and Taylor's discussion of aesthetics and gender in the work place (in the context of flight attendants), which looks specifically at "those particular aspects of women's work which takes place outside formal, contractual relations of exchange, yet upon which formal, contractual relations of commodity exchange depend". Tyler and Taylor's interpretation of aesthetics in the work place draws on "women's attributed nature, femininity and sexuality the commodification of women's Otherness". Thus, aesthetic skills can be seen as both an innate dimension of gender and as an area of skill which processes socialisation, education and training can develop and hone.

Westwood (2004) notes that in ascribing a 'soft skills' descriptor to labour with an emotional and/or aesthetic dimension, there is an implicit assumption that such skills are somehow less important than their 'hard' counterparts.

This is a view disputed in Bolton's (2004) argument that emotional work has a clear high skills dimension. Of importance in wider human resource terms is Westwood's comment that such skills, whatever their level of demand, "are a very long way from the kinds of skills that the UK's education system is used to supplying" which persists in a focus on "the processing and supply of more academic skills".

This indictment is applicable to many other countries and has particular bite in the context of tourism, pointing to a significant mismatch between education and training and the requirements of the contemporary industry.

Managing Diversity in the Work Place

Diversity in the tourism work place is not a new phenomenon, but full recognition of its impact and managerial implications in developed countries is relatively recent, driven by demographic, labour market and legislative change. Wood adopts an encompassing definition of diversity management when he talks of "a set of evolving philosophies and practices concerned with the utilisation of a variety of human characteristics, orientations and dispositions in satisfaction of ethical precepts and the pursuit of business goals".

In the context of this paper, our main concern is with the consequences of diversity in the tourism work place that have arisen through mobility in the form of labour migration, but we will also acknowledge the significance of other forms of diversity to contemporary HRM within the sector.

Indeed, as Adib and Guerrier (2003) rightly point out, it is rarely possible to consider the impact of any dimension within the diversity agenda in isolation in that, for example, ethnicity and disability are frequently closely associated with social class and economic status including labour market participation.

Governments in the developed world increasingly recognise the apparent benefits of labour migration to a country's economy. Home Office research shows that in the UK over a single year, migrants (including asylum seeks and refugees) contributed £2.5 billion to the UK economy.

Migrant workers can be beneficial to the economy in a multitude of ways: in particular, they are able to fill gaps in the domestic labour market and alleviate skills shortages as well as increasing the levels of employment which, in turn, helps to raise gross domestic product. Their age profile is such that they use less in the way of services but contribute to tax and national insurance payments which, in turn, help to finance future pensions.

The importance of labour migration to the work force of the contemporary tourism industry is well documented. Tourism businesses have long relied on a culturally diverse work force. Baum (2006a) traces examples of vocational mobility in the sector in Europe back to the 13th century and discusses the important role that, primarily, southern Europeans played in developing the culture and character of tourism operations in industrialised Europe in the 19th and much of the 20th centuries.

However, contemporary labour migration, within tourism in Europe, has received limited attention from researchers. Widespread labour shortages and other labour market changes resulting from the impacts of a combination of, among others, demographic, globalization and economic factors in Europe are leading tourism companies to hire new employees from a wide range of less developed and transition economy countries.

Traditionally concentrated in core, urban centres, multiculturalism within the tourism labour market is now a phenomenon that has reached geographically peripheral areas and has implications for the marketing of destinations such as Ireland which have depended significantly on images of people and place in their destination branding. The numerical impact of migrant labour on the delivery of tourism services in these locations is particularly noticeable.

As an example, it is estimated that there are over 250,000 non-Irish nationals employed in the economy of the Irish Republic or some 13% of the entire work force.

This figure reaches 17% in the Irish tourism industry and is up to 25% of the work force in key areas of hospitality work. This growth was stimulated further in 2004 following the accession of 10 new Member States to the European Union. It is estimated that new arrivals to Ireland from within the Union reached 50,000 in 2004, primarily from Poland. In addition, some 9000 work permits were issued to non-European Economic Area nationals.

The changing nature of labour markets in the tourism sectors of developed countries, as a result of increasing migration, raises issues that have been subject to analysis across a range of the social sciences. Conceptually, this discussion can be located within debate about different forms of mobility in contemporary society and their specific impact in the tourism context. The nature of mobility discussed here and its impact are less common in their analysis in that they are a form of migration (labour) that exists solely because of the presence of another form of mobility, that of tourism.

The issue under the microscope here also responds to Rosello's (2001) notion of the immigrant as guest in her consideration of hospitality and immigration in postcolonial France. If migrants are, themselves, guests in the communities in which they work, interpretative representations of the destination in that context may be provided for guests (visitors) by guests (workers). This context has the potential to place strain on understanding of working roles within the tourism sector and the nature of hospitality provided by those employed as frontline staff.

It is arguable that the widespread recruitment and use of migrant labour in the tourism industry of developed countries has acted to the detriment of real change within the sector's work place. The argument that the tourism sector cannot recruit to unfilled vacancies and, therefore, turns to external labour sources is predicated upon the assumption that the labour economics of the industry remain appropriate and need not change.

There are exceptions, as evidenced in good practice examples across the sector, but much of the industry operates on the basis of a labour economics model that depends upon high turnover, low pay, poor conditions and minimal investment in training. Accessing low cost but untrained migrant labour is likely to act as a dead hand with respect to change within the work place economics of the sector. As a consequence, many tourism businesses do not perceive the need to change.

They are not required to consider strategies designed to enhance labour productivity, notably through real investment in training and development, in order to reduce the numbers they need to employ at higher rates of pay because low cost employees remain readily available. This analysis accords with Riley and Szivas' comment that "by not recruiting fully trained workers, employers forego productivity in favour of lower labour costs". It is also consistent with Riley's assertion, based on conceptual rather than empirical evidence, but valuable here nonetheless, that "where unskilled labour is imported to fill a shortage, the effect is to deflate existing pay levels".

Notwithstanding the advent of minimum wage legislation in the buoyant tourism economies of countries such as Ireland and the UK, there is little doubt that the availability of migrant labour does allow tourism businesses to employ more untrained workers at lower cost than might have been the case had this source of employee not been available, thus imposing deflationary pressures on individual but possibly not total remuneration costs.

Our discussion thus far, in the context of diversity, has focused on culturally induced dimensions. The management of people in the contemporary tourism sector in many countries is increasingly either legally or morally bound to recognise diversity in terms of a far wider interpretation.

These manifestations of diversity are not wholly new in tourism and there is evidence of their recognition, to a limited extent, in early analysis of the sector. However, highlighting such diversity in today's tourism work place is both functionally and ethically important. Dimensions that merit acknowledgement in this context include:

- Gender and the evident and continuing institutionalised disparity that exists in the status and pay of men and women in the services work place. Services work in most societies is highly gendered and this universal reality across national boundaries and continental divides is clearly evident in the range of contexts that are addressed by Sinclair (1997) and her contributing colleagues. Women, as Toynbee (2003) clearly illustrates, often undertake the least desirable and lowest status work in hospitality and other evidence from elsewhere in the services sector suggests that gender has an underpinning influence on rewards, achievement and status in the work place. Likewise the culturally induced absence of working women in the services sectors of some countries is tempered by evidence of gradual change in, for example, Iran and Saudi Arabia. Some areas of gendered work in services can be seen to represent exploitation and degradation and, therefore, combating sex services, particularly in relation to children, has become a major concern of governments and NGOs in some countries. Some areas of services work have, historically, been a predominantly male preserve. Mills (1998) notes, with respect to airline pilots that "In the first two decades of commercial flying the characteristics of heroism and experience came to form a unique type of organisational masculinity—the pilot. Indeed, British Airways' earliest corporate image was that of the experienced, heroic and supremely confident pilot." While gender balance on the flight deck has improved, Mills notes that it was the late 1980s before British Airways appointed their first female pilot. Progress towards gender balance, in this area of high status services work, has been varied across different airlines but female pilots are commonplace today in many countries. Ali Khan (2004) even reports the appointment of the first female airline pilot in Saudi Arabia. However, this area of work remains masculine in its operating culture so that the experiences of female pilots can be challenging and degrading at times.

- Sexual orientation is a theme that has been addressed in services in terms of consumer markets. The experience of gay employees in the sector is not widely recorded except in anecdotal form. This may be because, as Wood notes, "gays and lesbians are not always visible, indeed adopting invisibility as a strategy is one way in which homosexuals cope with organisational life and avoid the disapprobation of those who possess animus against homosexuals".
- Ability and disability is an area of increasing interest in services. The services industry is frequently portrayed as an industry for the young, beautiful and super-fit and this projection is used to create the image of vibrancy, energy and fun. The services sector can be described as one that offers opportunity to members of a society across much of its ability and disability range. It is a sector that can accommodate the expectations and abilities of those with exceptional talent (in culture, entertainment, sports,

technology, entrepreneurship as examples) as well as those in most communities who face challenges of a different sort in terms of physical or intellectual ability.

- Age in the sense that services work is frequently perceived to be an area for the young and historic data in developed countries certainly bears this out. However, changing demographics in wealthier countries means that traditional sources of labour are no longer so readily available, creating the potential of opportunity for more mature workers, returners to work and those retired from first careers. As we have already seen, this solution is, in part, countered by the availability of low cost and young workers from overseas.
- Social inclusion reflects the capacity of services, as a sector for employment, to provide opportunity to potential workers from across a wide social and economic spectrum. This capacity is not always delivered in what is a growing labour market contradiction within the sector, that of widespread employment vacancies in services existing alongside endemic and longterm unemployment within communities in both cities and in rural areas. A partial explanation can be drawn from the aesthetic demands of the industry in that some sectors of services impose implicit or overt entry barriers based on appearance, cultural cache and education upon those seeking work and many of those from socially excluded communities do not meet such criteria.
- Motivation and choice, in terms of why people choose to work and also factors that underpin voluntary, unpaid work in services.

Uncritical claims for the virtue and value of diversity in the work place must be put forward with some degree of caution. The aspiration of effective diversity management in the tourism work place can easily be blinded by what Wood calls "the worthiness of the concept" which belies the rather more pessimistic consensus of the research literature. Furthermore, as we have argued with respect to the employment of migrant labour in the tourism sector's of developed economies, their impact, while making sound short-term business sense, also has the effect of deflating remuneration, permit the continuation of variable working conditions and allowing employers to fudge investment in skills development. If this is true with respect to one form of diversity in the work place, may be necessary to question whether some of the other forms of diversity touched on here are also adopted with similar objectives.

Conclusions

We started this paper with a fairly damning assessment of work and working lives in tourism, arguing that, in many respects, Wood's bleak (1997) assessment of the industry remains substantially unchanged in many countries, both developed and less developed.

We have considered themes wherein wider contextual change can be identified that has a direct impact upon people and their management in the tourism sector and we have considered the consequences of such changes. The evidence points, unsurprisingly, to conclusions in the form of a curate's egg and, indeed, contradictions in terms of practice across the industry. For example, we have evidence of the gentrification of tourism skills from Nickson and Warhurst (2007) while, at the same time, ready access to low cost migrant labour, both legal and illegal, permits many tourism businesses to sidestep this trend and to ignore issues of productivity, skills development and general work place enhancement.

As in other areas of work, it is clear that polarisation is taking place within tourism work, but the criteria of distinction relates to the branding and image of the work rather than to its technical or professional status. "Cool" work is equated with style, fashion and consumer branding (bars, night clubs, boutique hotels, creative venues) while "uncool" includes the work of drudgery in the sector (cleaning, popular service) and also some glamour work from the past, airline cabin crew, particularly with some newer, lowcost airlines.

Another example of contradiction is that vocational and educational opportunities for most young people in developed countries are such that many areas of tourism work are much less obvious and attractive longterm career options than they might have been 20 years ago. At the same time, growth in tourism in developing countries means that the sector has become an important source of employment for those previously dependent on subsistence living so that what is, ostensibly, the same work in a technical sense is constructed in very different ways across social, cultural and economic contexts.

It is true that, at an organisational level, human resource practices in tourism have changed in many developed countries and in most larger operations. This change has been driven by a combination of the effects of commercial, legislative, ethical and external environmental pressures.

At the same time, tourism remains a sector within which, worldwide, very poor employment practices persist, incorporating both minimal compliance with the law and transgression beyond legally accepted behaviour.

Some of the changes over the past 20 years that are considered here, notably the mass mobility of economic and political migrants from the world's poorer countries, have allowed tourism work and employment to remain firmly located at the margins of many societies in terms of benefits and status and has acted counter to attempts to reform and modernise the sector with regard to its employment practices.

In the final analysis, the conditions of work in tourism are attributable to the outcomes of market force pressures, temporised in part and in places by government and wider societal interventions.

In parallel to our bleak assessment of the work environment, it is important to recognise that insatiable and growing demand for low cost tourism services, across the globe, means that consumers must also take responsibility for pressurising operators into undesirable, marginal or even illegal employment practices. It is self-evident that downward pressures on the overall cost of tourism (low cost airlines, aggressive tour operators, electronic distribution, deregulation) encourages the use of low cost labour and, to an extent, may also deflate expectations of service and product quality.

Growth projections for tourism, over the next quarter of a century, are such that it appears unlikely that we will see fundamental change in this environment in the foreseeable future.

Human Resource Module of the Tourism Satellite Account, Update to 2006

The aim of the Human Resource Module (HRM) is to provide timely and reliable statistics on the human resource dimension of tourism. It serves as a useful planning and forecasting tool for policy makers in the tourism, employment and training areas. Various tourism-affiliated agencies, academics, and decisionmakers in tourism will also be able to use it for research and analysis, planning and development.

Travel Services accounted for 47 thousand jobs in 2006, up 1.3%, following a 5.9% gain in 2005. This industry group accounted for only 2.6% of all jobs in tourism. The average hourly compensation for jobs in this industry group was above average ($21.56 per hour versus $17.95), as were the hours worked (1,805 hours per year versus 1,559). Travel counsellor was the predominant occupation, accounting for 42% of the industry's employee jobs.

Jobs, Hours and Earnings in Tourism Industries

A total of 2.8 billion hours was worked in tourism industries in 2006, accounting for 9.7% of the 29.1 billion hours worked in the economy overall. This reflected an average 1,559 hours of work per year, somewhat less than the economy-wide average of 1,738 hours. The lower hours of work reflected the higher proportion of part-time jobs found in tourism. It is interesting to note that the average annual hours worked increased slightly in 2006 in tourism industries, but were unchanged for the economy overall. In Retail Trade, a sector characterized by a high proportion of part-time jobs, like tourism, the average annual hours of work per job fell from 1,584 hours in 2005 to 1,566 hours in 2006.

Profile of Employees in Tourism Industries

The HRM includes details on three characteristics of employees namely, gender, age group and immigrant status. The following highlights some of the HRM results according to these demographics.

Women held 920 thousand employee jobs in tourism industries in 2006, an increase of 22,000 from 2005. These gains were mostly full-time and accounted for nearly half the job gains in the sector. Among women, the number of employee jobs held by those aged

45 and over increased the most in 2006 (+3.5%). Among men, on the other hand, jobs held by those aged 25-34 increased the most (+3.9%). The number of jobs held by women and men aged 35 to 44 hardly changed. Women were notably under-represented in Other Transportation, holding only 26% of the employee jobs.

Conversely, 68% of jobs in Travel Services were held by women. Women were more likely to be working part-time than men. They also earned less. Women working in tourism industries earned $19,100 in 2006, compared to $30,500 for men.

There was significant variation in women's wages and salaries, with jobs in Air Transportation paying the most ($42,269) on average, and jobs in Food and Beverage Services paying the least ($14,632).

Youth aged 15 to 24 years held 658 thousand employee jobs in the tourism industries in 2006. These young workers were more likely to be working in part-time jobs than other tourism workers, accounting for two-thirds of all the part-time work in the sector. Their wages were also considerably lower.

For example, the average hourly wage among workers aged 15-24 was $8.82 in 2006, just over half the average across tourism industries. Over 1997 to 2006, the number of jobs held by younger (15 to 24 years of age) and older (45 + years of age) employees in tourism has grown significantly, averaging 2.8% and 4.8% per year, respectively. Over the same period the number of jobs held by 25 to 44 year olds has declined.

Immigrants (persons born outside Canada) held 344 thousand jobs in tourism industries in 2006, or 20% of employee jobs. They were more likely to be employed in Travel Services and less likely to be employed in Recreation and Entertainment compared to non-immigrants. Immigrants were also more likely to be older: 18% were between 15 to 24 years old, compared to 44% for non-immigrants. Over 40% of immigrant workers belong in the 45+ age group.

Immigrants working in tourism industries were more likely to be men (53% versus 43%) and more likely to be in full-time jobs (72% versus 58%) than their non-immigrant counterparts. These results have been quite stable over 1997 to 2006. On average, immigrants worked longer hours than their non-immigrant counterparts, 1,755 hours per year versus 1,485 in 2006. This was the case for both men and women and for full-time and part-time jobs, across the period covered by the HRM.

Immigrants also earned higher annual wages and salaries on average ($28,769 versus $23,112 in 2006), although this reflects the fact that the immigrant labour force in tourism industries is older and that older workers earn more than younger workers 6: Human resources for travel and tourism Learning outcomes.

By completing this unit candidates will develop knowledge and understanding of human resources procedures and issues relevant to travel and tourism organisations. They will also develop an understanding of the recruitment process and the skills required in an interview situation. Candidates will produce evidence to meet the unit assessment objectives in order to show that they understand:

- the responsibilities of the human resources department in a travel and tourism organisation.
- how travel and tourism organisations manage their human resources.
- the recruitment process.

Candidates will also demonstrate their practical skills in interview techniques.

Assessment Objectives Knowledge, Understanding and Skills

Describe the responsibilities of the human resources department in a travel and tourism organisation Human resources department responsibilities:

- human resources planning.
- recruitment and selection.
- training and development, e.g. induction, mentoring and coaching.
- internal and external training.
- dismissal, redundancy, promotion, demotion, transfer.
- support and advice, e.g staff and line managers.
- policies and procedures, e.g grievance, disciplinary, equal opportunities, maternity, paternity, sickness.

- contracts, terms and conditions, holidays and hours of work.
- adherence to legislation, e.g race, religion, gender, gender identity, sexual orientation, disability or age (equality and diversity).
- staff welfare.
- ethical issues.

Explain how travel and tourism organisations manage their human resources Organisational structures:

- flat, tall Management styles.
- formal, informal Motivation of staff.
- motivation theories.
- job enlargement, enrichment, rotation.
- pay, bonuses, benefits.
- appraisals.

Leadership:

- styles (democratic, autocratic, laissez-faire).
- importance of clear targets.
- communication channels.

Explain how travel and tourism organisations manage their human resources;

- line management Teamwork.
- team roles.
- targets.
- importance of effective communication.

Chart the Recruitment Process

The need for staff:

- staff turnover.
- organisational growth.
- internal change.

Examples of recruitment:

- internal.
- external.

- use of agency.
- headhunting.
- advertising.

Stages of the recruitment process:

- job analysis (production of job description and person specification).
- attracting candidates (timing, different methods and their benefits).
- short listing (from CVs and application forms).
- selection interview (planning, the panel, good techniques).
- testing (psychometric and aptitude).
- appointing (contracts, terms and conditions).
- evaluation of process.
- equal opportunities issues.
- induction.

Costs:

- of poor recruitment.
- poor performance.
- impacts on team.
- advertising, staff time.

Demonstrate interviewer and interviewee techniques Interviewer:

- planning.
- questioning techniques.
- format and style of interview.
- use of interview record sheets.
- awareness of legislation regarding equality and diversity.

Interviewee:

- production of curriculum vitae.
- planning and preparation for interview.
- knowledge of organisation and job role.
- awareness of dress code.
- nonverbal communication.

- dealing with questions.
- asking appropriate questions.

Assessment

This unit is centre assessed and externally moderated. In order to achieve this unit candidates must produce a portfolio of evidence showing that they have met all of the assessment objectives. Portfolios of work must be produced independently. They will need to be made available, together with witness statements and any other supporting documentation, to the OCR Visiting Moderator when required.

Centres must confirm to OCR that the evidence produced by candidates is authentic. An OCR Centre Authentication Form is provided in the Centre Handbook and includes a declaration for assessors to sign. It is a requirement of the QCA Common Criteria for all Qualifications that proof of authentication is received.

Guidance on Assessment and Evidence Requirements

This unit aims to develop candidate's knowledge and understanding of the role of the human resources department and its importance within the organisation. The unit also aims to develop the skills required to perform effectively in an interview situation.

This unit has links with Unit 4: Customer service and selling skills in travel and tourism, Unit 8:

Planning and managing a travel and tourism event, Unit 9: Living and working overseas, Unit 11:

Career planning for travel and tourism, Unit 12: Developing skills through work experience in travel and tourism, Unit 13: Working as an overseas resort representative, and Unit 27: Working as airline cabin crew.

Links with a selection of travel and tourism organisations are encouraged for the delivery of this unit. Centres may wish to establish these. Alternatively, candidates may be able to research organisations, either individually or in small groups, share information and make comparisons. Information may also be provided through a case study, visits, talks, work experience or alternative. Ideally, organisations from different sectors of the industry and different types of organisation will be used to highlight different procedures and practices.

It is envisaged that such links with organisations will highlight the fact that the role of the human resources department varies from organisation to organisation and that management techniques and recruitment practices vary enormously. Classroom discussion of the different practices should be encouraged. However, it is recommended that underpinning knowledge of all areas is provided prior to organisational visits.

This will enable candidates to make comparisons and comment on good practice. There is a wide selection of printed and video material available on all aspects of human resource management.

When developing candidates' understanding of management techniques, tutors should draw upon candidates' experience of being 'managed' at work experience, within a work place and even within the classroom. Where candidates have worked in teams, they should be encouraged to consider whether the teams worked well and if so why. Tutors may wish to use the Belbin questionnaire to demonstrate the different team roles and the fact that a range of roles within a team is important.

It is envisaged that this unit will be used to develop candidates' awareness of the recruitment practices and the necessary preparation needed to gain employment within a travel and tourism organisation.

Candidates should chart the stages of the entire recruitment process, with explanatory notes of each stage. Again, contact with organisations will highlight differences and possible 'short-cuts' taken by organisations. Candidates should be encouraged to discuss these and comment on good practice. An understanding of the recruitment process can be used to encourage candidates to consider the need for their own applications to be professional and the costs involved in recruiting one person.

When preparing for Assessment Objective 4, candidates should be encouraged to produce curriculum vitae and complete job application forms to a professional standard. They could collect and evaluate job descriptions and person specifications. The paperwork used to shortlist candidates should be made available to candidates. Candidates should develop an awareness of their own body language. Self-reflection on skills gained and those requiring further development should be encouraged. It is anticipated that the practical activities used to develop candidates' interview techniques both as an interviewer and interviewee will help their preparation for their own interview situations, on completion of the course. Candidates can work in pairs or small groups for the assessment of Assessment Objective 4, with each candidate taking a turn as the interviewee and interviewer or interview panel member. Tutors are encouraged to video these interviews and candidates should be encouraged to self-evaluate. This could be cross-referenced with Unit 11: Career planning for travel and tourism.

Candidates may provide portfolio evidence for all of the assessment objectives in this unit using a range of presentation techniques. This may include assessor testimony/witness statements logbooks, diaries, the use of video, audio and presentation software, posters/charts, written work. Where video and/or audio evidence is provided this must be supported by assessor testimony/witness statements. Where candidates demonstrate competence, centres should record skills demonstrated on appropriate recording documentation.

8

Employment of Tourism

Introduction

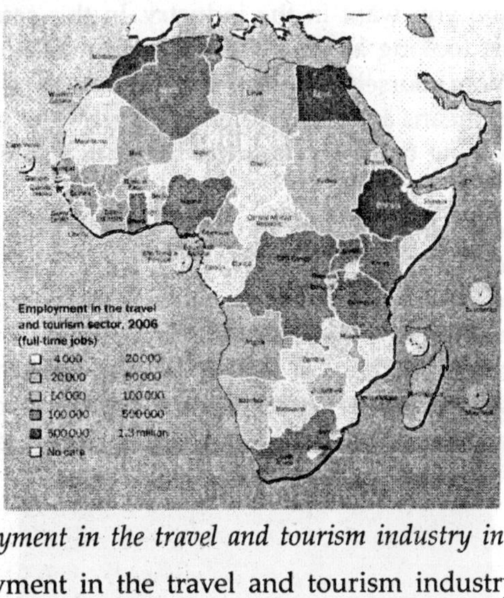

Employment in the travel and tourism industry in Africa

Employment in the travel and tourism industry in Africa. About 6.3 million people work in the travel and tourism industry in Africa, where tourism is highly dependent on natural and cultural environment. However, since travel & tourism touches all sectors of the economy, its real impact is even greater.

Preparing for Employment in Travel and Tourism

Activity

In the last session, work was focused on how recruitment and selection is used in organisations to attract effective people into jobs in the travel and tourism sector. Building on an understanding of how people in the real world make progress through their careers in the sector, you will have learned from completing work on a series of tasks:

- The stages involved in recruiting staff into jobs that you selected.
- That you can produce a flowchart of the process.
- The documents needed, such as a job description and person specification.
- The strengths and weaknesses of your chances of getting into the selected job.

Higher grades were available if you started an action plan for getting the job you want in the industry. In this session, you're going to start looking at the skills you will need to develop in order to promote yourself in a positive fashion during a job selection process. That means analysing someone's interview performance and then showing that you could do better by using self-selling skills.

If you've made it through the initial pre-selection stage to be invited for an interview, you know you stand a chance of getting the job if you perform well at interview. Some people complain that interviews are too highly pressured situations for them to show themselves in the best possible light. But in truth, good interviewing skills are very rarely natural-they have to be learned and then sharpened by experience. Let's see how one individual handled a particular interview.

Can you help your career take off in the right way?

A Dream Job and a Nightmare Interview

Tarjani felt nervous. She had been looking at the email she had received from the airline, saying she'd got through to an interview for her dream job: member of cabin crew on the London to Singapore long-haul service. But she hadn't found out much about the airline or the country she would be visiting regularly. Her friend Murali had warned her that she had better be well prepared for the interview, as he knew that the company were pretty hot on getting the right people in as cabin crew. But Murali had gone off with his mates for the evening and Tarjani didn't really know where to start.

Unfortunately, the interview was the next day and she still hadn't done much preparation, expect for rereading the job advert. She hadn't kept a copy of her application, or the documents the company had sent through-the job whatsit and person thingy-as she had been in too much of a rush to get the application sent.

She was still going through her wardrobe, deciding what to wear for the big day tomorrow, when it occurred to her that she would have to catch the bus to the place where the interviews were being held. Murali wouldn't be able to give her a lift-he wouldn't be back at his place until well after she had to leave to get to the interview.

Suddenly, she remembered that she didn't have any credit on her mobile, so couldn't check the bus times or order a taxi if she needed one. That phone box down the road was still out of order, so she'd have to spend all her time this evening going through the timetables online. That took ages, because she always forgot to favourites the right Web site. She was in a right state and had to stay up really late, as there was no way she could sleep with all the stuff she hadn't done on her mind.

The next day was one that Tarjani would like to forget, but didn't think she would be able to for a while. Later, when she talked to Murali, the sorry tale emerged:

- She'd overslept and missed the bus that would have got her to the office where the interviews were happening.
- Although in the end she was just in time, she was so flustered that she barged into the wrong office, interrupting another interview that was going on. So embarrassing!

- She'd thrown on some clothes which would have been OK if they weren't so creased they looked like she was on her way back from a festival.
- The first question in her interview asked her to say what she knew about the company: doodly squit, as it turned out. She couldn't even get the name of the airline right.
- The other questions weren't much better. She hadn't realised that they would be so in-depth. "What would you do if a passenger was rude to you because for safety reasons you wouldn't allow him to see the flight deck?" She hadn't seen that one coming.
- She thought she was on firmer ground with her answer about her qualifications. But she'd forgotten the name of a couple of modules on her college course. Well, it was nearly a year ago. And surely they'd got it all on her application? That didn't go down too well.
- To cap it all, she caught her heels in the hem of her skirt as she got up at the end of the interview and nearly fell over. She felt such an idiot and the four interviewers all had a good laugh about that. She'd just scowled at them as she left.
- As she left the offices, it started to rain. Disappointed and soaked, she eventually got home after missing another bus.

Murali agreed with Tarjani's analysis: she wouldn't be hearing from them again. "Next time you'll be better prepared," he said. She couldn't help feeling angry with him for deserting her just before her big moment. I mean, if you can't count on your best friend to help you through that, who can you rely on?

Task

Using the experience of Tarjani, who quite clearly blew her big chance at the job of her dreams, write a script for an interview that goes somewhat better. Base the interview on your own choice of job, selected in an earlier session, or one that you have only recently identified.

Track the progress of how you would prepare for the interview, making sure you cover the following important aspects of promoting yourself positively.

About the Organisation

- How is it structured?
- Where are the teams of staff located?
- How is the organisation presented in the media?
- Why do you want to work for them?

Practical Points for the Day

- Have as normal an evening as possible before the interview day.
- Don't stay up late the night before. If you've prepared well, you've got nothing to fear.
- Eat a meal before leaving for the interview.
- How will you get yourself ready for the interview?
- Prepare clean, ironed and appropriate clothes to wear.
- Plan your journey to and from the interview.
- Make sure you get to the interview with plenty of time to compose yourself.

It's your big day-don't miss the bus!

Revise Your Application

- Read through what you said about yourself in your application.

- This means always keeping copies of everything you sent.
- Interviewers only have this information about you, so make sure you know what you said.

Anticipate Questions

- Think about the likely questions you are going to be asked.
- How will you answer them?
- Ask someone beforehand to think up some really tricky questions and work out what you might say in response.

Practice What you will Say

- Practice your interview technique by writing a script of things you might want to say.
- Read these through (in private or with someone you trust!) and listen to how you come across.
- Make sure that you can make your key points fluently, by concentrating on practising them out loud.

Use the Opportunity

- Remember that an interview is not just about an organisation finding out about you.
- It's also an opportunity for you to find out if you'd like to work for an organisation.
- Think up some really good questions, which will show that you've really thought about the job and where it could lead you.
- Practice asking these out loud before the interview itself

Tourism = Employment: Is India Capitalising?

At several trade and global events over the years, the travel and tourism industry has been highlighted as an important economic employment generator. Veterans have voiced their opinion on the same. It is certain that travel and tourism, if properly encouraged can play an important role for economic stimulus and building consumer confidence. Travel fuels business growth, makes entertainment possible and sustains rural destinations.

It also strengthens trade by boosting income for the poorest countries, as well as for global suppliers. Taking all these factors into consideration we need to recognise the value of travel and most importantly its capacity to generate jobs. The tourism sector in India did witness an increase in employment numbers from 44.7 million to 51.1 million during the period 2004-05 to 2006-07 however, we need to cash in more on this potential. Taking India and its cultural diversity into consideration, we have diverse offerings and also the talent of the youth and artisans which need to be tapped. Every state has diverse tourism opportunities but still the focus is on the regular. This gives us an opportunity to augment the much talked about domestic tourism, which certainly needs a short in the arm. Apart from a few players in the industry who have tried to bring a new flavour to domestic tourism, this sector yet needs to be aggressively marketed.

Encouraging domestic travel is good for consumer confidence; international travel has the added value of strengthening trade flows. Action to boost trade promotion, simplify regulation, build infrastructure and rationalise taxes, in turn incites companies to invest, innovate and stimulate demand. This kind of public–private sector collaboration should be strongly commanded within and between all states, as it can help build resilience and buoyancy across economies.

Tourism Employment & Opportunity

CDS' innovative TEMPO model is a collaborative system organized to build the capacity of micro, small, and medium size enterprises to access new markets and B2B linkages, more fully participate in public sector planning, and more convincingly sell the assets they have to offer to the tourism industry.

TEMPO is an 'intrapreneurial' model, and programs that follow it focus on assisting local businesses to provide services demanded by tourists at market rates and international standards. The programs utilize donor funding to build capacity of local businesses and perform asset audits and value chain analyses to determine the goods and services on offer versus market demand from tourists. They then become collaborative nonprofit enterprises that link high-performing local businesses into international booking and reservations systems.

This combination of services that provides capacity building for businesses in the tourism industry and facilitates entry into real-time reservations systems is the stand out added value of TEMPO versus other tourism development programs.

Activities within the TEMPO model that create sustainable and sustaining tourism enterprises include:

- Demand Surveys,
- The CDS Inventory and Asset Audit System,
- The CDS Tourism Products Registry,
- Value Chain Analysis,
- Strategy and Action Planning,
- Capacity-building and Partnerships,
- Competitive Grants,
- Product Development,
- Digital Content Development for Marketing and Sales,
- Linkages to Wholesale and Retail Tour Operators and Other Channels.

Tourism Employment

Overall View

On average, 1.1% of persons employed in the EU work in the tourist accommodation sector.

In 2007, more than 9 million persons were employed in the hotels, restaurants and catering (horeca) sector in the EU; this equals 4.2% of all persons employed. The highest number of jobs in this sector was observed in Spain (1.45 million), followed by Germany (1.43 million). However, when taking into account the size of the labour market, the largest shares employed in the horeca sector were found in Malta (8.3%), Spain (7.1%), Greece (6.9%), Austria (6.4%) and Cyprus (6.3%).

About one out of every four persons employed in the horeca sector works in an enterprise providing tourist accommodation (hotels and similar accommodation, campsites, etc.), giving a total of 2.3 million employed in 2007. At the height of the tourist season, i.e. in the third quarter of the year, the number of persons employed climbs by an additional 10 percent to an estimated 2.5 million. In relative terms, this means that 1.1% of all the employed in the European Union work in the tourist accommodation sector.

The Member States showing the highest share of employment in tourist accommodation were Malta (5.3%), Cyprus (3.2%) and Austria (2.3%). Not surprisingly, these are also the top three Member

States in terms of tourism intensity, i.e. the number of nights in collective tourist accommodation divided by the number of inhabitants. The sections which follow take a closer look at the pattern of employment in the tourist accommodation sector, compared with the horeca sector and the labour market as a whole.

By Gender

The share of female employment in the tourist accommodation sector is high at 60%.

The share of full-time employment in the tourist accommodation sector is not much different from the share in the EU-27 economy as a whole. About four out of every five persons are employed on a full-time basis. Looking at the hotels and restaurants sector as a whole, this is the case for only 72% of the persons employed (or 69% when excluding the tourist accommodation subsector). Only in the Czech Republic does part-time work tend to be slightly more common in tourist accommodation (8%) than in the horeca sector as a whole (7%).

Looking at the country data, big differences can be seen, ranging from almost no part-time employment in the tourist accommodation sector in Bulgaria or Romania to a rate of 60% in the Netherlands. In general, the figures for this sector reflect the full-time/part-time breakdown in the economy as a whole. Countries with a high share of part-time employment in short-stay accommodation, such as the Netherlands, Denmark (44%), Norway (38%), Germany (32%) or Sweden (30%), also have around 25% or more part-time workers in the whole labour market, compared with the EU average of 18%.

The tourist accommodation sector is a major employer of women. On average, 60% of the EU labour force in this sector consists of female workers, who make up only 45% of the persons employed in all economic activities in the EU. In terms of creating job opportunities for women, the accommodation sector scores even better than the hotels and restaurants sector as a whole – where female employment stands at 56%.

The differences across the European Union are relatively small, although slightly more pronounced than for the economy as a whole, where in nearly every country the share of female employment deviates from the EU average of 45% by no more than a few percentage points. Among the countries for which data are available, more than two out of every three persons employed in the tourist accommodation sector are female in Romania (72%), Norway (71%), Poland (70%), Finland (70%) and Germany (69%). Malta (38%) and Italy (49%) are the only countries where women do not take the majority of the jobs in the tourist accommodation sector. But, together with Greece, these two countries also have the lowest female participation rate in the economy as a whole.

The analysis by gender with the full-time/part-time breakdown. The proportion of women working full-time is much higher in the accommodation sector (75%) than in the rest of the economy (68%) or, more specifically, than in the hotels and restaurants sector as a whole (64%).

Among men working in this sector, 90% have a full-time contract, which is slightly less than the overall average for men (92%). Only in the Nordic countries – Denmark (50% versus 36%), Sweden (51% v. 42%) and Finland (27% v. 19%) – are significantly more women working part-time in the tourist accommodation sector than in the economy as a whole. On the other hand, a significantly higher proportion of women are working full-time than in the economy in general in Austria (69% versus 59%), Portugal (96% v. 83%) and Switzerland (59% v. 41%).

The lowest rate of full-time employment in the EU can be observed in the Netherlands, for both male (59%) and female (28%) workers, but this Member State also registers the lowest overall average rate across the EU for both men and women.

The shaded/patterned sections of the pie charts, the share of part-time employment. In both the tourist accommodation sector and in the labour market as a whole, slightly less than 20% of persons employed works on a part-time basis, 19% and 18% respectively. In both cases, women account for around 80% of these part-time jobs. Out of 100 persons employed in the EU, 4 are part-time working men while 14 are part-time working women. For the tourist accommodation sector this is 4 and 15 respectively.

The situation with full-time employment is more pronounced. Women occupy 56% of full-time jobs in the accommodation sector.

Indeed, out of 100 persons employed in this sector in the EU, on average 81 work full-time, of which 45 are women and 36 are men. On average in the economy women account for only 37% of full-time employment.

By Age

43% of those employed in the tourist accommodation sector are under 35 years old.

Both the hotels and restaurants sector as a whole and the tourist accommodation sector offer job opportunities to a young work force. Indeed, with 48% of persons employed in hotels and restaurants and 43% in the tourist accommodation sector younger than 35 years, both have a much younger age profile than the rest of the European Union labour market, where only about one in three of those employed is under 35.

This observation at EU level also applies to most of the Member States for which data on the age profile of employment in tourist accommodation are available. In most of these countries, the share of the two youngest age groups taken together lies 10 or more percentage points above their average share in employment in the economy as a whole.

Under-35s make up more than half of the employees in the tourist accommodation sector in Slovakia (58%), the Netherlands (56%), Sweden (56%) and Norway (56%). In all four countries, this share exceeds the average for the whole economy by around 20 percentage points. Cyprus is the only Member State where the age profile of employees in tourist accommodation is less young, with under-35s taking just 28% of the jobs in the tourist accommodation and 33% in the horeca sectors, whereas their share in the economy of Cyprus as a whole stands at 37%.

Only in Greece and Spain, two countries with a big tourism industry, does the age profile in the accommodation sector appear to be not significantly different from the age profile in all economic activities taken together.

At the other end of the age distribution, employment opportunities for persons aged 55 or more tend to be more limited in tourist accommodation (11%) than in the labour market (14%) overall. However, it must be underlined that reliable data are available for only a few countries, partly due to the low probability of including older persons employed in this sector in the sample for the survey used to collect the data.

By Education Level

The data in the previous sections revealed that tourist accommodation in particular employs younger and female workers. A third socio-demographic group strongly represented in this sector are persons with a lower level of education, i.e. persons who completed lower secondary education at most. That 36% of employees in the tourist accommodation sector did not complete upper secondary education, compared with a general labour market average of 25%.

For all countries where data on employment broken down by educational level are available, the conclusion that the tourist accommodation sector employs relatively more persons with a lower level of education holds true.

The biggest deviations from the average for the economy can be observed in Switzerland, where the share of lower educated persons in tourist accommodation is more than double their share in the whole labour market (36% versus 16%). Other countries where – compared with the entire economy – this sector offers jobs especially to less educated persons are Germany, Sweden, Norway and Denmark. Portugal (71%), Cyprus (24%) and Hungary (14%) are the only countries where there seems to be no noticeable difference (Portugal being the country with the highest share of employees with a low level of education in the European Union).

These findings are in line with the statistics on ICT use in enterprises, which indicate that the tourist accommodation sector does not require a high level of e-skills from most staff. Instead, only 36% of the employees in this sector use computers in their daily work, compared with almost one out of every two employees (49%) when considering all economic activities. Among the branches covered by the Community survey on ICT usage and e-commerce in enterprises, only the construction sector has a lower penetration rate for ICT at the place of work than the hotel and accommodation sector.

By Job Status

The accommodation sector does not differ significantly from the rest of the economy in terms of full-time/part-time breakdown.

However, considering the duration of the jobs and the average stay with the same employer, the sector appears to offer less stable jobs than the rest of the labour market.

The proportion of those having a temporary job rather than a permanent job is more than twice as high in the tourist accommodation sector (where 30% of the jobs are temporary) than in the economy as a whole (14%).

In all the countries for which data on the duration of jobs are available, the accommodation sector performs relatively poorly. The largest discrepancies between this sector and the economy as a whole can be observed in Greece (59% permanent jobs v. 89% in the whole economy), Italy, Sweden and Bulgaria.

The more limited availability of permanent jobs can be linked to the seasonal nature of tourism. Indeed, Greece, Italy, Bulgaria and Malta also appear to have the largest variation in number of persons employed between the peak and the trough quarters.

The discrepancy in terms of share of permanent jobs between the tourist accommodation sector and the economy as a whole is particularly small – not more than 3 percentage points – in Hungary, Finland, Denmark and Spain.

The lowest shares of permanent jobs in the tourist accommodation sector can be found in Poland (58%), Greece (59%) and Sweden (61%). In the case of Poland, however, this is not exceptional, as this is also the Member State with the lowest proportion of permanent jobs in the economy as a whole (72%).

Another indicator of stability of employment is the average stay with the same employer. That staff turnover is much higher in the accommodation sector – with an average stay with the same employer of slightly over 6 years (76 months) – than in all economic activities taken together (121 months, in other words more than 10 years). Comparing the accommodation sector with the rest of the economy at the level of the Member States, the average stay is less than half as long in Greece and Sweden. On the other hand, the discrepancy seems to be smallest in Portugal and Spain.

Seasonal Variation

Tourism activity varies strongly in the course of the year. In every Member State, occupancy in collective accommodation (expressed as number of nights spent by tourists) is at least twice as high in the peak tourism month as in the quietest month. Logically, the countries with a short tourist season have the highest seasonal variation in nights spent. In Greece and Croatia, the number of nights spent in collective accommodation is respectively 13 and 35 times higher in August than in the low season in January.

The quarterly data, that the number of tourism nights is 2.5 times higher in the third quarter (the peak quarter) of the year than in the first quarter (the trough quarter). With a ratio of "only" 1.2, employment in this sector tends to be far less affected by seasonal influences.

On average, the seasonal variation is only half as pronounced in the hotels and restaurants sector as a whole as in the tourist accommodation subsector. In only four countries (the Czech Republic, Denmark, the Netherlands and Norway) employment in the latter subsector seems to be less volatile over the year than in the horeca sector.

In the economy as a whole, seasonal fluctuation is relatively limited– but this robust aggregate can, of course, hide strong seasonal variations in certain branches of the economy. Within the tourist accommodation sector, the highest seasonal fluctuations in employment are observed in Greece and Croatia.

In both these countries, the level of employment in the peak quarter of the year is nearly double the level in the trough quarter and 30% to 35% higher than the annual average. At the other end of the spectrum, there is no significant seasonal variation in employment in Denmark, the Netherlands and Norway, although the number of nights spent by tourists is two to three times higher in the peak season than in the low season.

Based on data for ten Member States (accounting for 65% of employment in the tourist accommodation sector in the EU), the seasonal variation in employment separately for full-time and part-time jobs. The two types of employment contract tend to have a different seasonal pattern. While both are relatively low in the first quarter, part-time employment seems to be the main contributor to the seasonal needs in the second quarter.

In the third quarter, full-time jobs appear to fill the additional needs on the tourist accommodation labour market (although it is not clear from the data whether these are additional full-time posts or an increase in weekly working hours to bring existing part-time posts up to full-time level).

By Region

Regions with high tourist activity tend to have lower unemployment rates. Tourist activity can have a negative impact on the quality of life of the local population in highly touristic areas. However, the influx of tourists can also catalyse the local economy, including the labour market.

The top regions (at NUTS 2 level) in the European Union in terms of number of nights spent by tourists per capita of the local population and takes a look at the unemployment rates in these regions. In order to take into account structural differences across the EU, the regional unemployment rate is compared with the unemployment rate at national level.

Although tourist activity will, of course, not be the only factor affecting the unemployment figures, That in all but three of the 20 most popular tourist regions listed, the unemployment rate lies below the national average. Two of the three regions where this does not hold true, namely the Canary Islands and Corsica, are island regions relatively remote from the mainland.

The Community statistics on tourism provide no data on occupancy of collective accommodation below the NUTS-2 regional breakdown.

However, at a more detailed regional level the number of bedplaces in tourist accommodation in comparison with the local population figures can be used as a proxy for the intensity of tourist activity in the region– assuming the capacity eventually accommodates tourist visitors.

That in most of these tourist areas the unemployment rate is lower than the national rate. Two of the most significant exceptions to this finding are the Greek islands Zakynthos (Zante) and Kerkyra (Corfu), both part of the Ionian Islands. As shown above, Greece tends to have a highly seasonal tourism industry.

This seasonal component possibly distorts the comparison as the unemployment figures are an annual average. In Rügen, Germany's number one region in terms of tourism intensity, the unemployment rate is nearly 10 percentage points higher than the German average. In this specific case, the comparison is affected by the fact that Rügen is in Mecklenburg-Vorpommern, the Bundesland with the highest unemployment rate.

Total Employment

The analysis in this paper mainly focused on the tourist accommodation sector, not on the entire tourism industry. In general, the breakdown into economic activities used in official statistics does not single out the tourism sector as a whole.

In particular, apart from a few core tourist activities such as tourist accommodation or the activities of tour operators and travel agencies, most tourist activities can be filed under sectors of the economy of a broader nature. For instance, restaurants can cater for both tourists and locals or transport companies can provide services to tourists but can equally well run freight or commuter operations.

To overcome this measurement problem, the European Union, together with international organisations active in the field of tourism statistics (the UNWTO, UNSD and OECD), has been fostering development of a framework that will allow accurate measurement of the tourism industry and comparison with other branches of the economy.

Taking the concepts, definitions and aggregates of the System of National Accounts as a starting point, this statistical instrument called "Tourism satellite accounts" (TSA) should allow valid comparisons with other industries and also between countries or groups of countries. Part of these TSA cover employment in the tourism industry. Unlike the analysis in this paper, the TSA figures are not limited to the tourist accommodation sector, but also include tourism-related activities of other branches, such as the food and beverage serving industry, passenger transport or culture, sports and recreation.

Currently, national, non-harmonised data are available for a handful of Member States. These estimates for 10 Member States. The contribution made by the tourism industry to total employment ranges from 3.4% in the Czech Republic to nearly 10% in Slovenia. In Spain the tourism industry accounts for almost one out of every eight jobs (12.0%) in the economy.

Based on the aggregate data for these 10 Member States, the share of the tourist industry in total employment appears to be around 6.2%. Employment in the accommodation sector accounts for around 1.1% of the labour market, or approximately 2.3 million jobs. From the TSA estimates, total employment in the tourist industry can be estimated to be five to six times higher, with somewhere between 12 and 14 million employed in the EU. Once again, it must be stressed that these preliminary figures are based on non-harmonised national data from only 10 Member States.

China to Boost Tourism Employment to 100 Million by 2015: Report

China's tourism industry is expected to employ 100 million people by 2015, state media reported Thursday, meaning one in every 14 Chinese will work in the sector then. The government will introduce various policies to help the industry reach the goal, which marks a steep increase from the 60 million currently employed in the industry, the People's Daily said.

Authorities will adopt measures to facilitate job hunting and subsidise training of new staff, according to a statement posted on the National Tourism Administration's website Wednesday.

They also plan to launch a campaign to expand tourism infrastructure in less developed areas, the administration said.

Labour Minister Tian Chengping said earlier this year that the employment;

Employment in the Tourism Industries

- Two possible points of view on Employment.
  - * from a perspective of supply (persons employed) and
  - * from a perspective of demand (jobs),
- A person might have more than 1 job.
- A job might be occupied by more than 1 person.
- No one to one relationship between jobs and employed Persons.

Tourism Employment vs. Employment in the Tourism Industries

- Labour is a factor of production, and as such, related to a production process, not to a product, and even less so to the consumption of a product by certain category of consumers (a visitor);

- Employment in an establishment, and thus in an industry, can be observed and measured:
- Employment associated with tourism consumption can only be estimated via an explicit or an implicit model.

The basic recommendations: measuring employment in the tourism industries.

The units of measurement

* Number of jobs,
* Number of employed persons,
* hours worked (which should be included???),
* Equivalent full time job.

What do we want to know?

- For each tourism characteristic activity:
  * Number of jobs (monthly? Yearly? Peak and low?) by
- Gender.
- Status in employment.
- Qualification.
  * Number of employed persons,
  * "Quality of the job",
- Permanent.
- Seasonal.
- Direct contract/through an employment agency.
- With/without social insurance.

Sources for measuring employment in the tourism industries;

- From the supply side: household surveys; main difficulties.
  * Significance at the detailed level of activities,
  * Comparability of measurements overtime,
  * Geographical coverage; issue of rural area or small villages,
- From the demand side: surveys of economic activities; main difficulties.
  * Snapshot at a given moment in time,
  * Relationship of this snapshot with supply statistics,
  * Non permanent activities; seasonality,
  * Use of employment agencies.

Tourism Creates Employment Opportunities

Culture

Tourism creates opportunities of employment in the smallest and most remote communities. The Eastern Cape is one of the privileged provinces which has been awarded such an opportunity.

This task of alerting people to the possibilities is led by a non-government organisation called Fair Trade in Tourism South Africa (FTTSA) which is working towards a fairer, participatory and sustainable industry in South Africa.

One of its specific objectives is to contribute towards the Black Economic Empowerment programme and also to assist community-based and other emerging tourism enterprises to access niche markets.

Projects in the Eastern Cape include the Mehloding Community Tourism Trust in the northern Alfred Nzo District Municipality; Pondoland Community Trust and Tshezi Trust in OR Tambo District Municipality; the Kwam Emakana township homestays in Cacadu District Municipality, and the Nqileni Community Trust in Mbashe Local Municipality.

The Mehloding trust is one of the successful projects led by the NGO. The community owns the Mehloding adventure hiking trail and some homestays for tourists. This was an underprivileged community due to the lack of employment opportunities but FTTSA has sprinkled some nourishing water on the economic and social condition of the community.

Thozamile Xaki, a community tour guide, said: "We learn more about the environment and we gain entrepreneurship skills. This gives us as the community the urge to plough and preserve clean water for our tourists and it encourages us to start our own businesses." The projects have created job opportunities to impart skills to those who lack them and also recognition for Mehloding but above all the activities draw tourists to Mehloding.

The beautiful nature-preserving community has caught the attention of many tourists throughout the many years of its existence.

Nomthandazo Mnyameni, another community tour guide, said she has witnessed change in her community in terms of recognition and their knowledge on how to approach other NGOs when they need any kind of assistance. Even though this project is alive and advantageous, it does not really cover all the community's needs in terms of giving all of them suitable jobs, nor has it employed all the jobless.

Jabu Manyathi is not employed in this project. She said the project had given jobs to some and imparted skills for those in need. One still has to stand up and do something for oneself in order to survive. Jabu said she was not satisfied with the communication channels between the organisation and the community members that are not employed on the project.

9

Tourism in Modern World

Introduction: Need for Global Economic Development

The theme of the 2001 IAF Congress was "Meeting the Needs of the New Millennium", reflecting the fact that humans' most urgent need at the start of the 21st century is undoubtedly the continuation of economic growth. This is the only means by which the great majority of the world population can lift themselves out of the poverty in which they live.

The conventional definition of economic growth has been justly criticised. In order to be more useful it needs to be improved by including the preparation of national balance sheets and government accounts according to standard accounting principles, the use of factors to measure 'quality of life', the valuation of unpaid domestic and child-rearing work, accounting for environmental destruction, adjustment of market exchange rates to allow for 'purchasing power parity', and other improvements. New measures such as the "Genuine Progress Indicator" (GPI) are being developed, but they require further work before they can be relied upon.

Although economic measures may not yet be a satisfactorily precise definition of the standard of living, large-scale differences such as that between 'G7' countries with average incomes of about \$20 000/yr and developing countries with average incomes of \$1000 or less per year are undeniable. As a result of worldwide economic growth to date, more people live at higher standards of living than ever before; middle-class populations in many previously impoverished countries are growing rapidly; and average life spans have grown rapidly in every country in the world over the past two decades. However, this is not a cause for complacency since, thanks to unequal distribution of income and population growth, very large numbers of people still live in poverty.

The longterm effects of economic growth are impressive: in round figures, growth at 2 3% per year raises incomes by 100% in 25-35 yr, and by 1000% per century. Poorer countries growing at 7% per year can double their average incomes in just 10 yr, and grow by nearly 1000% in a single generation. However, achieving continuing economic growth in the world economy requires appropriate policies in both poorer and richer countries.

Unfortunately, governments in both democratic and non-democratic countries are continually tempted to follow policies that hinder economic growth, as analysed in depth in recent decades in the field of 'Public Choice' economics.

In particular, politicians in democratic countries can often win electoral popularity by implementing policies to 'protect' companies in difficulties. The economic effect of such policies is strongly negative: instead of flowing to new activities with good growth prospects, resources are wasted preserving economically incompetent companies that should be reorganized-thereby delaying needed restructuring of the economy.

This problem has been particularly notable in Japan where, during the 1990s, the government borrowed more than $1 trillion to support a large number of unprofitable companies. As a result there is substantial overcapacity in 'mature' industries such as construction, department stores, real estate, retail banking, car-making, steel-making, shipbuilding, distribution and others, while the number of new companies has declined substantially since 1990.

Predictably, this has aggravated the recession caused by the bursting of the economic 'bubble' of the late 1980s to become the worst recession in 50 yr-with continuing deflation, shrinking of the economy and ever-rising unemployment. In order to understand what policies would be more effective in sustaining economic growth, it is useful to understand the pattern of global economic development.

Pattern of Global Economic Development

While there are many details that are the subjects of ongoing research, the large-scale pattern of business and economic development through the 20th century is not the subject of significant dispute. One of the most fundamental underlying trends is that as poorer countries develop economically they progressively 'take over' industries in which low labour costs are a significant advantage, and export their products to richer countries. Employment in these relatively low-productivity activities is thereby lost from the rich countries. In parallel, the familiar processes of automation and improving business practices continually reduce the number of employees needed to produce a given quantity of goods and services. However, these trends have not caused rising unemployment overall because the displaced employees are reemployed in new industries which are continually being created.

The process of global economic development is thus one of continuous change, involving the decline and failure of companies as well as the birth and growth of new ones. As a consequence, for most people it is not possible to improve their standard of living without accepting change in their working lives. In addition, the timing of economic booms and recessions depends on many factors including chance discoveries leading to innovation, the whims of entrepreneurs and the vagaries of political decisions. Although economic growth can be hindered by government policies, the underlying process cannot be stopped-at least not without preventing people from trying to improve their standard of living which is not desirable. In the simplest terms, some people use their heads to work out ways of achieving the same results with less effort. This human creativity, specifically in inventing machines improving business practices (including expanding trade), and developing new popular services makes the productivity of work grow continuously, decade after decade, enabling everyone's incomes and standards of living to rise progressively.

World economic growth also requires international flexibility and agreement on rules of 'fair play'. For example, the rapid economic growth achieved by Japan from the 1960s until the 1980s caused considerable trade friction with the then more advanced countries as it changed the pattern of global specialisation-even leading the French Prime Minister Cresson to describe Japan as "France's number one enemy". Thus Japan's rapid growth depended on the richer countries' willingness to make adjustments to facilitate it, which Japan in turn is now required to show towards later developing countries.

However, as a measure of how much more adjustment in the structure of the world economy is going to be required, note that the combined populations of India and China are 20 times the population of Japan, and their average wages are just a small percentage of Japanese wages today. Consequently the adjustments in the pattern of global specialisation that will be required to accommodate the growth in these countries' shares of world trade will be proportionately many times larger than was required for Japan. The recent rapid growth of exports of clothing from both countries, and of food products, light manufactured goods and motorcycles from China, and bicycles and software from India, is just the beginning of this long process of adjustment. In principle the growth of exports resulting from such differences in labour costs will not end until average incomes in these countries reach broadly the same level as in the richer countries. (The current loss of competitiveness of certain industries in Korea Taiwan and other southeast Asian countries, as their average incomes rise relative to those in China, are examples of this process.). For humanitarian reasons, as well as from the wish to reduce friction between richer and poorer countries, we must hope that poorer countries' economic development continues successfully. But, as an inescapable corollary, to the extent that these countries' participation in the world economy grows through the 21st century, proportionately greater innovation of new industries will be required in the currently more advanced countries. If this is insufficient, unemployment will increase very substantially, and/or average incomes will fall proportionately because of inexorable competition from countries with lower average incomes.

Overall, as the human effort needed to produce the same output of goods and services becomes less and less through technical and managerial progress, and unless humans generate more total output and consume more goods and services, the total amount of work needed will fall. In this case, unless the remaining work is shared out through shortening average working hours (and reducing wages proportionately), more and more people will become unemployed. During the 20th century demand did not reach such a limit; instead, although employment in many older industries shrank drastically in the richer countries, the continuation of economic growth was stimulated by the creation of new industries.

Creation of New Industries

During the 20th century, as the number of people in economically more advanced countries who worked in such fields as agriculture, horse-drawn transport, steam-engines, mining, textiles, clothing and many other traditional activities declined, a wide range of new industries arose which re-employs those displaced. These included car manufacturing and associated activities (such as oil production, refining and distribution and road construction and maintenance), electricity generation and distribution, the film, radio, television and video industries, aircraft manufacturing and operation and associated activities (such as airport construction and operation and air traffic management), telecommunications, computers, tourism and an ever-growing range of leisure industries, including many sports activities.

During the 20th century also, government activities expanded from <10% of GNP to some 40%-though this trend has more-or-less stopped or even begun to reverse in most countries with the recent moves towards privatisation. This new trend has been stimulated by work in the field of 'Public Choice' economics, which has provided the theoretical explanation for the fact that, in general, government activities are economically very inefficient, as outlined for instance in.

It is a sine qua non for continuing economic growth in the 21st century that the rich countries continue this process of creating new industries which will employ people displaced from older industries as they progressively automate and migrate to lower-cost countries. During the 20th century this process created high-productivity employment for hundreds of millions of people around the world, and enabled many more people in developing countries to gain employment in exporting and importing businesses, thereby facilitating their economic growth. It is a key desire of companies in poorer countries today to be allowed to increase their exports to richer countries, but these are restricted by international treaties designed to protect relatively uncompetitive activities in the richer countries, in order to reduce local unemployment. For example the governments of the USA and the EU subsidise the production of many agricultural products, thereby reducing the market for imports from cheaper countries, and they also subsidise the export of agricultural surpluses, providing a second blow to poorer countries' price-competitive agricultural industries. The G7 countries also limit clothing and textile imports from poorer countries.

The development of new industries has another important aspect, namely the 'leading sector' effect: as investors anticipate the future profits that they expect to be earned in new industries, market prices of relevant companies' shares rise. This attracts more investment to these companies, helping them to grow faster, while the 'wealth effect', whereby shareholders spend their new (anticipated) wealth, spreads the benefits of expansion to other sectors of the economy.

This process was seen particularly clearly in the late 1990s in the USA, when share prices of many companies related to the major innovations of the Internet and World Wide Web grew by hundreds and even thousands of percent. As shareholders became wealthy, at least 'on paper', they increased their spending on a wide range of goods and services including houses, cars, restaurants, travel and leisure, thereby greatly stimulating the general economy. Unfortunately, in this particular case, much of the rise in share prices of 'new economy' companies was distorted in an economic 'bubble' in which investors had become unrealistically optimistic. Consequently the companies in question did not achieve the high level of profits that stockbrokers' analysts were predicting, and their share prices have since fallen steeply to date, destroying several trillion dollars of the 'wealth' that had been anticipated. (Controversy continues over the relative blame attributable to failures of business ethics, stockbrokers' conflicts of interest, auditors' standards, market regulation, media reporting, economic policy and investor caution.)

Today the need for new industries is particularly urgent because of the serious imbalances in the world economy. These include the decade-long recession that has led to the highest unemployment in Japan for 50 years, with continuing deflation and negative economic 'growth'; continuing double-digit unemployment in much of continental Europe as well as in Russia, Southeast Asia, South America and many other countries; and a deepening recession combined with an unsustainably high trade deficit and private indebtedness in the USA. The fundamental reason for this deflationary condition of the world economy is the excess capacity in many older industries and insufficient investment in the establishment and growth of profitable new industries, which alone can create new employment for those no longer needed in mature industries. The record US trade deficit of more than $1 billion per day, first reached during the 'Clinton bubble', is a measure of many US industries' lack of economic competitiveness: toys, clothing, electrical goods, steel, televisions, personal computers and mobile telephones are just some of the industries in which fewer and fewer US-based manufacturers can match global competition. The only way in which the currently richer countries can maintain higher average incomes than currently less-developed countries is through working with higher productivity: people earning higher incomes cannot compete with people using the same technology and know-how but working at significantly lower incomes. The solution to enabling those in already rich countries to maintain or increase their standards of living while also enabling poorer countries to grow rapidly, is for companies in G7 countries to work at newer activities that poorer countries cannot yet perform. The need for this was explicitly recognised in a 2001 article in the Washington Post: "What this country needs is a really good $500 billion technology-something to reignite popular enthusiasm and the economy".

What, then, are the new industries that are expected to generate new fields of large-scale high-productivity employment? It is important to note first that commentators' inability to predict future industries is no evidence that they will not arise: almost no-one in 1902 could even imagine, let alone predict, the rise of passenger air travel, nor a fortiori its growth to its current world-changing scale. Economic commentators today predict growth in employment in many areas of the information industry (although it is important to recognise that the growth of the Internet is also eliminating work in many related fields); in biotechnology, including the use of genetic information in agriculture and medicine; and in activities aimed at environmental preservation.

Many new opportunities could also arise through restructuring the incentives created by the government-imposed pattern of taxation and subsidies. For example, in many countries employment is heavily taxed and large companies are subsidised, while the use of non-renewable resources and environmentally damaging activities are lightly taxed or even subsidised. Reversing these undesirable distortions could increase the quantity of employment in many different fields, including particularly recycling activities. An important clue to the identity of other fields in which new jobs will arise in rich countries can be found in the 'Engel coefficient', which is defined as the proportion of peoples' income spent on food (although alternative definitions based on expenditure on 'necessities' are also used). The average Engel coefficient in any country falls progressively as it develops economically; in G7 countries it is now typically <25%. Further economic growth in such rich countries depends less on providing for consumers' real 'needs' and more on satisfying their 'wants'. Broadly speaking, this explains the relatively rapid growth of leisure-related industries. Although many people feel that there are more 'important' things in which to invest than leisure industries, once average productivity reaches the level in the G7 countries, most basic needs of the society can be satisfied by a fraction of the workforce-for example agriculture typically employs <5% of the workforce. Thus there is no longer enough 'essential' work to employ more than a fraction of the population in richer countries.

One problem that arises in low-Engel-coefficient societies is that the demand for nonessential goods and services is relatively unstable, since by definition their consumption can readily be cut if necessary. This inherent instability is seen clearly in the demand for tourist air travel which periodically falls sharply as a result of heightened concern about the risk of terrorism. Another example of this instability is that as the number of two-, three-and four-car families increases, sales of used cars can grow rapidly at times of recession, leading to dramatic falls in the demand for new cars.

The truth of the 'human condition' at the start of the 21st century is that economic development has progressed so far in the

G7 countries that, if the average standard of living is to continue to rise, there is an urgent need for the growth of major new industries, most of which will probably be leisure services broadly defined. The reason for this is that in order for a new industry to grow to large scale it must provide services that will be purchased by a large proportion of the middle-class population-most of whom already possess most of the goods they 'need'.

Arguably the most significant industrial development of the 20th century was the development of passenger air travel from zero in 1900 to 1.5 billion passengers per year in 2000. Among other effects, this development has helped the hotel and restaurant industries to reach their present scale, employing some 60 million people or 3% of the world's total labour-force, and some 6% in Europe. As a pointer to the future growth potential, a survey performed in 2001 showed that the majority of middle-aged and older Japanese do not wish to purchase any more goods; the main service they wish to buy is foreign travel-which has notably been booming even during the current recession.

Until 2001 the aviation industry was predicting 100% growth over the next 20 years, although airlines' increased costs for security and customers' fears of terrorism may reduce this. However, it should be noted that tourism is already having damaging environmental impacts as a result of ever-growing numbers of tourists visiting popular destinations. It is not clear that this activity can reasonably grow by a factor of 1000% as would be necessary by the time-perhaps 2100?-when most of the world population attains a middle-class lifestyle which includes foreign travel.

Some commentators, mostly in the richer countries, take the view that most of those living in the presently poorer countries will remain poor forever. However, living standards are rising in every country, and the desire for material comfort is strong everywhere that living standards are low. While attaining a 'middle-class lifestyle' in the same form as seen today in G7 countries for a world population of perhaps 10 billion people would cause many industries-energy, construction, cars, agriculture, waste disposal-to degrade the environment severely, it must be anticipated that technological progress will greatly ease currently foreseeable problems. The application of even only presently foreseeable advances in already existing fields-such as genetic engineering and hydroponics in agriculture, energy efficiency and non-fossil (solar) energy, city planning, and Internet-based tele-commuting, to name but a few-holds such clear promise that simple extrapolations based on multiplying existing economic activity by increased population numbers without allowing for technological improvements are unrealistically pessimistic. As a result it may be that the main limits to the potential for terrestrial economic growth are political ones. It is clearly in the self-interest of the already-rich countries to try harder to help overcome these in order to reduce the friction that would be inevitable in a globalized world with continuing gross inequalities in living standards.

Whatever the longer term future, assuming that economic growth will continue for at least a few more decades, the popularity of leisure travel in low-Engel-coefficient societies raises the question of what other newer destinations people could travel to. Tourist destination development is proceeding rapidly around the world, but a new possibility which has received ever-increasing attention is passenger travel to space, or 'space tourism'. It is now clear that this idea is not only not fantasy, but it is a promising candidate to grow into a major new activity as economically valuable and socially significant as passenger air travel.

Economic Potential of Passenger Space Travel

On the 'demand side' of passenger space travel, market research performed in Japan, Canada, the USA, Germany and the UK, and summarised in has shown that there is enormous pent-up consumer demand. It is sometimes suggested that this demand is fictitious; for example a recent letter to Aviation Week & Space Technology stated: "People were already travelling in the early days of aviation-by trains boat and car. They had a reason for travelling and infrastructure to support them when they reached their destination. The aeroplane became another mode of transportation. The reasons for travelling do not exist for space. No one is visiting relatives, emigrating nor going to business meetings. And there is no infrastructure in space".

However, it is a mistake to have preconceived ideas about people's reasons for wishing to travel to space, which are obviously different from reasons for travelling on Earth. The market research referred to above shows consistently that a large proportion of the middle class population of the richer countries does want to go to space, and that their major reason for wanting to do so is to be able to look back at the Earth. The fact that all of the 400 people who have been to space to date say that it was the greatest experience of their lives probably has some connection with this immense popularity. While there is a great need for more market research, and it will remain uncertain how many people will actually travel to space until the service becomes widely available, there is no justification for denying facts shown by market research.

Furthermore, contrary to what the above letter states, there is infrastructure to support travellers-a partly assembled space station which was sufficient for the first customer, Dennis Tito, to describe the Russian section as "paradise". The second piece of infrastructure for space travellers, Mir Corp's 'Mini-Station', is due to become operational for an investment of $100 million. And as launch costs fall to a few hundred dollars/kg as passenger traffic grows, it will be possible to assemble even very large accommodation facilities in orbit at a cost acceptable to hotel companies.

On the 'supply side' of passenger space travel technical studies by the Japanese Rocket Society (JRS), Dietrich Koelle, Ivan Bekey, Bristol Spaceplanes, Buzz Aldrin and others have shown that the cost of developing the required vehicles and infrastructure would be a small fraction of the $25 billion that G7 taxpayers already pay every year for government space activities. The great potential of passenger space travel for 'space commercialisation' has also been acknowledged in reports published by Nasa; the American Institute of Aeronautics and Astronautics (AIAA) which concluded: "In light of its great potential public space travel should be viewed as the next large new area of commercial space activity"; and the Japan Federation of Economic Organisations, among other organisations.

One particularly interesting conclusion of the Nasa report namely that "generally available trips to orbit and weeklong stays in low Earth orbit hotels now can be seen as certainly feasible" gives a further indication of how large the economic impact of space tourism may become. This is because in all market research to date most people say they would like to spend several days or a week or more in orbit, rather than only a few hours or a day. Thus in addition to economical launch vehicles the demand for space tourism will also drive the construction and operation of accommodation in orbit-that is space hotels.

The only detailed professional study of the potential development of passenger space travel published to date is that of the Japanese Rocket Society (JRS) briefly reviewed in. (A large number of other papers from the pioneering JRS study are available in the library of the six major JRS reports published as of 2002 are available only in Japanese.)

According to the JRS scenario, the number of customers would reach 700,000 per year 17 years after starting the development of the ' Kankoh-maru' passenger vehicle, with a return flight price of some $20,000 per passenger.

The JRS cost estimates are in line with those of Koelle and Bekey. Extrapolating from this, when the number of guests reaches one million per year after perhaps 20 years, there will need to be accommodation for more than 10,000 people in orbit, and several thousand staff will work in orbit. Since no one has identified any other space activity that offers anything approaching this level of demand, we reach a conclusion that is still not widely appreciated-the hotel industry will probably become the largest employer in space.

From the economic point of view it is very significant that the development of orbital accommodation will lead to the participation of a wide range of associated industries, thereby greatly expanding the number of different industries involved in space activities including particularly such consumer-oriented activities as construction, interior design, hotel management, catering, fashion, entertainment and sports.

This will have the effect of bringing the economic energy of the consumer economy to bear on space activities, which are cutoff from this source of economic growth, except for certain information services.

In addition to stimulating innovation in these many different fields, the growth of space tourism in this way could also exert a 'leading sector' effect, whereby an expansionary economic influence will diffuse through the economy as direct investment and optimism lead to increased shareholder wealth. Furthermore, the increase in employment and economic growth which the development of passenger space travel causes directly in more advanced economies will in turn reduce the pressure for protection against imports from less developed economies. Such a scenario is strikingly different from the effect of existing governments' non-science space activities which, sadly, contribute very little to the economy or employment, despite the very large financial resources they consume.

Low Economic Value of Space Agencies' Activities

The desirability of initiating passenger space travel might be less if space agencies were engaged in work that was of great economic value or urgency-but they are not. Some 20% of their budgets are typically used for scientific research, including astronomy and Earth observation, which can be assumed to have value per se. However, the remaining 80%, some $20 billion per year, is used for the development of technological systems and technologies for such purposes as "space infrastructure development". The economic value of the results of this expenditure can be considered in two parts, direct and indirect.

Direct Economic Value

The definition of economic value is the present value of future profits to which an activity gives rise. Since space agencies' investment mostly does not lead to commercially profitable activities, it has far less economic value than normal business investment. The difference between commercial activities and space agencies' activities is shown in Figure 1. In round figures when a company invests $1 billion it typically generates commercial sales revenues of some $1 billion per year, from which the cumulative profits over several years exceed the initial investment by a sufficient margin to satisfy investors and increase the assets of the company. (For example, $1 billion investment might generate profits of $3 billion over 10 years, from which $2 billion would be repaid to investors, and $1 billion would add to the company's assets.) By contrast, the expenditure of some $20 billion per year by government space agencies on non-science activities generates little or no increase in commercial space activities: employment in space activities is currently shrinking, rather than growing cumulatively, as would result from commercial investment on this scale.

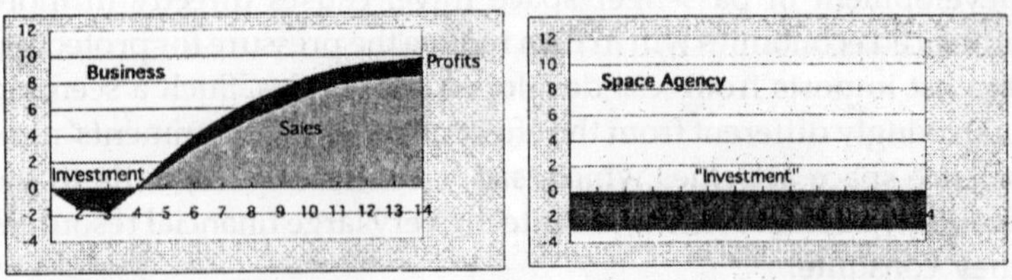

Figure 1. Contrast between Business and Space Agency Activities.

For example, the development and operation of expendable launch vehicle systems are heavily loss making; such launchers never repay their development costs, and depend in many cases on continuing government funding of periodic 'upgrades'. At the time of writing, the most recent of many articles describing the lack of demand for satellite launch services states that, of the three main launch vehicle manufacturers: "Arianespace, the only company that discloses its annual earnings, posted a loss in 2001 for the second straight year..." and predicts that because "the market could remain flat for the next 10-20 years..." one of the three companies may disappear in the anticipated 'shake-out'.

Following the conventional definition of economic value given above, the ' International Space Station' (ISS) project has very little economic value: almost no companies want to pay to use its facilities, and their total contribution will represent a small fraction of its running costs alone, let alone repaying taxpayers' investment of some $50 billion. The probability of researchers on board the station making a valuable scientific discovery must also be judged to be low: research in microgravity has been underway for more than 30 years, and there is little expectation of any major discoveries in the near term, particularly since the microgravity environment on board the station will be of low quality. This and the station's very high cost led many science research bodies, including the US National Science Foundation and the British Science Research Council, not to support the project. In 2001, as the latest step in the ISS's ever-growing cost and ever-shrinking capabilities, Nasa's announcement of further 'cost growth' of $5 billion led to it becoming the subject of a special investigation by the US government's General Accounting Office. Upon the departure of its then administrator it was decided to appoint the deputy director of the Office of Management and Budget (OMB) as his replacement.

(It is perhaps worth noting that accounting is not a mysterious activity. When the managers of a $15 billion per year organisation choose to use accounting systems that allow them to be 'surprised' by cost over-runs as large as $5 billion, this is surely not accidental-it is done because it is in their economic interest to obscure the truth.

In this, space agency managers' behaviour is entirely consistent with the economic analysis of government bureaucracy pioneered by Niskanen. Because of the incentives which a bureaucratic organisation creates for its staff, they are motivated primarily to increase their budget; they have no motivation "either to know or seek out the public interest or to act in the public interest". Until the 'crisis' of 2001, successive Nasa administrators' policy of having such inadequate accounting information was successful in preserving its budget; and it seems very unlikely that Nasa or its management will suffer any significant cost-certainly nothing approaching that experienced in commercial companies when their accounts are revealed to be untrustworthy, such as the 'carnage' among 'new economy' companies in the USA in 2001-2002.)

Indirect Economic Value

Advocates of larger budgets for government space agencies frequently argue that government spending on space is much more beneficial for the economy than other forms of economic activity, thanks to the useful inventions arising from the development of space-related technology. The original source of this idea was a study performed during the 1970s by Chase Econometrics, which claimed to find such an effect. In a recent citation members of the US Congressional Research Service in 1998 wrote: "Studies by Chase Econometrics Inc., and the Midwest Research Institute in the late 1980s determined that every Nasa R&D dollar produced $5-$9 in economic activity".

However, it is rarely reported that when Chase Econometrics tried to reproduce their work in 1980 they concluded that: "productivity changes from Nasa R&D spending proved not to be statistically different from zero". Hertzfeld studied the issue in detail and concluded: "due to theoretical and data problems with the macroeconomic model and data sets available, this approach to finding aggregate economic returns to R&D expenditure is difficult at best, and probably impossible". Other studies of particular technologies developed at Nasa which have subsequently been used in new products are said to have shown reasonable rates of return. However, such studies do not enable any conclusions to be drawn concerning the relative value of alternative innovations that would have arisen if the same funding had been applied in other fields, such as marine engineering, electrical engineering etc.

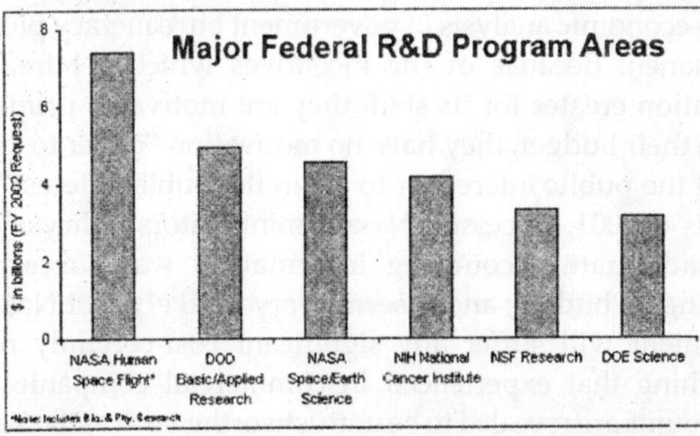

Table 1: Major U.S. Federal R&D Program Areas

In this context the bar chart presented to the US Congressional Science Committee by Sean O'Keefe, when Deputy Director of the OMB during 2001, is of interest. This shows that Nasa's budget of $15 billion per year is twice the combined research budgets of the US National Science Foundation (NSF) and the US National Cancer Institute (NCI). Since scientific research funded by these organisations has contributed to many of the Novel prizes and scientific advances which US researchers generate, the lack of Novel prizes or major technological advances arising from Nasa's work-let alone twice the annual output of the NSF and NCI combined-is striking.

Seen in this light, the claim that US government spending on Nasa projects (including the $5 billion cost-growth during 2001) is particularly valuable for the economy is not credible. It appears rather to be a convenient myth that serves the economic interests of the government-funded space industry. Much more credible is the 'common sense' view that Nasa's expenditure of more than $100 billion during administrator Goldin's 1992 2001 tenure, during which employment in the space industry grew not at all and passenger space travel was starved of research funding (as discussed below), was a serious misuse of economic resources which could have been used much more productively on other activities.

Space Agencies' Anti-space Tourism Policy

In view of the low economic value of space agencies' current activities, it is very unsatisfactory that they are making no attempt to realise or even evaluate passenger space travel. In this the agencies do not simply show a lack of enthusiasm-they appear to have deliberately delayed progress towards this economically valuable objective, and even to have concealed valuable information from the public.

For example, the largest government space agency, Nasa, is required by US federal law to "encourage, to the maximum extent possible, the fullest commercial use of space". In its 1998 report, 'General Public Space Travel and Tourism', Nasa confirmed that space tourism is a realistic objective; that most people will be able to take a trip to space; that suborbital space travel (similar to that experienced by the first American to travel to space, Alan Shepard) is easily feasible using long-available technology; and that passenger space travel is likely to grow into a major commercial use of space. The report also included a long list of recommendations as to how to encourage this commercial use of space. However none of the recommendations in this report have been implemented, and no funding at all was allocated to advance the possibility-out of the $56 billion that Nasa has spent between that report's publication and time of writing. This behaviour is clearly contrary to Nasa's obligation to "encourage, to the maximum extent possible, the fullest commercial use of space".

It is worth noting that Nasa's 'space tourism report' can be judged the most economically valuable report Nasa has ever published, since it describes what is likely to become the largest commercial activity in space, and steps to realise it. It is therefore of particular interest that the then Nasa administrator Goldin refused to allow the report to be made available via Nasa's website for over 3 years. The author spoke to both Goldin in 1999 and then deputy associate administrator Graver in 2000 at public meetings at which they both stated (in recorded sessions) that NP-1998-03-11-MSFC would be put upon the Nasa website. However, this simple step did not take place until 2002.

Early in 2001 Nasa administrator Goldin attempted unsuccessfully to prevent the US citizen Dennis Tito visiting the international space station; his high-profile campaign was widely reported in the media. Yet the 80% popular support shown for Dennis Tito in US opinion polls provides a good indication of the great popularity of passenger travel and the misguidedness of Nasa's stance on this matter. Subsequent events during 2001 included the announcement that Goldin would not continue as Nasa administrator; testimony requested by the Subcommittee on Space and Aeronautics of the Congressional Science Committee from Nasa deputy associate administrator W. Michael Hawes on 26 June concerning Nasa's work relating to space tourism; and the appearance on Nasa's internet website of its space tourism report after over 3 years delay. Also during 2001 newly appointed Nasa Chief of Staff Courtney Stand drafted a plan for the agency under which it was proposed that Nasa would "provide commercial projects with engineering support for private-sector development of commercial manned spaceflight vehicles for commercial space tourism". (It is perhaps worth noting that the main supporter of space tourism in the US government today is the associate administrator for Commercial Space Transportation in the FAA. As the first head of the then Office of Commercial Space Transportation within the Department of Transportation Stand could be expected to take a more commercial approach.)

The selection of Nasa during 2001 as the fourth-worst-managed activity within the US government, and the recently initiated probe into its extraordinary mismanagement of the ISS project provide further testimony to the very poor value-for-money that US taxpayers receive in return for $15 billion per year-over and above Nasa's deliberate delaying of the development of passenger space travel services. The growing political disenchantment with this behaviour is reflected in the recent comment that "space spending is moving from the back burner to completely off the stove".

Other Countries' Activities

Other countries' government space agencies also have responsibility for commercialisation of space activities, but they take a similar stance towards passenger space travel. For example the European Space Agency (Esa) joined Nasa's unsuccessful attempt to prevent Dennis Tito visiting the international space station, and has likewise provided almost no funding whatsoever for research on the economic potential of passenger space travel. The senior staff of Esa and their political paymasters do not want to know about the commercial potential of passenger space travel, any more than their counterparts in Nasa and the US Congress, exactly as Niskanen's work describes.

Uniquely among G7 countries' space agencies, the British National Space Centre (BNSC) invests in neither expendable launch vehicles (such as the European Ariane) nor the international space station, since it is required to focus on space science research and activities with potential to be commercialised. However, in 2000 it was criticised by the UK Parliamentary Trade and Industry Committee for investing some 1 billion Sterling over the past decade in remote sensing systems that have generated far less commercial revenue than planned, and for actively discouraging any British government investment in research aimed at realising passenger space travel. The BNSC staff responsible for this stance, Director-General Colin Hicks, Deputy Director-General David Leadbeater and Director of Policy and Finance Alan Cooper, ignored the Committee's suggestion to perform some analysis of its feasibility. They have still provided no justification for their decade-long prevention of funding of work towards passenger space travel-which is clearly contrary to the BNSC's stated objective "to help industry maximise profitable space-based business opportunities".

Space agencies' negative behaviour towards the largest commercial opportunity in space can be termed a 'Conspiracy of Silence'. The economic reasons for their acting so strongly against the public interest in this matter are discussed in, and some of the 'cultural' reasons why the heads of space agencies unanimously refuse to permit any work to facilitate passenger space travel are discussed in the appendix to. Because of government space agencies' organisational structure making them responsible for commercialisation presents a conflict of interest with their own economic interest in survival and expansion, since it would mean handing over some of their operations to private companies.

They resolve this conflict, predictably, in their own interests by suppressing the most promising commercial application, which is ipso facto also the most threatening to their own interests. Nasa, Esa and other countries' national space agencies also exert a strong influence on the news media, being a near-monopoly source of information about space activities. This has helped to delay, though not to prevent, the growth of interest in passenger space travel in the mass media. By contrast, Russian companies have now already profitably carried two space tourists to orbit, and are currently planning an orbiting 'mini-station' for tourism accommodation at a cost of $100 million. This is particularly noteworthy since, at the time of writing, Nasa's mobile exhibition 'Starship 2040' is publicising the idea of a small module being feasible for space tourism in 2040. 'Starship' is smaller than the first US space station 'Skylab' that operated 70 years before this date. Together with the suppression of the 1998 Nasa space tourism report until July 2001, this can only be seen as deliberate 'disinformation' designed to mislead the US public, media, government and others about the potential for space tourism. In view of the potential for passenger space travel described above, it is clearly greatly against the public interest that space agencies are knowingly resisting progress in these ways in favour of continuing their existing activities despite their low economic value.

Future Scale of Space Tourism Industry

As discussed above, meeting the needs of the new Millenniums, or at least of the early 21st century, requires the development of major new industries in the more advanced countries.

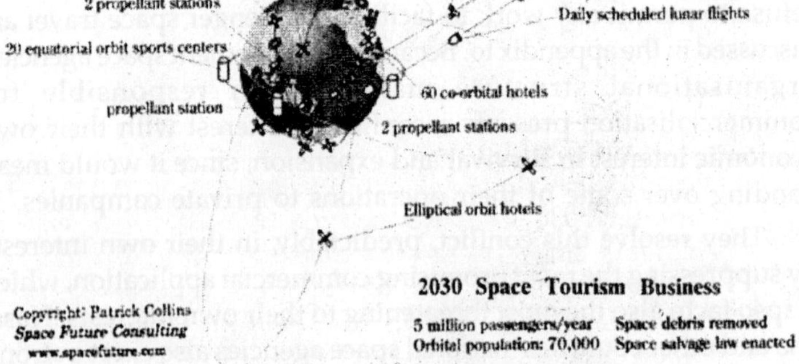

Figure 2: Feasible Space Tourism Scenario

Failure in this would lead to a further rise in the already high levels of unemployment worldwide, with corresponding undesirable social effects. In view of this need for new industries to facilitate continuing global economic growth, it is interesting to consider how large a scale passenger space travel might eventually reach and how much it might ultimately contribute to world economic growth. As described above, the unique potential of passenger space travel was acknowledged by Nasa, the AIAA and the Keidanren as long ago as 1998. Since none of these organisations has made any further attempt to investigate or assess the scale of this opportunity during the four years since these reports were published (during which time government space agencies have spent a further $100 billion on economically unprofitable activities), the author outlines a simple estimate in this section.

Although some critics have claimed that space tourism will be no more than a pastime of the very rich, the basic scenario of the Japanese Rocket Society is aimed firmly at serving the middle-class market, and leads to some 700,000 passengers paying a little more than $20,000 each for return flights to orbit in the 17th year. Further growth to reach, say, 5 million passengers in the 30th year as discussed in would require an annual growth rate of some 16% which is not unrealistic by comparison with growth rates seen in other popular services. This would give a scenario like that shown in Figure 2.

Several comments are worth making about this figure.

(1) On this scenario, some 40 million people would have visited space by 2030, that is perhaps 2% of the middle class of that time-yet market research has shown that most middle class people (that is, more than 50%) would like to make a 'space trip'. Consequently this scenario certainly does not seem over-optimistic in relation to the potential market.

(2) The cost to taxpayers to realise this scenario would be far less than the $750 billion that they would have to pay through 2030 for space agency activities on their existing budgets, since most of the investment would come from the private sector. The economic value of the scenario, based on the difference in expected profits, would be about $1 trillion higher.

(3) Several million people would be directly and indirectly employed in related activities, and tens of thousands of people would work part-time in space as hotel staff.

(4) Such a scenario makes some people uneasy as they think that leisure industries are not 'important', and that people should be doing more 'serious' work, like making machines or buildings. But, as described above, the G7 countries have made such progress that producing necessities does not keep many people busy: a smaller and smaller proportion of the population can produce all that is needed, and a growing proportion work to provide services that are 'wants' rather than true 'needs'. The growth of service industries in turn creates demand for manufactured products-as the demand for tourist air travel creates a massive market for the aerospace manufacturing industry. Thus the growth of passenger space travel as shown would stimulate a genuine 'renaissance' of the space industry, after the post-cold-war period of stagnation and shrinkage.

In addition to its economic value as a popular consumer service, making space travel available to the general public would have great social value. Thanks to its well-known inspiring and educational value it would seem highly desirable in comparison with many other 'unnecessary' activities that are proliferating in rich countries, such as the use of recreational but often addictive drugs, gambling and pornography, to mention a few.

For some years there has also been talk of a "crisis in aerospace" because of the sustained decline in interest among young people in working in the industry. The author's proposal that the development of passenger space travel would also resolve this problem by putting work in space engineering at the forefront of a popular new industry was published as a 2001 editorial in Aviation Week & Space Technology.

For simplicity, if it is assumed that the progressive fall in service price thanks to increasing scale of operation is balanced by growth in demand for more expensive services, average expenditure of $20,000 per passenger would give a turnover of some $100 billion in 2030. How much further passenger space travel services might grow depends on many factors; however it does not seem likely to be limited by a lack of demand in the foreseeable future. In addition to the great popularity of the activity itself, there is enormous scope for provision of even more interesting experiences in space with the development of progressively more advanced hotels, orbiting sports centres, lunar hotels and other facilities, as discussed in the references in. As an example, growth of 8% per year after 2030 would lead to a turnover of $1 trillion per year in 2060, that is some 50 million passengers per year (less than two weeks' of air travel passengers today). As a different way of looking at the potential, a rough estimate of the potential cumulative market.

Cumulative revenue of $40 trillion is equivalent to some 2 billion people travelling to space once each. Although this may seem a large number, we note again that aviation has already reached 1.5 billion passengers-i.e. equivalent to one quarter of the world population every year. Criticism of this suggestion by staff from government space agencies, by those indirectly funded by space agencies or by others in such terms as that it is "unconvincing" or "pure guesswork" could of course be readily answered if agencies were to devote even as little as 1/10 000 of their annual budgets to study the possibility. It is also interesting to consider how a correct prediction made in 1902 about the future scale of passenger air travel during the following century might have been received, at a time when the main form of transport was still horse-carriage, and no one had even flown in an aeroplane. Talk of "millions of passengers per day" and "one billion passengers per year" would surely have been dismissed not as "guesswork" but as sheer madness. Yet, by contrast to the nonexistence of aviation in 1902, crewed space travel has been under way in 2002 for more than 40 years already, making the projection of future passenger space travel services-based on known technology and market research data-far less uncertain.

The low cost of access to space that would be brought about by such large-scale space tourism would also lead to other forms of economic development in space which are not possible at present high launch costs. Many writers of both fiction and nonfiction have described futures in which human activities spread far beyond Earth-a genuine 'Space Age'. The fundamental reasons why this has not happened yet are because the cost of access to space is too high, and there is very little demand for the services utilising space that are currently being offered. By bringing costs down by providing services for which there is known to be a very large consumer demand, space tourism uniquely offers the promise of realising these longterm possibilities. Even if the possibility of realising this scenario was estimated to be only 1%, space agencies should still be investing tens of millions of dollars/year to investigate it. The fact that they devote nothing to this work is proof that they are not trying to maximise the growth of commercial space activities, despite their legal responsibility to do so.

'Opening the space frontier' is a phrase used in the literature published by government space agencies-but despite spending $25 billion per year they offer taxpayers no such prospect. The research-oriented activities funded by government space agencies are of little value for commercialisation, which is the key to enabling space activities to contribute to economic growth. The fact that the development of consumer-oriented commercial services in space is likely to be far more effective than government 'space development' activities at bringing about economic development in space should not be surprising-and it should be particularly obvious to economic policy makers.

Imperative for Economic Policy

Space activities generally receive little or no attention from economic policy makers for a number of reasons: they are very small-scale by comparison with commercial industries; they are largely government-funded; and they show little prospect of significant growth-at least according to government space agencies' forecasts. In truth, economists should know better than to rely on the views of government monopoly organisations concerning either costs or future prospects, since they have a well-understood tendency to have excessively high costs, to avoid risks, and to resist innovation, in pursuit of their own economic interests. However, although these problems of government organisations are well-known within both business and the economics profession, it is easy for government organisations that use large budgets for public relations to appear impressive and authoritative to non-specialist members of the public, including many journalists and politicians. And it is notable that both journalists and politicians-and indeed most of the general public-tend to accept the statements of space agencies as definitive even in matters of cost.

Sadly, government space agencies have avoided proposing that space activities could have economic value commensurate with their costs. On the contrary, the way in which they are structured and funded gives them a strong economic interest in exaggerating the difficulty of space activities, playing down future prospects, avoiding risks, and minimising the public's expectations by such means as ignoring proposals for passenger space travel, in line with Niskanen's description. Before being appointed Nasa Administrator, O'Keefe himself drew attention to the unsatisfactory form of many of Nasa's stated objectives, such as to "chart our destiny in the solar system" which do not allow the measurement of success or failure. In this way, by reducing the likelihood that they will receive criticism for having 'failed' in their work, space agencies thereby maximise the likelihood of continuing to receive funding.

To date, government space agencies have spent some $1 trillion of taxpayers' money. But whereas commercial investment on that scale would have created businesses earning revenues of some $1 trillion per year, commercial space activities today are roughly one 50th of this. Even allowing for the fact that 10-20% of this funding is for scientific research, and perhaps $1/2 trillion spent in the early decades was explicitly for political purposes, the return on investment is still < 10% of what commercial activities would achieve. If space agencies were genuinely motivated to achieve economic benefit for taxpayers, then in view of this extremely poor economic performance they would be urgently investigating potentially promising new commercial opportunities. Since passenger space travel is recognised to have the potential to grow into a major new service industry similar to passenger air travel space agencies' unanimous refusal to investigate it, despite being required by law to promote commercial space activities, shows that space agency leaders do not want to know about the potential of passenger space travel, and moreover that they do not want the public to know about it either.

In view of space agencies' economic interest in maintaining government funding of their existing activities, it seems likely that they will continue to refuse to do anything to help the development of passenger space travel until they are compelled to do so. Unfortunately the interests of the politicians who control their budgets are very similar to those of the agencies themselves, as Niskanen explains. Consequently reform will require intervention from outside existing arrangements, which will take time.

From the economic point of view, a particularly damaging effect of the present situation is that, until such change occurs, it will remain very difficult for private companies to raise funding to develop passenger space travel services. Major aerospace companies are 'captives' of space agencies, in the sense that they cannot do any independent work that might jeopardise their chances of continuing to receive large, low-risk contracts from them, while small companies lack the credibility to raise the funding they need in financial markets, since financiers tend to accept the 'conventional wisdom' about space which comes from government space agencies. This problem has been documented in such cases as Beal Aerospace Inc. Stopping their project to develop a lowcost satellite launch vehicle in 2001 because of competition from Nasa, and difficulties caused for other companies trying to raise funding for similar projects by public comments from space agencies.

Macroeconomic Viewpoint

From the macroeconomic point of view, in the absence of detailed analyses demonstrating errors in the Nasa report and similar published work, it is clearly desirable that passenger space travel services should be developed as soon as possible. This is because in 2002 the major blocs of the global economy are sinking into recession simultaneously, and the severe overcapacity in many older industries, combined with a serious lack of profitable new industries creates a real risk of a prolonged depression.

Historians and economic policy makers must not forget that the slide towards the second world war gathered pace through the depression of the 1930s when unemployment reached 20% in many countries. If current high levels of unemployment rise even higher in the coming years, they may lead to dangerous impatience in many regions of the world. It is already clear that in some of the poorest countries religious extremism can seem attractive by comparison with a life of impoverished unemployment, from which escape is hampered by G7 countries' protectionist trade barriers against their cheap exports. These trade barriers are motivated by the high unemployment in richer countries caused by the lack of new industries (as discussed above).

It would be economically beneficial to taxpayers if economic policy makers insist that our accumulated space engineering capabilities be used for activities with greater economic value than government space agencies' current unprofitable ones. As they operate today, instead of contributing to economic growth, government space activities are a hindrance to it-by using $20 billion per year of taxpayers' funds on activities which have an annual rate of return close to minus 100%; by indirectly preventing companies from developing lower-cost launch vehicles; and by deliberately hindering the growth of the activity which they have themselves confirmed is the most economically promising use of space-passenger space travel.

As described above, if present budgets continued and passenger space travel services were not developed as proposed in Figure 2 above, the net loss to taxpayers from continuing the present pattern of government space activities for several more decades would be around $1 trillion. This would be a terrible miscalculation of economic resources-particularly at a time of inadequate economic growth-and the quicker it is remedied by prioritising the development of passenger space travel the more the space industry will contribute to world economic growth, and thereby to 'Meeting the Needs of the New Millennium'. In addition to this economic cost, there would also be an incalculable human cost: in unnecessarily prolonging the poverty of hundreds of millions of people in late-developing countries; in postponing the development of an exciting new goal for the young in the currently richer countries; and in aggravating the risk of global conflicts through high unemployment. If government space agencies were genuinely trying to "encourage, to the maximum extent possible, the fullest commercial use of space" they would obviously investigate this potentially major new business opportunity in depth. But instead, they are currently suppressing discussion of this possibility by refusing to provide even the smallest funding to study it, despite having endorsed it in print. Economic policy makers should act to correct this serious policy failure as soon as possible. Another cost of this policy of deliberate neglect is that it ensures that there will inevitably be a further delay before passenger space travel grows to a large scale. Although it seems possible that passenger space travel could grow to reach a scale of $1 trillion per year later in the 21st century, turnover during the next 10 years will clearly be limited, and even with vigorous growth it seems unlikely to be measured in more than tens of billions of dollars by the 2020s.

How best to stimulate the development of passenger space travel services is a separate question, which has been discussed elsewhere. Some preliminary actions can be simply described: following the first recommendation in senior staff of space agencies should speak formally, positively and often about the economic importance and social value of developing a vigorous, commercial passenger space travel industry; they should also establish well-resourced offices tasked with encouraging the development of passenger space travel; and they should collaborate closely with the aviation industry in realising this goal. The latter action will require significant restructuring since government space activities have little relevant contact with aviation. Yet the vast experience of the airline industry is essential to realising passenger space travel. To the extent that space agencies do not participate effectively in implementing these and other economically beneficial changes to their existing activities, taxpayers will benefit economically if space agencies' budgets are cut-both directly by making large savings in subsidies to high-cost activities with little economic value, and indirectly by reducing misinformation about the potential for space commercialisation in general and passenger space travel in particular.

The chapter has described the potential economic benefits from developing passenger space travel services, which could contribute greatly to the continuation of peaceful world economic growth. By contrast, the vision of the future offered by government space agencies, based on continuing government domination of space activities centred on a crewed mission to Mars, is tragically narrow-minded and would merely preserve space agencies' near-monopoly status rather than contribute to economic growth. In view of the potential economic importance of passenger space travel in creating a major new field for economic expansion it is most unfortunate that little progress is being made today in developing this promising new consumer service industry, mainly because governments spend some $20 billion per year on a range of unprofitable 'space development' activities and nothing at all on work that would help to realise passenger travel. Claims by space agency leaders that they are fulfilling their legal responsibility to encourage space commercialisation are disingenuous at best.

The sooner that policies are implemented to accelerate the development of passenger space travel, the sooner the space industry will be able to claim honestly that it is contributing to meeting the needs of the 21st century-rather than holding back world economic growth by suppressing a new field with great business potential. For government space agencies and the politicians responsible for their budgets to continue to remain silent concerning their potential contribution in this area at a time of growing economic difficulty worldwide would be a shamefully wasted opportunity. It is highly desirable that economic policy makers should be informed of the opportunity for economic growth that is being wasted by government space agencies. They will then be in a position to implement policies to bring about the attractive future shown in Figure 2, thereby creating a wealth of new business opportunities for the innovative leaders who are so sadly lacking in space agencies.

Sampling and Non-sampling Error

Due to various constraints, the authors believe a small amount of sampling error exists in the survey data. First of all, error was introduced in the sample by interviewing the first person who answered the telephone on each call. Although, in many cases, the person who answered chose to pass the call on to another, in the majority of cases the initial respondent completed the survey. An example of the error that can be introduced by doing this is that, in western households, women are statistically more likely to answer the phone than their male counterparts. In order to produce a sample that better represents the population, one needs to select a respondent randomly from all the individuals who reside in each household. This can be accomplished, for example, by asking to interview the person in the house with the next birthday. This procedure or others like it, however, considerably complicate the survey procedure and increase the time needed to take the sample. A comparison of the sample taken in this study with national statistics of gender and age shows very little difference in composition, and therefore this type of sampling error is considered small. Further details concerning the representativeness of the sample are discussed later in the paper.

The largest source of sampling error in a telephone survey can usually be attributed to non-response. This arises because many people are not at home when called (54% of the numbers dialled), and many individuals (48% of those contacted) choose not to participate in the survey. This survey was administered during selected periods of time during the week: Monday-Friday from 5 pm to 9 pm, and on Saturday from 11 am to 7 pm. These set time-frames were chosen to reduce non-response due to refusals, and to increase the likelihood that more people in each household would be at home to answer the phone. It is recognized however, that calling during specific time periods can exclude certain portions of the population who may be doing shift-work, or certain age-groups who may not typically be at home during these time-periods. Calling on Saturdays and also on the Labour Day holiday may have helped to reduce this error. Possible ways to determine if biasing is present include making call-backs to numbers where there was no answer, and interviewing individuals who refuse to do the survey on their first option by coaxing them with some type of reward. These measures however, were considered unnecessary in this case because of the nature of the survey. All in all, it is very unlikely that significant error has been introduced into the data with the sampling method used. Non-sampling error for this study is considered to be very small since the interviewing sessions were conducted in a highly controlled manner. The use of computer programs to dictate the survey text so that each participant received exactly the same information, as well as to collect, process, and analyse the data, decreased the possibility of error being introduced in these processes to a minimum.

The Survey

The survey consisted of 17 questions and took approximately four minutes to complete. Respondents who were not interested in travelling to space had a much shorter survey to answer that took only half the time. The first section of the survey collected basic personal information on the respondent, as well as information concerning interests and travelling preferences. The second half of the survey began with the following space tourism concept statement: Consider for the moment that it is possible to travel to space as a potential vacation alternative. Imagine that people are able to go to there using a means of transportation similar to a planed The respondent was then asked would you be interested in travelling to space-yes or noway If the respondent answered no, they were queried as to why. If they responded yes, the survey continued with more specific questions concerning a space trip. Several open-ended questions in the survey stimulated many interesting opinions and comments from the respondents, which suggests that many people have given considerable thought to the idea of travelling to space for themselves. In the future, a more detailed analysis of the results of this survey will be published, and those comments will be given further attention. For the present, the following paragraphs briefly describe the studious main findings.

Survey Results

Table 1 shows the overall distribution of the survey participants by age and gender, and compares them to the US population as a whole. (Adding the figure in the variant column to the corresponding age group yields the percentage of that group in the overall US population, census data-1990.

Table 1: Breakdown of surveyed respondents with comparison to the US population

Gender	Male	Female	Total	Male Var	Female Var	Total Var
20's	11.4%	13.8%	25.2%	0.6%	-2.1%	-1.5%
30's	10.5%	12.5%	23.0%	1.7%	-0.2%	1.5%
40's	7.4%	11.6%	18.9%	1.7%	-2.2%	-0.4%
50's	5.7%	8.2%	13.9%	0.5%	-1.6%	-1.1%
Over60	7.2%	11.8%	18.9%	1.8%	-0.3%	1.5%
Totals	42.1%	57.9%	100.0%			

It has been assumed that the Canadian population distribution is similar.) The distribution by age matches the overall population very closely; none of the five age groups considered is over-or under-represented by more than 2.2%, confirming the representativeness of the sample in this respect. The distribution by gender, however, is significantly different, with women over-represented and men under-represented by 6.3%. In the following, wherever necessary, the figures are adjusted to compensate for this.

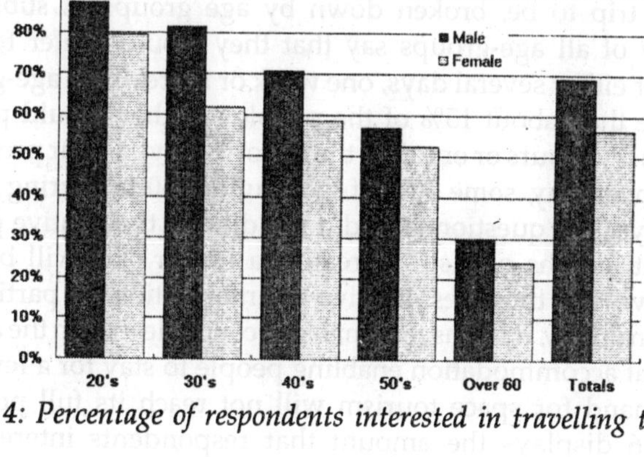

Figure 4: Percentage of respondents interested in travelling to space

Figure 4 shows the basic level of interest in travelling to space, broken down by age and gender. As an overall average, more than 60% of the population say they are interested, with a higher proportion of younger people being interested, as one might expect. The overall average figure is comprised of more than 75% of those under 40 years old; 60% of those between 40 and 60; and more than 25% of those between 60 and 80.

It is notable that in every age group men were more interested than women, the average difference being about 10%. This is rather different from the results of the survey in Japan, where no significant difference was found. This may be due to the fact that many US astronauts are military staff, whereas all the Japanese who have visited space are civilians.

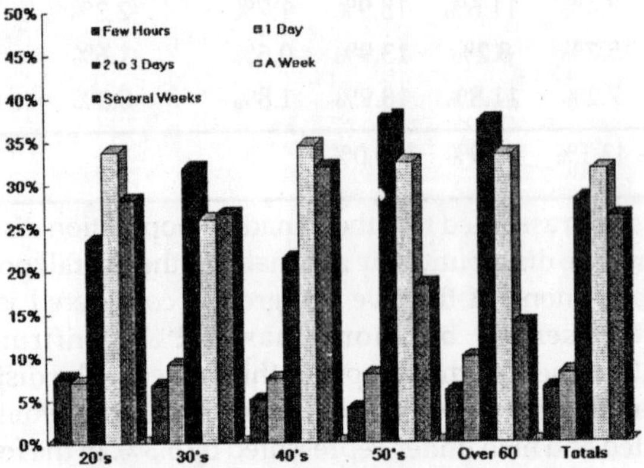

Figure 5. Preferred length of space trip

Figure 5 shows the length of time participants would prefer a space trip to be, broken down by age groups. A substantial majority of all age-groups say that they would prefer to go to space for either several days, one week or more. In all age-groups, no more than about 15% of the people say they would prefer a visit of a few hours or one day; the majority have a clear preference for a longer stay, some 30% of those under 50 preferring several weekdays. The questionnaire did not discuss the relative price of different lengths of visit. In reality, a longer stay will be more expensive, but these results give no information on participants price-sensitivity. It seems reasonable to conclude that, in the absence of orbital accommodation enabling people to stay for a few days, the demand for space tourism will not reach its full potential. Figure 6 displays the amount that respondents interested in travelling to space would be prepared to pay for a trip, expressed in months of salary. The first point to note is that there is little difference between the various age groups on this variable. At the upper end of the range, it is interesting that 2.7% of those wishing to visit space (representing almost 3 million people) say that they would pay three hearsay salary. Clearly for these people travelling to space is a very strong desire.

10.6% (representing 11 million people) say they would pay one year's salary, which is still a very substantial expense. 18.2% of participants (representing 19 million people) say they would pay 6 months salary, and 45.6% (representing 48 million people) say they would pay 3 months salary.

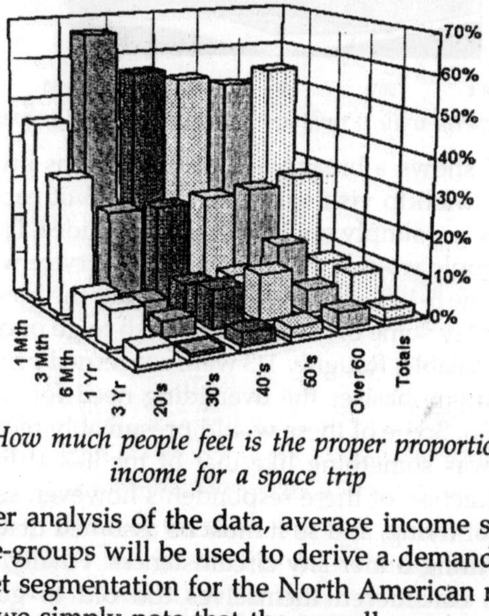

Figure 6. How much people feel is the proper proportion of their income for a space trip

In further analysis of the data, average income statistics for different age-groups will be used to derive a demand curve and study market segmentation for the North American market. For the present we simply note that the overall average income for North Americans is approximately $2,000 per month, or $12,000 for six months salary, and $24,000 for a year. In addition, two thirds of those wishing to visit space said that they would like to do so several times, not once only. Consequently, even allowing for a substantial gap between consumerism intentions and their actions, space travel could clearly become a $multi-billion per year market in America alone. 10% of the above estimate is still more than $60 billion in funds that people say they are willing to spend on a space trip.

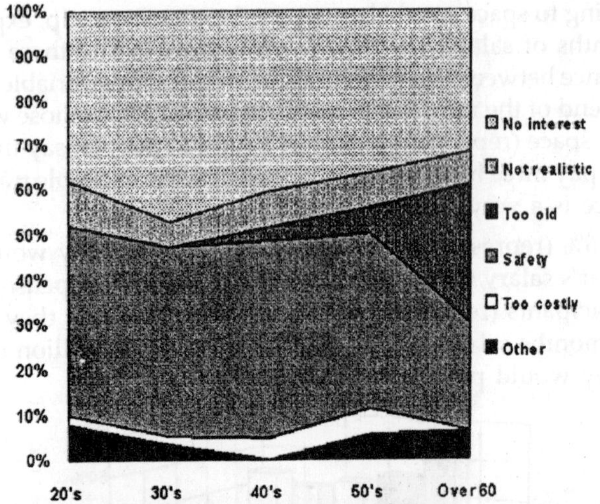

Figure 7: Reasons why people are not interested in travelling to space

Figure 7 shows a breakdown of the reasons given by those who did not wish to visit space. Roughly 1/3 of each age group said that they are simply not interested in the idea. It seems likely that these people would not go, even if the service was available. However, some 5-10% said that they consider the idea unrealistic, and presumably some of these would wish to go once the service was really available. Roughly 1/3 were concerned primarily about safety, which emphasises the overriding need for reliable space transportation. Some of these would presumably reconsider once the service was something like that of toadies airline travel. A substantial fraction of these respondents however, said that they were afraid of flying, and so it must be assumed that they would remain unwilling under any circumstances. Finally, most of the people who considered themselves too old to go, were still interested in travelling to space if it had been available when they were young. Overall, it seems that the average of 60% interested in visiting space could grow to 70% or more in the event that a regular service became available.

A weakness in terms of complete consistency between all respondents is suspected by the authors in terms of the personal interpretation of the space tourism concept statement. Since the respondent was free to envision what the space trip and vacation would entail, it was felt that in some cases the respondent thought that they might be travelling to faraway places or planets on their trip. Whenever questions arose as to where they might be travelling on a space trip, it was suggested by the interviewers that these trips would be mainly in orbit around the Earth.

Although some misinterpretation may be present, it is felt that most respondents had a clear picture as to what would be involved; a vacation orbiting the Earth or slightly beyond. Discussions with the interviewees during and after the study attempted to elicit information concerning this issue. If bias is present due to the lack of clarity involved, it could move the results in either direction, but probably not by a substantial amount.

International Comparison

One of the more interesting aspects of this study is that it enables a comparison of data to be made between different national markets. It appears from these results and others that the desire to travel to space is consistent with the popular idea that people of all cultures are intrigued by, and eager to experience living in space for themselves. Here we briefly compare the results of the two similar studies carried out in Japan and Germany.

A survey using a similar format was recently carried out on 200 people using the two airports in Berlin, of which the results will be published in detail in the near future. The data are particularly interesting in being the first such market data to be collected in Europe. Because airport users are a well-characterised economic group, the results allow us to draw conclusions about the middle and upper income group of the German population, and also reasonably firm conclusions about western Europeans as a whole. In combination with the American and Japanese data, Figure 8 shows the comparison of the amounts that people said they would pay in these four countries. More detailed analysis is required to draw precise comparisons, but the similarity between the North American and German data is striking. The figures for Japan are noticeably higher.

In comparing the American results with the earlier data on the Japanese market, we must make allowance for differences in the circumstances of the two surveys that might lead to differences in the results. A significant difference between the two survey procedures was that in the telephone survey participants were given minimal information about what form the service would take. It was clear from comments made by some respondents that they were envisaging something rather similar to a flight in an existing launch vehicle, and at the other extreme, dreaming of a trip in a futuristic starship.

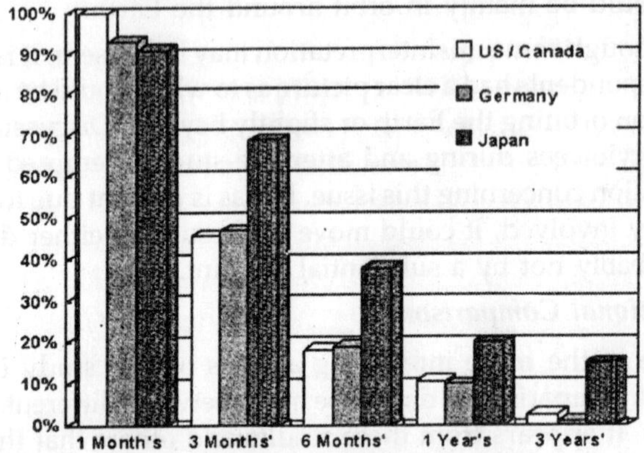

Figure 8: Comparison of the amount people would pay in several countries

In the Japanese survey however, participants were given an illustrated pamphlet explaining that the service would be rather like air travel today, and passengers could stay in an orbital hotel. It is to be expected that this would increase the attractiveness of the prospective service. Another difference is that Japanese personal savings are considerably higher than Americans', and consequently Japanese people may more easily envisage a rather large expense for a particularly desired activity. Other potentially significant differences are the 2-year difference in the dates of the surveys, the difference between a written and a verbal survey, and recent media events in the countries concerned. Thus, at the present early stage of this market research, it would seem premature to claim that even such an apparently major difference as that in Figure 5 is real, either as representing a significant difference between the countries concerned, or in terms of the data being in error.

More striking than this possible difference is surely the fact that people from such different countries, approached in such different ways, answer the basic question of whether they wish to visit space with such a high similarity. A large majority of young people, a majority of the middle-aged, and a substantial minority of people in their 60s and 70s say that they wish to visit space, and many are prepared to pay several months salary to do so. We can surely conclude that personally travelling to space is an almost universally popular ambition.

Index

O

P

R

S

T

❑❑❑